ELIJAH
AMONG
US

UNDERSTANDING AND RESPONDING
TO GOD'S PROPHETS TODAY

JOHN LOREN
SANDFORD

Chosen Books

A Division of Baker Book House Co
Grand Rapids, Michigan 49516

Published by Chosen Books
A division of Baker Publishing Group
P.O. Box 6287, Grand Rapids, MI 49516-6287
www.chosenbooks.com

Fourth printing, March 2007

Printed in the United States of America

Library of Congress Cataloging-in-Publication Data
Sandford, John Loren.
    Elijah among us : understanding and responding to God's prophets today /
John Loren Sandford.
        p.   cm.
    Includes bibliographical references and index.
    ISBN 10: 0-8007-9303-X (pbk.)
    ISBN 978-0-8007-9303-6 (pbk.)
    1. Prophecy—Christianity. I. Title.
BR115 . P8 S255 2002
231.7′45—dc21   2002000367

To my wife,
Paula
For 51 years
my loving and faithful partner

CONTENTS

7

PART 3   PURPOSES AND TASKS
          OF PROPHETS TODAY

FOREWORD

BY DR. BILL HAMON

WHEN I BEGAN WRITING my first book, *Prophets and Personal Prophecy*, in 1983, I did a thorough search to find books written on present-day prophets. The only significant book I found on the subject was *The Elijah Task* by John and Paula Sandford. Now in *Elijah Among Us— Understanding and Responding to God's Prophets Today*, John again brings much wisdom and maturity to ministering the prophetic. He not only gives scriptural proofs and examples, but his many illustrated life experiences also make the prophetic real and understandable.

John mentions 1988 as the year of the prophets and the emergence of modern-day prophetic ministry. I agree that the modern prophetic movement was sovereignly birthed into the Church in October of 1988. At that time, God began bringing forth a company of prophets in the spirit and power of Elijah to fulfill Malachi 3:1, 4:5–6 and Isaiah 40:3–5. Just as John the Baptist fulfilled the "prophet Elijah" prophecies for Christ's first coming, so now a company of prophets are fulfilling those "prophet Elijah" prophecies by preparing the way and making ready a people for Christ's second coming.

During my almost fifty years of being a prophet and ministering prophetically, I have known many prophets. I have seen "the good, the bad and the ugly." Thankfully, my years of experience in prophetic ministry have witnessed 90 percent of the good and only 10 percent of the "bad and ugly." There have been, and still are, a few false prophets operating in the church. However, many who are called false are really just immature saints who do not fully understand how to properly administer their prophetic gift.

9

Elijah Among Us can help prophetic ministers function properly in the Church. John Sandford is fully qualified to write on this subject. He is a father in the faith and a pioneer of prophets and prophetic ministry. John and Paula have proven their credibility by many decades of consistent, quality prophetic ministry. From what I have learned and experienced, I can say that this book is not just for those who want to be prophetic, but it is for everyone who wants to minister the life of Christ. It is especially beneficial for those who desire to minister with wisdom and maturity.

I highly recommend this book for all Christians and particularly for those who minister to others. Great blessings and benefits will be obtained by any who read and learn from this work. Thanks, John, for sharing all this knowledge and life-giving experience with us. God bless you and all who read this book.

Dr. Bill Hamon
Founder/President/Bishop of Christian International Ministries Network
Author of five books: *The Eternal Church; Prophets and Personal Prophecy; Prophets and the Prophetic Movement; Prophets—Pitfalls and Principles;* and *Apostles, Prophets and the Coming Moves of God.*

ACKNOWLEDGMENTS

IN SOCIOLOGY CLASSES at Drury University in the late forties, I learned that the discovery of how to store food delivered mankind from incessant hunting and gathering and enabled culture to arise. Likewise, communication through speech and the ability to remember first gave mankind the capacity to retain knowledge and improve by experience. I have never so greatly appreciated the truth of those teachings as during the writing of this book!

On May 25, 2001, during the time of writing, I suffered a heart attack. My cardiologist, Dr. Dean Hill, informed me that ten years ago doctors would not have known how to do an angioplasty or insert a stent. I was grateful to have both of these procedures. The alternatives—open-heart surgery or weakness without surgery—would have incapacitated me and caused our publishing date to be long delayed. But these relatively simple new procedures and the subsequent enforced cancellation of our traveling schedule gave me opportunity to complete the manuscript *before* our deadline. So, my first thanks are to the medical staffs of Kootenai Memorial Hospital in Coeur d'Alene, Idaho, Sacred Heart Hospital of Spokane, Washington, and Lewisville Medical Center of Lewisville, Texas, and to the researchers whose works have so rapidly advanced knowledge in the medical field.

As it was, from Memorial Day until November 7, I was in hospitals ten times, due to complications with reactions to medicines and the need for insertion of a pacemaker! Preventricular contractions and an extremely low heart rate caused fatigue and necessitated the pacemaker, which was installed just this week on November 6, 2001. The writing of this book has been the most intense, even dangerous, spiritual warfare I have ever endured—from beginning to end! Not only did I experience attacks upon

11

my health, but frequent, odd computer crashes, crazy interruptions of on-line procedures, lost bits of manuscripts and books from which quotes were to be taken, etc., ad nauseum. The devil surely does not want this book published! Therefore, my second thanks are to the countless intercessors who responded to so many calls and prayed for me faithfully through it all. It could not have been accomplished without your persistent support.

Thirdly, I am vastly impressed by the rapid maturing of the Body of Christ in these days. Knowledge and wisdom other prophets have shared with me personally and through their books have been an immeasurable help in amassing the information shared here—especially whatever wisdom has filtered down.

Usually, Paula and I write together, so most of our books have been joint projects. This book, however, has been my sole essay. Nevertheless, had it not been for her incessant care for my health and sometimes frantic intercession, this book could never have found expression, much less completion. In January 2001, we celebrated our fiftieth wedding anniversary, and I am inexpressibly grateful to God that He brought us together. He knew we had to be a team, though this time the writing is mine.

Bob Dilley of Odyssey Tek, our local computer expert, has been invaluable. This crazy computer insists on doing what this computer illiterate tells it to do, and Bob has faithfully rescued me from countless errors. With the help of a friend, I managed to delete the entirety of chapter 9 just after writing it under an anointing that could never be recaptured. Bob Dilley brought in special software and worked diligently for several days until he finally recovered the chapter. And he set up a special shared folder in his office server, giving Grace Sarber, the editor, and myself access, thus avoiding what often occurs when long e-mail transmissions garble manuscripts.

My thanks to Grace Sarber, editor for Chosen Books, who faithfully plugged away at making my often erudite ramblings interesting and understandable for common lay readers.

And my thanks to my fifteen-year-old grandson, Jacob. How in the world do these youngsters know what they do about computers? Numbers of times, when I couldn't figure out how to do something on the computer, he came and said, "Oh, that's easy, Granddad," and just instantly did it! Miraculous!

I want also to thank two of our sons, Loren and Mark. Mark, who wrote A Complete Guide to Deliverance and Inner Healing with me, read the entire first draft and tackled me about many expressions, suggesting wiser and more scriptural ways to say things. Loren added advice, especially concerning chapter 1 about the possibility of true prophets making errors.

Finally, how could anyone sufficiently thank our wonderful Lord?! Days on end, I wrote under His powerful anointing, delightfully surprised at what He poured through me into my recalcitrant computer. Again and again, He pulled me up out of sickness and desperate tiredness and filled me with energy and perseverance to write. How steadfast His love has been during all this time! Everyday, His still, calm voice encouraged me as He strengthened me to continue. What a wonderful Lord He is! We have the best boss in the world!

I love what He is doing, as He is raising His end-time prophets and preparing His Church for His return. I am grateful for your faith as you read. Your response is my reward, if serving Him were not enough.

INTRODUCTION

MANY FRIENDS HAVE PLED with us to write a sequel to *The Elijah Task*. Paula and I have never felt led to do so—until now. Since Paula is engaged with other projects, writing the sequel falls to me.

When *The Elijah Task* was published in 1977, Paula and I predicted the rise of the prophetic office. Though individual prophets had been emerging for a number of years, neither individuals nor the office gained much notoriety until 1988. Then at a conference held in a large Vineyard church in Denver, more than three thousand pastors and leaders from all over the world watched and listened as John Wimber showcased the prophets. This event catapulted prophets into prominence.

Subsequently, many conferences that highlighted prophets were held throughout the Church, giving personal prophecies to thousands. People began to rush for seats, hoping to be called out and given a word from the Lord. Although it was wonderful that God's prophets were once again being recognized and respected in the Church, problems arose. For example, many were not prepared to know what to do with such prophets or their prophecies, or how to interpret their words. In addition, the importunity of people threatened to turn prophetic utterances into divination, and many stopped listening for themselves, wanting simply to hear from the prophets. Later in this book, I will address these problems and, I hope, bring some clarification. But for now, suffice it to say that while Paula and I were pleased that at last prophets were arising, none seemed as yet fully to comprehend the office, and certainly no one had begun to manifest its fullness.

The giving of personal words is only one of the functions of a prophet established in the office, and though important, it may in fact be one of the least and most dangerous of a prophet's functions. Even though the

1988 Vineyard conference made the Church once again begin to recognize prophetic gifting, it seemed that none, other than Paula and me, were teaching about all the prophet's other functions, of which there are more than twelve major and a host of other minor. Several prophets did speak about and manifest a few of the other functions, but not many.

In the years since 1988 we have waited and watched anxiously, hoping that prophets would begin to mature into the fullness of the office. But too few have grasped that prophets are anything more than those who give personal words to individuals. Several have begun to act in some of the prophetic functions, such as those who have led in the area of spiritual warfare, notably Peter Wagner (though he does not think of himself as a prophet), Cindy Jacobs, Chuck Pierce and Dutch Sheets.

Before the November 2000 presidential election in America, Dutch Sheets called the Body of Christ into fervent intercessory prayer that God's man be elected as our nation's leader. That calling of the Body into intercession, and giving it direction in prayer, is a major function of the Lord's prophets.

John Paul Jackson has written *Selling Your Children's Souls*, which reveals the demonic nature of Pokemon and admonishes Christians, especially parents, to reject all Pokemon materials; and *The Veiled Ploy*, which exposes the Jezebel spirit—a spirit with a lust for power—and how it undermines and destroys leadership and creates division in churches, families and organizations. Cindy Jacobs has written *Deliver Us from Evil*, revealing how insidiously occultism has invaded our lives and endangers our children. These are prophetic books, much needed and timely in their appearance. They exemplify a major function of prophets—to protect the Body by teaching, intercession and prophetic proclamation.

Cindy Jacobs has written another prophetic book, *The Voice of God*, which teaches how to listen and how to discern. This is another major function of prophets: to prepare the way of the Lord in the hearts of His people. Cindy Jacobs also has written *Possessing the Gates of the Enemy*, and John Dawson has written *Healing America's Wounds* and *Taking Our Cities for God*. These are prophetic books that call the Church into intercession, reconciliation and spiritual warfare for the healing of the nations. And, of course, I have written the prophetic books *The Elijah Task* and *Healing the Nations*.

We could continue to catalogue other selected prophetic works. But no one as yet, or so it seems to me, has comprehended the fullness of what it is to be an Elijah prophet of the Lord. I do not know that anyone could write a book that encompassed the total fullness of the office, but the Body has a crying need to understand more of what the prophetic office entails. The Body needs to know how to respond, to inform by discernment, to raise up a standard that may beckon more to the calling, to increase awareness, to instruct many budding prophets lest they think their yearnings and endeavors eccentric or irrelevant, and especially to fulfill the function of forerunners in laying a plausible track for others to follow.

For these reasons, and simply the impelling of the Holy Spirit, this book has been gestating in my heart. It has begun to thrust its way so much into consciousness day by day that I have to write, if only to relieve the pressure in my mind and heart. We hope you will find it helpful.

May God bless you, and keep the fruit.

PART 1

HISTORY
OF THE
PROPHETIC
OFFICE

ONE

THE BIRTH
OF THE PROPHETIC OFFICE

THE PROPHETIC IS THE ONLY ONE of the five offices that has a long and scripturally detailed history. The other offices—apostles, evangelists, pastors and teachers—have very little history, if any, prior to the New Testament. Apostles are not mentioned in the Old Testament. Evangelists are not spoken of specifically as such, though Jonah was sent to Nineveh, and Jeremiah "came from Topheth, where the LORD had sent him to prophesy" (Jeremiah 19:14). In both cases the prophets were sent to prophesy destruction for sins. Nineveh repented and turned to the Lord. In this instance, God's acting among people served to evangelize them. Another example of this is the story of King Nebuchadnezzar, who after seven years of eating grass—just as Daniel prophesied—recognized there is no God besides the Lord (see Daniel 4:34–37). But such happenings throughout the Old Testament were results of prophetic endeavors, not the work of evangelists sent as such. Pastors are mentioned, but only as "shepherds after My own heart, who will feed you on knowledge and understanding" (Jeremiah 3:15) or as shepherds who fail to feed the flock, with whom God contends (see Ezekiel 34). But the pastoral office is not developed. The same is true for teachers. Only the prophetic office has a long and developed history.

That fact is important. History is the battleground for the control of people's minds. What we know of our history declares to us who we are, what we are to do and how we are to behave while doing it. Our view of history controls all of our thinking, impels our feelings and calls forth our motivations. Demagogues take control of multitudes by reciting biased and false histories. White lynch mobs were generated by volatile speeches detailing histories of violations supposedly committed by black people.

Our view of history forms our self-image and thus our self-confidence; it leads to the release or blockage of talents and skills. Knowledge of history warns of the pitfalls of the past. The old adage is too often true that "Whoever does not know history is doomed to repeat its errors." Most importantly, our history informs us positively, guiding us on the stable track of mankind's good experiences. A generation without a solid knowledge of history must reinvent the wheel for itself.

Christianity began with a new template to form each of the other four offices, as there was no significant history upon which to build, but we do not have to invent the prophetic office. We have only to rediscover what the prophetic office was, how it developed and what that means for us today. But before we embark upon the historical quest for the prophetic office, it would be wise to clear up some areas of confusion.

"Prophets of the Moment" and Prophets Called into the Office

First, there is a vast difference between a prophet of the moment and one who stands in the office. All are called to prophesy: "Now I wish that you all spoke in tongues, but even more that you would prophesy; and greater is one who prophesies than one who speaks in tongues, unless he interprets, so that the church may receive edifying" (1 Corinthians 14:5). But not all are called to be prophets. One who interprets or presents a word from the Lord in a meeting is called a "prophet of the moment." That is not to be confused with one who is called into the office permanently. True prophets are called to wear a mantle that cannot be removed. A prophet is a prophet 24 hours a day, 365 days a year, for every year of his life! His body—and all he is—is given to the Lord, a living sacrifice that is his spiritual service of worship (see Romans 12:1).

A prophet of the moment is employed by the Holy Spirit for that moment to deliver a word from God to His people. When the word has been

22

presented, the messenger has no more responsibility for it or to it than any other of its hearers. Prophets of the moment are to weigh their words, but they do not carry the burden and authority resident in the heart of a prophet called into the office. "Let two or three prophets speak, and let the others pass judgment" [other versions say "weigh" what is said] (1 Corinthians 14:29). The burden of informing the pastor and elders for the protection or blessing of the congregation concerning that word is far more explicit and fraught with greater consequences for the prophet who stands in the office. The instruction given to teachers applies just as well to prophets: "Let not many of you become teachers [or prophets], my brethren, knowing that as such we will incur a stricter judgment" (James 3:1). The higher the office, the stricter the level of responsibility and judgment.

A Prophet Is Fallible

Some have thought that a prophet's word must always come true or he is not a true prophet, and that in the Old Testament the penalty for a prophet's error was always death. In the day of the prophet Micaiah, King Jehoshaphat of Judah wanted to know whether or not he and the king of Israel should go up against the king of Syria (also known as Aram). Several prophets said, "Yes, go up against him." But Jehoshaphat asked if there was another prophet of whom they might inquire. The king of Israel called for Micaiah. In the meantime the prophet Zedekiah made horns of iron and said, "Thus says the LORD, 'With these you will gore the Arameans [Syrians] until they are consumed'" (1 Kings 22:11). All the other prophets agreed and told the kings that the Lord would prosper them and give Ramoth-gilead into the hand of the king of Israel (see verse 12). When Micaiah came, after some exhorting by Jehoshaphat to tell the truth, Micaiah told them the true word that Israel would be scattered on the mountains and the king of Israel would be killed (see verse 28). Micaiah explained that the Lord Himself had sent a deceiving spirit to speak through the mouths of the other prophets (see verses 19–23). Micaiah's prophecy came true, and the four hundred other prophets were proven wrong.

But the prophets who had brought deceptive words were not slain. Neither were the prophets in Jeremiah 23 and Ezekiel 13 slain for their lying visions and words but only castigated severely.

23

Sometimes prophets were indeed killed, as in the case of Hananiah (see Jeremiah 28:15–17), although he was not put to death by men but, it seems, by the Lord. And in Deuteronomy 13, the command was given to put an erring prophet to death. But read verses 1–5 carefully. The Word says the prophet's prophecy was true: "and the sign or the wonder comes true" (verse 2). It was not for false prophecy that death was decreed. It was for false teaching: "But that prophet or that dreamer of dreams shall be put to death, *because he has counseled rebellion against the* LORD *your God*" (verse 5, emphasis mine). By the way, if you look again at Jeremiah 28:16, you will see that Hananiah died because he "counseled rebellion against the LORD." Our Lord is not so strict or unjust as to put any and all prophets to death for errors. Death was required only for very serious matters, such as leading God's people into rebellion.

Some persist, saying that a true prophet's word must always come true, for this is one way to judge whether or not the prophet is true. Such teachers would do well to read the Word of God more thoroughly before speaking. Paul said, "For we know in part and we prophesy in part" (1 Corinthians 13:9). As the Amplified Bible puts it, "For our knowledge is fragmentary (incomplete and imperfect), and our prophecy (our teaching) is fragmentary (incomplete and imperfect)." This verse humbles us to realize that even the best of our prophecies are incomplete. No one can encompass all the truth or fully express it. God's thoughts and ways are high above ours. *But incompleteness is not necessarily error.*

Critics could say, possibly with some justification, that we have not yet addressed adequately the question of whether or not true prophets can err. Micah 3:5–7 speaks to true prophets who make mistakes:

> "Thus says the LORD concerning the prophets *who lead my people* astray; when they have something to bite with their teeth, they cry, 'Peace,' but against him who puts nothing in their mouths they declare holy war. *Therefore it will be night for you—without vision,* and darkness for you— without divination. The sun will go down on the prophets, and the day will become dark over them. The seers will be ashamed and the diviners will be embarrassed. Indeed, they will all cover their mouths *because there is no answer from God.*"
>
> EMPHASES MINE

The Lord is saying that because the prophets are leading the people astray by their errors, He is going to stop giving them visions and stop speaking to them. Had these been false prophets, He would not have been giving them visions or talking to them in the first place! The fact that He says there will be "no answer" implies that He has previously been giving them answers. So, it is clear that He is addressing true prophets who have been making mistakes. But note: These prophets are not killed. They are punished by the Lord's silence; He will not speak to them again.

Earlier I mentioned a more precise text: "Let two or three prophets speak, and *let the others pass judgment*" (1 Corinthians 14:29, emphasis mine). Paul was trying to establish order in church meetings. In the process, he revealed something crucial about prophets. That is, that they can err. Paul advised that when two or three have spoken, the others are to examine what was said. Throughout this book we will see that the Church needs to seek God for clear interpretations of what His words through prophets mean. But Paul's instruction here goes beyond mere pondering of true words from God. He uses the words *pass judgment*. If prophets' words could always be depended upon to be truly from God and without error, there would be no need for such an admonition. Knowing that prophets can make mistakes, wanting the Body to be cautious, Paul advised that each word be judged. Paul would not have given the instruction to judge each word if prophets' words were always without error. Because we who are prophets are fallible and can err in what we say, we need one another and we need humility to hear each other's corrections.

In His wisdom, God does not grant anyone's desire to be absolutely correct all the time. That would endanger any prophet's flesh through pride and self-reliance, and tempt the Body of Christ to honor and follow the servant rather than the Master. Deuteronomy 13:3–4 says that when prophets err

> "the LORD your God is testing you to find out if you love the LORD your God with all your heart and with all your soul. You shall follow the LORD your God and fear Him; and you shall keep His commandments, listen to His voice, serve Him, and cling to Him."

Prophets err because all are cracked vessels, no matter how full our sanctification in Him—God has nothing else to use.

Occasional errors do not prove that an individual is a false prophet. Doctrinal errors and continually wrong prophecies certainly prove that the prophet is immature and could possibly lead to the conclusion that he is false. The word *false* should perhaps be reserved for those who have no real intention of being true, whose hearts are perverse, who are only faking what it is to be a prophet for vainglory or some other base motive, or who stubbornly cling to false concepts or doctrines. Those who are trying to be true but err in their words or doctrines—whether sometimes or even often—should be regarded as immature prophets, improperly instructed, needing the discipline and instruction of older and wiser servants.

Bishop Bill Hamon, one of the foremost prophets of today, says the same in his book *Prophets and Personal Prophecy:* "An inaccurate word from a prophet does not prove that person to be a false prophet; all human beings are fallible, and the inaccuracy may simply have been the result of immaturity, ignorance, or presumption."

Bishop Hamon also wrote these words of wisdom we all might heed:

> In discussing false or inaccurate prophecies undue emphasis is often placed on the standard for prophets without considering the need for accountability among the rest of the five-fold ministries. Are any of the other ministries held to a requirement of one hundred percent accuracy in all their pronouncements? No doubt "Thus saith the Lord" demands a greater accountability because of the authority claimed in the utterance. But this does not do away with the need for accountability in a teacher's doctrine or a pastor's counsel. The apostle James notes particularly that teachers will be held to a higher standard of accountability (James 3:1).
>
> All too often we employ a double standard. If a healing evangelist prays for a hundred sick and dying people, and two are miraculously healed, everyone is excited and shares the report of the two without mention of the ninety-eight who walked away as sick as they came. On the other hand, if a prophet ministers to a hundred people, and ninety-eight of them receive a specific, accurate word, you can be sure that folks will tend to remember the two prophecies that were inaccurate.

The word *prophet* comes from the Hebrew word *nabi,* in plural *neviim,* meaning "speaker" or "speakers," one whose mouth has been touched to speak for God. From this some have derived the idea that a prophet is one who foretells the future or speaks of things only God could know. Many foolishly run to prophets hoping to hear a word about what is going to happen in the future, especially their own. Though prophets sometimes do foretell, much of their task has nothing to do with speaking publicly about the future, or even with oral speaking at all. The Old Testament prophets spoke for God through all they did, as when Jeremiah wore an ox yoke, Isaiah went naked and barefoot, Hosea married a prostitute, and Ezekiel bore the iniquity of Israel and Judah on his own body. When prophets are called to speak, it is about anything God wants to address—the past, present or future, revealing things hidden or merely speaking of what is mundane and well-known. We need to be careful that our importunity does not tempt prophets to become diviners.

Back to the Beginning

To understand the history of the prophetic office, let's begin at the very beginning, before history was. In the Garden of Eden Adam and Eve could "walk and talk with God and jest, as good friends should and do" (from an old Latvian hymn). Their hearts and spirits were perfectly attuned to His. They read accurately His intentions behind everything He said. They could leapfrog in conversations, not having to complete sentences because they had already grasped what was meant. When Genesis 3:8 says, "They heard the sound of the LORD God walking in the garden in the cool of the day," I doubt that was the first time He had come. That was probably His custom and delight, to visit with His children in the soft glow of the evening sun.

But then Satan tempted Adam and Eve, and in the process disengaged their spirits from the Lord's gentle, loving nature and filled them with his own guilt and distrust. Sin separates. When God came as usual, nothing was as usual or would ever be again. The very God of love and forgiveness came walking in the cool of the day—and they fled from Him! If their spirits had not become defiled with Satan's rebellious inability to trust, they could have run to Him, exclaiming, "Oh, Father, we disobeyed Your command! We've eaten of that tree You said not to. Please forgive us." God might then have gathered them into His arms, as we do when our children come, tearfully confessing something they have done wrong. But fear and guilt, and Satan's defilement, had broken their ability to read His Spirit, or trust His words.

When God called to the man and said to him, "Where are you?" (Genesis 3:9), do you think He did not know where Adam was? Of course He knew. In His own polite and gentle way, God was giving Adam the opportunity to come and confess. Note that He did not call them both, but only the man, and not by name. Sin causes us to lose our names, which stand for our birthright and destiny.

But Adam replied with the first human lie in history (not the first ever—Satan had already lied to Eve several times): "I heard the sound of You in the garden, and I was afraid *because I was naked;* so I hid myself" (verse 10, emphasis mine). He was afraid because he had sinned and could not trust God to understand and forgive. From then on, each time God tried to elicit repentance and confession, Adam and Eve passed the buck, "The *woman* whom *You* gave to be with me, she gave me from the tree, and I ate" (verse 12, emphasis mine); Adam blamed both God and Eve. Eve passed the buck to Satan, "The serpent deceived me, and I ate" (verse 13).

Gone was the restful enjoyment of each other. Adam's and Eve's hearts were filled with Satan's lying ways, and their spirits became defiled with his spirit. They were unable to commune in true communication, which can only occur where mutual trust embraces hard truth and acceptance enables understanding. Fellowship had fallen, like the scattered shards of a once beautiful mirror. God could no longer communicate with Adam and Eve. They had become incapable. Now they had to be expelled from the Garden.

Man Is Separated from God

From that time forth, as mankind spread across the earth, few, if any, could communicate with God accurately until the time of Noah. But once mankind left the Ark on Mount Ararat and spread across the earth, none could hear God, and none knew His loving nature. Nowhere did mankind understand God and embrace Him for who He is. Everywhere men caught fragile and often mistaken glimpses of God's nature. None could visit with Him; none could comprehend His words and attitudes as Adam and Eve had done in the Garden.

Imagine the loneliness of God! Those of us who have children can catch a tiny glimpse of it. How our hearts would hurt if our own children continually fled at our approach and misunderstood our compassionate words as judgment and accusation! Sometimes that does happen in occasional confusions, and it hurts every time. But what if it were all the time, with every child? How crushing to our hearts! Multiply that by the millions of lost children who wander the earth in confusion and darkness, and you begin to sense only a smidgen of the grief that has beset our heavenly Father's heart as the years and centuries have gone by after the fall from the Garden.

All Part of God's Plan

Yet even in the depths of this tragedy, Satan did not slip one up on God or win a victory. God foreknew, before He ever created the earth, what Satan would do and how Adam and Eve would succumb. He knew that all of mankind would lose the ability to listen to Him, that all would misunderstand His nature, and that all would wander in darkness and confusion. He knew that we would catch only little glimpses of truth, falsely fearing Him because true fear born of trustful awe had died.

From the ground plan of creation, before anything appeared, God planned that at the right time in history He would come to one particular people and through them He would begin, electively, purposefully, progressively, to reveal who He is. He came to Abraham and told him he would be the father of many nations, but that his people would have to endure four hundred years of slavery in Egypt before He would bring them back to the land He promised Abraham (see Genesis 15:12–15). Then He came to Moses and said, "I AM WHO I AM" (Exodus 3:14). Not some local little deity, not a bull, a dog or a mountain, but the God of all that is, the one and only supreme God who alone can say "I AM; besides Me there is no other."

He brought the Israelites out of captivity and led them to Mount Sinai, where He entered into a covenant with them: If they would be His people, He would be their God. If they would be a light to all the nations around them, He would give them a land of milk and honey (see Deuteronomy 6). God wanted to be able to point to Israel and say to all the nations, "Look, there you will see My nature, there you will see who I am." Through these chosen vessels He would end the long drought of loneliness and begin to build a people with whom He could have fellowship. Through their witness He hoped to reach out into the darkened world and say, "Here I am. Come and meet Me."

If the Hebrew people were to be a light to all, they had to know how. What would be the rules? So there on Mount Sinai He gave them the Ten Commandments and all the other rules so carefully laid out in Leviticus and Deuteronomy. If they would follow these rules, they would live long and be a prosperous people—and God would have the demonstration group that would reveal Him to all the rest of mankind.

But continually, Israel fell away from the Lord. They were not the light. They succumbed and became as bad, if not worse, than all the nations before and around them. But God knew they would lay the groundwork of understanding and practice into which He could send His own Son, our Lord Jesus Christ, through whom, once and for all, He would reveal who He is. "Have I been so long with you, and yet you have not come to know Me, Philip? He who has seen Me has seen the Father" (John 14:9).

The plan is still the same. Now it is Christians who are to be the light: "so that you will prove yourselves to be blameless and innocent, children of God above reproach in the midst of a crooked and perverse generation, *among whom you appear as lights in the world*" (Philippians 2:15, emphasis mine). God wants to say to this crooked and perverse generation, "There, in the lives of Christians, I have revealed Myself. Be what they are, and you will know Me."

If that were not burden enough, now God has expanded the plan! Not only does He want to say to all the nations of earth, "Look. See My Christian people. There you will see who I am," He wants us to be His demonstration to all the principalities and powers in the heavenly places, "so that the manifold wisdom of God might now be made known *through the church* to the rulers and the authorities in the heavenly places" (Ephesians 3:10, emphasis mine). Whew! What a task!

We, too, may fail. We do not seem to be much of an example right now. But to the degree that we succeed we will have laid the groundwork for the Second Coming of His Son, through whom He will establish the way of His Father for all upon the earth, "for they will all know Me, from the least of them to the greatest of them" (Jeremiah 31:34). That is the revelation of the mystery of God's plan (see Ephesians 3:9).

Prophets and God's Plan

Where do the prophets fit into this plan? When I was a boy, my mother carefully gave me the "ten commandments and statutes" of gardening. You never plant without first carefully preparing the soil. Plant beans in rows eighteen inches apart, three inches deep and three or four inches apart in the row. Sow corn in hills, three grains to a hill, several inches deep, eighteen inches apart. And so on. I knew what was required of me to garden. But that was not enough. I needed to be able to talk with my parents to know how many rows of this or that to plant, which plants to put in what part of the garden, how they wanted the crops rotated, etc. Similarly, it could not be enough for the Hebrew people to have the Ten Commandments and the statutes of God. They needed to talk with God for the details of decisions, for directions, for fellowship and for worship.

God wanted all His people to listen to Him, to talk back and forth with Him. But the people had seen the fire and smoke upon the mountain. They had seen Moses go up the mountain as normal as any and return with his face glowing like a flame and his hair and beard as white as snow. So "they trembled and stood at a distance. Then they said to Moses, 'Speak to us yourself and we will listen; but let not God speak to us, or we will die'" (Exodus 20:18–19).

Right there was the birth of the office of the prophet.

In Genesis 20:6–7 prophets were mentioned for the first time in all of history. "Then God said to [Abimelech] in the dream, 'Yes, I know that in the integrity of your heart you have done this, and I also kept you from sinning against Me; therefore I did not let you touch [Sarah]. Now therefore, restore [Abraham's] wife, *for he is a prophet, and he will pray for you and you will live*'" (emphasis mine). Note that the very first instance of a prophet's being mentioned in the Bible is in the context of healing: "Abraham prayed to God, and God healed Abimelech and his wife and his maids, so that they bore children" (verse 17). One of the most important functions of prophets even today is to bring God's healing wherever they go. (More about this in chapter 5, "Healing.") But apparently, this was an isolated incident. The prophetic office had not yet been established. It was not until later, in the desert with Moses, that the *raison d'etre* (reason for existence) for prophets became known: to listen to God for the people.

Today, it is still the same. God wants to have fellowship with His children, and He wants us to listen to Him. But some will not and others seemingly cannot learn to hear Him. Prophets are, therefore, needed. But even if all could and would hear, God would still need prophets, because in His wisdom He speaks to His prophets on issues that He does not reveal and discuss with every one of His people, issues such as direction, rebuke, warning, judgment. The office is needed for all those matters that are of more than personal concerns—larger matters for churches, denominations, tribes, states, provinces and nations.

In *Prophets: Pitfalls and Principles,* author Bishop Bill Hamon writes:

> The Holy Spirit whispering the thoughts of Christ within a Christian's heart is obviously God's ideal and divine order for communication. But what an individual has sensed in his or her spirit should be confirmed: God's counsel is that every word needs to be confirmed in the mouth of two or three witnesses (2 Corinthians 13:1). This is a critical role that can be fulfilled by the prophetic office.
>
> . . . Prophets are special to the heart of God. They participate in all of God's plans and performances on planet Earth. They are to prepare the way for the second coming of Christ by bringing revelation knowledge on the Scriptures that must be fulfilled before Christ can return. Thus the restoration of the prophetic ministry and the company of the prophets is the greatest sign of the nearness of Christ's coming.

Until that time prophesied by Jeremiah, a time in which all shall know Him, from the greatest to the least (see Jeremiah 31:34), prophets and their office are necessary—until the Perfect One comes, and prophecy, like everything else imperfect, shall pass away (see 1 Corinthians 13:9–10).

TWO

WARNINGS BEFORE SINS
ARE COMMITTED

ONE OF MY PROFESSORS, Rabbi Dr. Ernst Jacob of Drury University, led a course on Hebrew prophets in which he taught that in Israel a man could not be convicted of intent to do wrong unless he had been warned twice beforehand not to do it. Without that, having been caught in some wrongdoing, he could say, "I did not know." But if he were warned beforehand by at least two witnesses not to act in that wrong way, God's judgment would be just—he knew what he was doing and intended to do wrong. Prophets, then, were first of all God's witnesses, warning His people not to sin before they fell into it.

A major function of prophets in Israel was to call the people back to honoring their covenant with God. That meant the prophets continually thundered about the sins of the people—idolatry, following after the false gods of the time, setting up and worshiping idols, falling into the occult practices of their predecessors in the land (forbidden in Deuteronomy 18:9–14), and all the other breaches of the Ten Commandments common to mankind. Moses said God would raise up prophets for this very purpose:

"The LORD your God will raise up for you a prophet like me from among you [in each generation], from your countrymen, *you shall listen to him.* This is according to all that you asked of the LORD your God in Horeb on the day of the assembly, saying, 'Let me not hear again the voice of the LORD my God, let me not see this great fire anymore, or I will die.'"

DEUTERONOMY 18:15–16, EMPHASIS MINE

But the people did not want to listen to the prophets.

For this is a rebellious people, false sons, sons who refuse to listen to the instruction of the LORD; who say to the seers, "You must not see visions"; and to the prophets, "You must not prophesy to us what is right, speak to us pleasant words, prophesy illusions."

ISAIAH 30:9–10

The people did not want to be reminded of their sins and coming consequences. How true that is today as well, and what a pull it is on today's prophets to be expected always and everywhere to prophesy of blessings coming—and nothing of judgment!

Israel's Prophets Used Signs to Get Attention

The prophets, therefore, did strange things to get the attention of the people. For example, Jeremiah wore an ox yoke as a sign of slavery in captivity.

Hosea's Family Were His Witnesses

Hosea married a prostitute as a witness of the faithfulness of God toward faithless Israel. By her he had three children, each a sign to the disloyal nation. His first son was named Jezreel, a sign of destruction for sin in the valley of Jezreel (see Hosea 1:3–5). His daughter, Lo-ruhamah, "the not pitied," was a sign that God would no longer have compassion (see verse 6). And a second son, Lo-ammi, "not my people," signified that Israel would no longer be God's people and God would no longer be their God (see verse 9). Every time the Israelites saw the three children, they had more than two witnesses reminding them not to sin.

34

Amos Used Language As a Witness

Amos resorted to clever hermeneutics. He came from the Southern Kingdom at God's request, and seeing how resistant the people were, he began crying out, "For three transgressions of Damascus and for four I will not revoke its punishment" (Amos 1:3). The people perked up their ears, for here was a prophet denouncing their enemy, pronouncing the wrath of God for their enemy's sins. Amos continued to castigate Israel's enemies: "For three transgressions of Gaza and for four . . ." (verse 6), then Tyre (see verse 9), then Edom (see verse 11). Damascus lay northeast, Gaza southwest, Tyre northwest and Edom southeast. The prophet was calling down judgment on all nations around them! One can imagine the crowd growing, responding ever more fervently. But Amos was drawing a noose tighter with each pronouncement: "For three transgressions of the sons of Ammon . . ." (verse 13) just north of Edom, then Moab (see Amos 2:1). And then upon the hated sister kingdom: "For three transgressions of Judah and for four . . ." (verse 4). For those who did not catch on, it must have been an increasing celebration! God was going to get *all* of Israel's enemies! Now Amos had their full attention, and he sprang his trap: "For three transgressions of *Israel* and for four . . ." (verse 6, emphasis mine). The people were caught, listening to the stern words of God they had not wanted to hear.

Isaiah Employed Many Witnesses

Isaiah 1 is one of the greatest, most powerful speeches ever given in history. Isaiah pled with the Israelites to do good and to love justice, to return to faithfulness to God and to the covenant. He used many methods to serve as his "two witnesses" to warn God's people before they entered into sin.

The Prophet Himself As Witness

The marketplace of Israel was not like our nice department stores or even a K-Mart or Wal-Mart. Each morning the people brought their wares into the village square on their own backs or the backs of donkeys or camels. They spread out whatever they wanted to sell in as enticing a display as their limited resources enabled. Then they began to call out, like a modern circus barker, trying to attract customers. When prospective buyers came, no one thought of accepting the first price. Each item was haggled over, until both seller and buyer agreed on the price. Markets were noisy, dusty melees of moving, shouting, haggling people.

The marketplace was where the crowds were found, so that is where the prophets came. Picture a high parapet above the milling crowd, visible to all. Upon this prominent place a naked man appears and begins to shout at the heavens and the earth! Of course, no television existed in those days. Here was entertainment for a bored world. Isaiah caught their attention. He used his own appearance as his first witness to Israel to remind them that if they did not cease their sinning, they would go naked into captivity.

The Heavens and the Earth As Witnesses

"Listen, O heavens, and hear, O earth; for the LORD speaks, 'Sons I have reared and brought up, but they have revolted against Me'" (Isaiah 1:2). It was a custom among the Israelites to set up memorials, as when Joshua instructed his army to carry twelve stones out of the Jordan and set them up as a reminder of when the Lord rolled back the waters and the Israelites crossed over safely into the Promised Land (see Joshua 4:4–7). Similarly, Isaiah set up the heavens and the earth as signs to Israel. From then on, every time the inhabitants of the land looked up at the heavens or down at the earth, these familiar sights served as two witnesses, reminding them not to revolt against their Maker, their covenant God!

The Ox and the Donkey As Witnesses

"An ox knows its owner, and a donkey its master's manger, but Israel does not know, My people do not understand" (Isaiah 1:3). In the villages, people lived on the second floors of dwellings. Their animals' stalls were directly below. This was not only convenient for care, but the body heat of the animals helped warm the house above. In the morning, owners opened the stalls. The oxen and donkeys were trained to wend their way, unattended, through the crooked streets to the city gate. Laborers would take to the fields whatever animals were slated for work. Boys would herd the remainder to pastures for the day. In the evening, the laborers and boys would bring the oxen and donkeys back to the gate and release them. Each animal would then wend its way back through the city to its own stall and manger below the dwelling of its owner. The people thought themselves smarter than dumb animals. But Isaiah was saying that when animals are released, they go straight to where they belong, but when God releases you, you do not have the sense of a dumb beast to go where you should!

Now, every morning and evening, when the people saw their animals obediently going where they should, they had more witnesses warning them not to sin.

Bruises and Sickness As Witnesses

> Alas, sinful nation,
> People weighed down with iniquity,
> Offspring of evildoers,
> Sons who act corruptly!
> They have abandoned the LORD,
> They have despised the Holy One of Israel,
> They have turned away from Him.
> Where will you be stricken again,
> As you continue in your rebellion?
> The whole head is sick
> And the whole heart is faint.
> From the sole of the foot even to the head
> There is nothing sound in it,
> Only bruises, welts and raw wounds,
> Not pressed out or bandaged,
> Not softened with oil.
>
> ISAIAH 1:4–6

Israel was, during Isaiah's time, much like the United States or any other advanced nation. The people were prosperous and healthy, feeling confident and good about themselves. But the prophet spoke as though the future were already present, the bruises and unattended sicknesses of captivity already upon them. Now, every time the Israelites looked at their own bodies, especially each time a bandage was required, they had more than two witnesses reminding them of the dire fruits of sin.

The Land As Witness

> Your land is desolate,
> Your cities are burned with fire,
> Your fields—strangers are devouring them in your presence;
> It is desolation, as overthrown by strangers
> The daughter of Zion is left like a shelter in a vineyard,

37

Like a watchman's hut in a cucumber field, like a besieged city.
Unless the LORD of hosts
Had left us a few survivors,
We would be like Sodom,
We would be like Gomorrah.

ISAIAH 1:7–9

None of this had happened when Isaiah spoke. The people were dwelling in a sense of security and freedom from anxiety and worry, prosperous and strong militarily—like so many of our modern First World nations. Again the prophet spoke as though what is inevitable due to sin had already come to pass.

"The daughter of Zion is left like a shelter in a vineyard." When an owner planted a vineyard, he also planted a dense, thorny hedge around it to help keep foxes out. But cunning little foxes sometimes figured ways to dig and worm their way through the hedge. For this reason the Song of Solomon 2:15 says, "Catch the foxes for us, the little foxes that are ruining the vineyards, while our vineyards are in blossom" (other versions say "that eat the tender grapes"). The vineyard manager, therefore, built a hut, above the vines and sheltered from the hot sun by a thatch of leaves. Boys were assigned to watch from the hut. If a fox wormed through, they threw rocks at it to force it to flee. If that did not work, they chased and caught it, threw it out and patched up its entrance. In the fall, after the harvest was concluded, the vineyard turned brown and began to blow away, and the hut was left to crumble in the wind—a picture of total desolation.

Similarly, rodents invaded cucumber fields, so a small box-like structure was built and covered with leaves. Boys, shaded and hidden, were assigned to watch. Their job was to catch or chase away whatever rodents threatened the garden. Likewise, when the crop had been harvested, the field and the hut turned brown and began to blow away—another picture of devastation.

Each fall, when the harvest had been celebrated, the fields became two more witnesses, warning the people not to sin lest desolation and devastation become theirs.

The Past and the Future As Witnesses

"We would be like Sodom . . . [and] like Gomorrah" (Isaiah 1:9). The people knew Isaiah had been speaking of the future. Now he reminded them of the severe judgments of the past. The past and the future served as two more witnesses warning them. From verse 21 on, Isaiah continued to scold and, in the process, to create other witnesses to their consciences.

Modern Prophets Also Should Warn Before Sin

Prophets today retain the same function as these Old Testament prophets. They warn before people sin, hopefully to prevent sin and its results. If the people do not listen, the prophets' warnings ensure that God's judgments are fair and just. A tragedy, and a major reason for this writing, is that so many of today's prophets are unaware of this responsibility—though it truly pertains to their office. The Body of Christ today pressures prophets to speak only things that are positive, that "edify the Church," as though warnings somehow do not edify! Ezekiel 33:6 ought to resound in our ears: "But if the watchman sees the sword coming and does not blow the trumpet and the people are not warned, and a sword comes and takes a person from them, he is taken away in his iniquity; but his blood I will require from the watchman's hand." Prophets must beware: Jesus said that if the people were blind, they would not have sin, but now that they see, their sin remains (see John 9:41). Knowledge increases responsibility, and with it judgment.

On the other hand, some prophets think their job is to blast away at sin too harshly and too much of the time. We need to remember how gracious the prophet Nathan was with King David. He knew what David had done in secret, yet Nathan did not arrogantly or rudely denounce. He allowed David to convict himself, so that David's repentance could be full and true (see 2 Samuel 12:1–15).

It is an awesome thing to be burdened with the task of reproving for sin. Each time a prophet is called upon to do it, such a task ought to call forth the deepest self-repentance and humility of heart the Holy Spirit can muster in us. It takes no genius to see sin. Anyone can do that—it is all around us. It does require the Holy Spirit's wisdom to reprove in such a way that hearers are enabled to receive and repent (though it ought to be recognized that sinners can reject the most lovingly delivered corrections). The prophet's task is to give the Holy Spirit every possible opportunity to win souls to repentance and, thus, to freedom in Christ.

Many prophets do reprove for sin, and some quite rightly and graciously, but let us remember that it is an altogether different matter to warn *before* people sin. One can know sin *has* occurred either with or without gifts of revelation from the Holy Spirit. But only those inspired by the Holy Spirit can know when specific sins are being contemplated and warn beforehand. This is an extremely important function of prophets. God loves us and does not want any of us to fall into sin and trouble.

Years ago, I drove to a church in another city every Tuesday morning to spend the day counseling whomever the church sent to see me. One Tuesday while I was on the way, the Lord spoke to me: *I want you to tell the senior pastor that if he takes the trip he is planning, I will kill him!* I thought of the erring prophet Balaam and how the angel sent from God would have killed him if his donkey had not balked and shied away (see Numbers 22:22–35). I wondered why our gentle Lord would speak so severely, and I pondered and prayed all the rest of the way. I did not want to give that word of prophecy or even believe it could be a true word from God. The associate pastor was my friend. I decided to check the prophecy with him. He said, "John, I believe that's a true word from the Lord, and you should present it to him."

So I went in to see him and hemmed and hawed, trying to think of a way to give such a frightful word. Finally he said, "John, you've got a word for me, haven't you?" I said, "Yes. I believe I've heard the Lord say that if you take the trip you're planning to take, you'll be killed." The pastor did not go on the trip. Later it was revealed that he had been planning to use church money not for a conference as it was intended, but for a hunting and fishing expedition! I remembered then that he had done a few similar things earlier. God had waited patiently for repentance, but the pastor was planning to sin again. Discipline would have been necessary if he had done such a thing one more time. God loved him and did not want to have to lower the boom. Therefore, He spoke to His servant.

But note how carefully the Lord guided me. He led me to check with the associate pastor before giving that word. God observes protocol and expects His prophetic servants to manifest His own nature. In *Prophets: Pitfalls and Principles* Bishop Bill Hamon says that "pastoral compassion and prophetic purpose will sometimes be at odds, causing friction and even conflict within the local church between pastor and prophet. So a willingness to humbly seek God together to determine His desire for the congregation is critical for maintaining unity in the local church leadership."

What if I had remembered the pastor's previous misdoings and correctly deduced the sin he was contemplating, and then had thought it my mandate from God to stand up in the congregation as God's prophet, exposing the pastor before the people? What great unnecessary harm prophetic arrogance can do! In His graciousness, God wanted His pastor to be warned privately so that he might have opportunity to repent. God wanted the warning from the prophet to register in the pastor's heart that God does see and care about what he is doing.

Padre Pio, the famous Catholic saint who bore on his body the marks of the stigmata, was celebrating the Eucharist at the altar. Suddenly, he turned and approached a man at the rail and said (quietly, I think, so that none nearby could overhear), "How dare you think of murdering your wife!" Most likely that man's sinful scheming came to an abrupt end! And the blood of the Eucharist probably meant more that day than it ever had before!

God Knows Our Thoughts and Acts to Prevent Our Sin

How important it is that our loving Father God knows every thought we have! "You understand my thought from afar. . . . Even before there is a word on my tongue, behold, O LORD, You know it all" (Psalm 139:2, 1). Because He knows in advance, He can plan to meet us at every point of need. Most importantly, He can act to prevent us.

How wonderful it would be if every local church had within it at least a few mature prophets, able to keep confidences and act in wisdom and graciousness *before* people fall into trouble! Let us pray that our Lord will give to the Church today what He gave the early Church as documented in Ephesians 4:11–12: "And He gave some as apostles, and some as prophets, and some as evangelists, and some as pastors and teachers, for the equipping of the saints for the work of service, to the building up of the body of Christ."

THREE

CHANGES IN THE OFFICE

DURING THE COURSE of biblical history, the office of prophet has seen many changes. It is not that God's plan for the office changed, or that God changed. Our Lord is the same yesterday, today and forever (see Hebrews 13:8). Rather, as God's people came to know His loving nature more clearly, their relationship with Him changed and the prophetic office altered accordingly. Since the resurrection, our knowledge of Him, and thus the prophet's role, has changed even more dramatically. Consequently, the ways in which prophets have filled the role, as well as the ways in which God's people have responded to prophets, have also changed. It behooves us to know the changes, lest we view all prophets as though they were the same in every age.

The Seer and the Prophet

The Bible itself speaks of changes as the prophetic office evolved and matured. The title of the office itself changed somewhat. The writer of the first book of Samuel states, "Formerly in Israel, when a man went to inquire of God, he used to say, 'Come, and let us go to the seer'; for he who is called a prophet now was formerly called a seer" (1 Samuel 9:9). Shortly thereafter, 1 Samuel 10:5 says that Samuel told Saul he would "meet a group of prophets coming down from the high place," so apparently the title "prophet" had become common enough that the writer thought he should explain why Saul and his servant still thought of Samuel as a seer. Judging from Saul's and his servant's language in 1 Samuel 9:6–8, many of the people still spoke of prophets only as seers or as men of God.

Although Samuel knew he was a prophet of God, in the Lord's courtesy he did not correct Saul; he just said, "I am the seer" (1 Samuel 9:19). But five hundred years before Samuel, God spoke to Abimelech, calling Abraham a prophet. Thus, it is clear that until just before Samuel's time the common people referred to those who rose among them with gifts of insight and knowledge as "seers" or "men of God," though God always viewed them as prophets. As men learned more about the office of prophet and as the Holy Spirit revealed God's purpose in it, they began to adopt His name for it.

There is nothing uncommon about this. In many Psalms, for instance, God the Father, speaking through the psalmists, referred to Jesus Christ as His Son. For example, Psalm 2:7 states: "I will surely tell of the decree of the LORD: He said to Me, 'You are My Son, today I have begotten You.'" But during Jesus' life on earth the people called Him rabbi (Matthew 26:25, 49; Mark 9:5; 11:21; etc.) or teacher (forty-three times in the four Gospels) or prophet (seventeen times in the four Gospels). None knew Him for who He really was as the very Son of God until Father God spoke this reality aloud to Peter, John and James on the Mount of Transfiguration: "This is My beloved Son, with whom I am well-pleased; listen to Him!" (Matthew 17:5). On the Mount of Transfiguration God seeded the truth into the three, but even they, closest to Him, could not believe what they had heard. To be sure, God had already said exactly the same thing when Jesus was baptized (see Matthew 3:17), but none had been able to hear and retain; they still called Him everything else. Even after the resurrection, Cleopas and the other disciples continued to say He "was a prophet mighty in deed and word in the sight of God and all the people" (Luke 24:19).

The point is that until the Holy Spirit revealed, and experience had granted ears to hear and minds that could understand, none knew Jesus for who He is—and the same was true of His prophets. In the beginning the people revered Moses, but at that moment in history they did not know him as a prophet; they recognized him only as their deliverer and leader— and as a seer from God. Later on, they referred to him as one of the great prophets. God always knew him as His prophet, but the people did not.

The same is true today. Many are serving in prophetic ways, actually fulfilling the prophetic office in many of its functions. But all too often, the people do not know enough about the prophetic office to receive prophets for who they are. The Holy Spirit may speak, as God the Father did, even aloud, but people, like the disciples and the Israelites, have not had enough experience and training to be able to hear and retain. It is vital that the Church be informed and prepared to recognize and relate to her prophets for who and what they are. We, the Church, must be made capable of hearing when the Holy Spirit reveals.

Akin to the people of Samuel's day, we recognize the gifted. They called them "seers" and knew little of what they really were. We may call some "prophets," but most of us know little of what a prophet truly is. The evolution of the prophetic office is as much a learning process among the people as it is a call to the Lord's prophets themselves to mature into the fullness of what they are meant to be.

Prophets' Changing Revelations of the Nature of God

The prophetic office is also a growing revelation of God's character, as shown by the evolving messages of the prophets.

A God of Stern Judgment

In the beginning, the prophets were very stern. Samuel hacked King Agag to pieces in front of Saul (see 1 Samuel 15:33). Elijah slew the 450 prophets of Baal and the 400 prophets of Asherah (see 1 Kings 18:19, 40) and called down fire and burned up two companies of fifty soldiers of the king (see 2 Kings 1:10–12). And then, as we discussed in the last chapter, Amos tricked Israel into listening as he began each peroration with "For three transgressions of [name] and for four *I will not revoke its punishment*" (emphasis mine).

A God of Mercy

Later, prophets seem to have mellowed out. They began to speak more of the mercy of God—in Isaiah 40:1–2, for example, and in all the suffering servant passages from there on through Isaiah 66. Was it God who

44

changed? Of course not. We know He is the same yesterday, today and forever. But as the people lived with God through the centuries, God was able gradually to reveal more and more of His nature—which had been His plan from the beginning.

This is not too different from the way we raise our own children. In the beginning years we have to be more stern (though loving and compassionate): "Foolishness is bound up in the heart of a child; the rod of discipline will remove it far from him" (Proverbs 22:15). Discipline has to build into little children walls of self-control, awareness of others, the law of sowing and reaping, etc. We have to shape the minds and hearts of our children. "Train up a child in the way he should go, even when he is old he will not depart from it" (Proverbs 22:6). Later, our way of teaching and training our children changes. As they grow older, we are able to sit down and talk with them, as God did in Isaiah 1:18: "'Come now, and *let us reason together*,' says the LORD, 'Though your sins are as scarlet, they will be white as snow; though they are red like crimson, they will be like wool'" (emphasis mine).

Unfortunately, not enough of the Israelites received His fatherly corrections or matured in character and behavior. They were failing to be the example of light to the nations that God wanted them to be. But the centuries of recorded experience had laid the groundwork for God to allow more of His gentle and forgiving nature to be revealed through His prophets.

God could, therefore, command Hosea to marry a prostitute as a sign of His faithfulness to faithless Israel. He could lead King David, who learned of God's love and mercy firsthand, to proclaim the God "who pardons all your iniquities" (Psalm 103:3) and "is compassionate and gracious, slow to anger and abounding in lovingkindness" (verse 8) and whose "lovingkindness . . . is from everlasting to everlasting on those who fear Him" (verse 17). God could lead Isaiah to transform the Israelites' previous religious and ritualistic way of fasting into an expression of the loving nature of God: "Is this not the fast which I choose, to loosen the bonds of wickedness, to undo the bands of the yoke, and to let the oppressed go free and break every yoke? Is it not to divide your bread with the hungry?" (Isaiah 58:6–7).

Always before, in biblical lands, the gods of every other religion were perceived as capricious, mean-spirited powers who had to be placated or seduced into acting on one's behalf. For example, cult prostitution was used to induce the god to do something good, such as causing fertility. Gods were feared. One never knew when a god might do something harmful, just for his own selfish purposes or perverse pleasures—as even a casual reading of Greek mythology makes obvious. One gave to the gods as much to keep them away as to draw them near.

That mindset held mankind captive for centuries. All the people, even those who became believers in the true God, had imbibed into their minds and hearts apprehensions of gods from their first moments of life. For countless generations, false ways of thinking and reacting toward God had been structured into their minds, largely below the level of consciousness. From all of that hidden and not-so-hidden conditioning, the prophets had to break free, to represent a God not at all the same as the one those centuries of experience had built into the minds of the people.

Here and there, like beams of light piercing through a darkling fog, individual men and women began to break through and see clearly. *But it was the task of the prophets to proclaim the true glory of God's nature until the power of His Word could once and for all smash those strongholds of captivity.*

A God of Goodness

"Forerunning" was a major task of prophets (as we will cover in depth in chapter 16). Perhaps no work was more crucial than that of being forerunners in discovering the true nature of God and breaking the hold of darkness on the minds of the people. Prophets did this by prophesying the goodness of God to the people! Read the psalms of David with this in mind. Study the heart's cry of Job, as he struggled against the mindsets of his wife and his friends, trying to hold to belief in the goodness of God despite all that happened to him. See the picture of God's goodness blossoming from a bud to glorious beauty as you read the Book of Isaiah, chapters 40 to 66. What a work of progressive revelation and celebration!

Still today, it is a major work of prophets to receive fresh revelation of the nature of God and to proclaim it to the people. The prophet must intercede until the boxes into which we have tried to cram God are smashed. Only then can people's hearts and minds be set free, so that our spirits can once again soar freely into the heights of God.

Prophets' Revelations Change Our Preconceptions

"Build thee more stately mansions, Oh my soul," Oliver Wendell Holmes said in his poem, *The Chambered Nautilus*. The nautilus, or snail, builds itself a chamber. As it grows, it must break out of the old and build a new chamber, larger than the first, and then another and another. That is a parable of our evolution with our Lord. We build theologies and concepts and ways of doing things, and then, while the basic must remain intact, we must shatter that which has crystallized and now prevents growth, and build anew—only to do it all over again whenever the Lord calls us higher in Him.

Prophets are those who are most often called upon by God to bring the fresh revelations that shatter the walls of prevention, the hardness of heart that lock us away from change. This was their task in Old Testament days as they thundered against the Baals and other idols, proclaiming God's Word in order to shatter the strongholds of deceit that kept enthralling God's people.

So a primary work of prophets is to bring revelation that shatters the mental idols that hold people back from growing in the Lord. Paula and I experienced a struggle that is a mere small sample of what the Old Testament prophets were up against as the Lord called them to be instruments in His hand to break His people out of the old into the new.

We have been forerunners in the pioneering of inner healing, which is actually simply sanctification and transformation. But particularly in America, a truncated theology has become a powerful stronghold. That belief system holds that when we received Jesus we were made perfect. This is true positionally: "For by one offering He has perfected forever those who are being sanctified" (Hebrews 10:14, NKJV). The proponents of that theology, however, overlook those little words *being sanctified* and claim too much for the conversion experience.

Our conversion certainly accomplishes a great deal: our sins are washed away, our sin natures are dealt a death blow, we are given a new heart and a new spirit and the Holy Spirit, and we are restored to relationship with Father God and with each other in the Church. *But being born anew does not finish the work of transforming our nature—it begins it!* Holders of this incomplete theology want to believe simply that they are totally new creatures and that being born anew is all God requires of them for their salvation. They are fond of quoting, "If anyone is in Christ, he is a new creature; the old things passed away; behold, new things have come" (2 Corinthians 5:17). But they confuse conversion and salvation.

The word *salvation* comes from a root that means "healing," or "being healed into wholeness." Salvation is a long process. Peter wrote of this in the first chapter of 1 Peter. While telling the Christians that they would be tested in the fires of trials, he spoke of "a salvation ready to be revealed in the last time" (verse 5) and of "obtaining as the outcome of your faith the salvation of your souls" (verse 9). These people had already been converted, but here Peter spoke of their salvation as something they were yet to receive through the process of maturation in suffering. In addition, Paul said to "work out your salvation with fear and trembling" (Philippians 2:12). Believers in this theology want to escape the process of sanctification and transformation through tough experiences by claiming they have already arrived, though their lives still manifest the brokenness and sinfulness of their hearts.

This truncated belief system became a corporate mental stronghold, wielded by powers of darkness, to keep Christians from purifying our hearts of sinful practices that continually spring up in our lives (see Hebrews 12:15). Therefore, anyone who proclaimed the gospel of change in the inner heart faced prophetic warfare. People did not want to be told that evil practices and unforgiveness remained in their hearts. But Scripture has this warning: "He who separates himself seeks his own desire, he quarrels against all sound wisdom" (Proverbs 18:1). The Amplified Version says, "He who willfully separates and estranges himself [from God and man] seeks his own desire and pretext to break out against all wise and sound judgment." The powers of darkness were only too happy to use that stronghold of incorrect theology to cause Christians to persecute those of us who teach that after our conversion there are still factors in the heart that must be dealt with.

Paula and I were called heretical, Jungian psychologists, occult, unscriptural—anything that could serve to justify rejecting inner healing in order to flee from facing their broken hearts. We were battling against powers of darkness that were holding men's minds captive (see 2 Timothy 2:26).

I am thankful that more and more Christians are beginning to recognize the validity of and need for inner healing. They have begun to receive sanctification and transformation and minister it to others. The gospel of healing for the inner man is now exploding into the entire Body of Christ. God used the prophetic work of a few others and ourselves to bring revelation and to shatter mental strongholds that were holding back many from growing in the Lord. And God used this difficult process of proclaiming and suffering to write many things onto the hearts of us who pioneered the field.

The Change Wrought by Prayer

While wrestling against the stronghold of truncated theology, we discovered that such principalities and their corporate mental strongholds are not defeated by words alone; they require persistent, powerful prayer. Not much is said in Scripture about prophets and intercessory prayer, but anyone with even a modicum of experience in these matters knows prophets had to have been deeply involved in intercession.

Ezekiel Sets the Stage

In Ezekiel 4, we see the great change that forever altered the prophetic office. God commanded Ezekiel to set up a diorama, a small clay city representing Jerusalem. He was to portray God's siege against Israel for its sins. The Lord told him, "This is a sign to the house of Israel" (verse 3). Then came the dramatic change: "As for you, lie down on your left side and *lay the iniquity of the house of Israel on it; you shall bear their iniquity for the number of days that you lie on it*" (verse 4, emphasis mine). *This is the first time in all of history that God laid the iniquity of a people on one man!* This is what would be spoken of in the New Testament as "burden-bearing." "Bear one another's burdens, and thereby fulfill the law of Christ" (Galatians 6:2).

Burden-bearing is a part of intercession. Intercession is distinct from every other kind of prayer in that it always begins in the heart of God. It is God brooding over His creation as at the beginning, finding what has become null and void or what needs His creative or healing touch. Because we have free will, God seeks invitation, so He searches for someone who will respond in prayer and invite Him to do what He wants to accomplish.

Sometimes our part is quite detached. We simply hear God's heart and pray, and God acts. (See chapter 7, "Transforming Prayer for the Nations," in our book *Healing the Nations*, or any of the passages on intercession in Cindy Jacobs' book *The Voice of God*.)

At other times, we are involved in God's answer. Burden-bearing occurs when our Lord sees someone in trouble and uses His servants to identify with the spirit and heart and mind of the person. He then draws much of the person's burden to Himself, setting the person free. In His wisdom, He will not take the entire burden to Himself at one time: "For each one will bear his own load" (Galatians 6:5). He draws enough of the other's trouble to Himself to restore that person's ability to think clearly and to pray on his or her own.

Burden-bearers share with Christ as He does this. They empathize. God unites their spirits in love with those to whom He is ministering, so that they feel in their own hearts what hurting ones are experiencing and sense in their own minds what they may be thinking. It is not that they are mind reading or that they feel others' physical pain or sickness. Rather, identification in love enables them to experience what others are feeling *emotionally*, which also enables them to sense fairly accurately what others are thinking in their suffering.

Burden-bearing is not our work. It is the work of the Lord Jesus Christ. We are given the privilege of sharing His sufferings as He ministers (see Philippians 3:10). Burden-bearing is a major work of intercessors, commanded by God: "Bear one another's burdens" (Galatians 6:2).

And Ezekiel was the one called upon to be the forerunner, the pioneer who would lay down the entire plan of burden-bearing for the rest to follow, the track on which our freight trains could ride! The work of burden-bearing began right there in Ezekiel 4:4! This became the groundwork onto which the Lord Jesus would come as the Christ. God called Ezekiel "son of man" (Ezekiel 4:1). Jesus called Himself "the Son of Man." Jesus traveled purposefully the path laid down by Ezekiel.

> Yet it pleased the LORD to bruise Him;
> He has put Him to grief.
> When You make His soul an offering for sin,
> He shall see His seed, He shall prolong His days,
> And the pleasure of the LORD shall prosper in His hand.
> He shall see the labor of His soul, and be satisfied.
> By His knowledge My righteous Servant shall justify many.
> *For He shall bear their iniquities.*
>
> ISAIAH 53:10–11, NKJV, EMPHASIS MINE

Every Prophet Has This Calling

Since the obedience of Ezekiel, the office of the prophet has been dramatically altered. Now, every prophet's calling includes becoming a burden-bearer. Few prophets, fewer Christians and almost none of the general public know that as yet. "My people are destroyed for lack of knowledge" (Hosea 4:6).

Burden-bearing in intercessory prayer is perhaps the most important work of today's New Testament prophets. There are many true prophets who have never spoken a word from God. Most of any prophet's work is meant to be hidden, a burden-bearing in his or her own heart as the Lord moves to set His children free.

Prophets are to hear God's calling to intercede or bear burdens for a person, people, groups, tribes and nations, for situations and events, nature and natural disasters, etc. Note: They are not to do all the praying and bearing. Their task is to inquire of God. If He so orders, they are to call others into the work.

At that point, the prophet must inquire of the Lord: "Who is to join in prayer?" "How many?" "When?" "For how long?" "Specifically how?" etc. To me, this a primary way—if not *the* primary way—prophets are to fulfill their calling to edify the Church.

Hebrews 7:25 says, "He always lives to make intercession." Jesus is always interceding. If He were to cease, like the beginning of the television program "Mission Impossible," our world would self-destruct in a few seconds! Jesus lives in our hearts. What is He doing in there? He is interceding for us and for others. The natural life breath of every Christian is intercession and burden-bearing. There is perhaps no more crucial work for prophets in our day—or any day—than to hear God's call and direction for intercession, and to lead the Body of Christ in that work.

Tragically, many prophets do not even know what intercessory prayer actually is, much less burden-bearing, though that is the major work of every prophet since that day when God laid the iniquity of the house of Israel upon Ezekiel! How we pray that His prophets will grow beyond the giving of personal words—and every other prophetic task, important as they may be—into the primary reason for our existence!

Changes Brought by the Resurrection

Before we leave the subject of changes in the office, we need to address some of the changes that occurred when Jesus' death and resurrection changed everything on the face of the globe.

Prophets No Longer Stand Alone

Most of the time, prophets in the Old Testament appeared to be loners, standing against other prophets, priests and kings. Sometimes, however, they traveled in companies. Samuel told the soon-to-be-king Saul that

> "you will meet a group of prophets coming down from the high place with harp, tambourine, flute, and a lyre before them, and they will be prophesying. Then the Spirit of the LORD will come upon you mightily, and you shall prophesy with them and be changed into another man."
>
> 1 SAMUEL 10:5–6

Obadiah hid a hundred prophets from the wrath of Jezebel, the sorceress (see 1 Kings 18:4). And Elijah and Elisha appear to have been a part of such companies, as 2 Kings 2:3 seems to indicate when the sons of the prophets at Bethel said to Elisha, "Do you know that the LORD will take away your master from over you today?" And Elisha answered, "Yes, I know; be still."

But none of the prophets whose writings appear in the Bible are actually recorded as being among such companies. They seem for the most part to have been alone, often somewhere in the wilderness.

New Testament prophets are never again to be that alone. They are to serve *within* the Church, encompassed and supported by the Body. Sometimes they must stand against and rebuke, but now everything they say and do is to be tempered by the nature of the Lord Jesus Christ and by their respect for the company that surrounds them. They are to check what they hear with others before speaking.

Prophets No Longer Speak Without "Tempered" Words

Speaking truth in Old Testament times meant that one stated, without fleshly change and corruption, exactly what God had commanded one to say. That still pertains to the office. But now, Jesus has come and says, "I am the way, and the truth, and the life" (John 14:6). Old Testament prophets could speak in ways that seem to our Western culture to be rough and impolite. For example, when Elijah came to the widow of Zarephath, who said she had only a handful of flour left in the bowl, he said to her, "Make me a little bread cake from it first" (1 Kings 17:13)!

But in the New Testament experience, every word must be delivered within the nature of the Lord Jesus or, no matter how accurate it may be, it is no longer valid.

Prophets No Longer Bear Persecution Alone

Apparently, Old Testament prophets bore reproach and persecution alone. Today, a prophet fails his job if he thinks to play the role of a lone martyr. He is to share with a company of intercessors, who help to carry the burden with him.

Prophets No Longer Call People Back

Along with prophesying the coming of the Messiah, the Old Testament prophet's task was to call the people *back* to the standard of the laws and their covenant with God. Today's prophets call the people *forward* into whatever new thing God is directing.

Prophets No Longer Have an Old Base of Repentance

Then, as now, prophets call to repentance. But today, repentance has a different base. Repentance then was for breaking God's laws. That is still so today. But now repentance is much more for grieving the Holy Spirit, for hurting the heart of the One who loves us so much that He died for us. And even though Old Testament people possessed a tribal consciousness, repentance then was much more individual. Today, as Christians we are members of one Body. "And if one member suffers, all the members suffer with it; if one member is honored, all the members rejoice with it" (1 Corinthians 12:26). That takes repentance to a new level of corporate awareness, unknown in those days.

Prophets No Longer Use Archaic Methods

Old Testament prophets spoke by signs that today would land a prophet in an insane asylum or in jail for indecent exposure! In our generation a few intrepid souls have walked about the country bearing huge crosses as signs. But modern prophets have found other methods to spread the word. For example, when Dutch Sheets was hit with great sobbing grief and told by God to call the Church to pray fervently for God's man to be elected as our next American president, he used the Internet and e-mail—something unavailable to previous prophets up until this last decade.

Prophets No Longer Face Limits in Intimacy with God

Now prophets also call God's people into an intimacy with God that was previously unavailable. Jesus' death rent the veil and opened the way for every man into the heart of God, so New Testament believers have an opportunity for an intimacy with God that God's people in the Old Testament never dreamed of.

The Greatest Change of All

But the greatest change of all remains that of Ezekiel 4:4. Oh, that every prophet would hear the call and offer himself or herself to God as a living sacrifice, holy and acceptable, which is our reasonable or spiritual service of worship (Romans 12:1)! Oh, that every prophet today would be willing to bear burdens for the Lord at any hour of the day or night, being on call to intercede whenever God desires!

PART 2

FUNCTIONS
OF THE
PROPHETIC
OFFICE

FOUR

BLESSING

GIVING PROPHETIC WORDS of blessing to God's people is one of the most pleasant functions in the life of a prophet. Prophets bless people by declaring what God has done in people's lives, by pronouncing His present blessings and by predicting future blessings. Many prophets today who give personal words regard blessing as their primary task.

Many years ago a friend and prophet, Dick Mills, pronounced to our ministry that God would give us land beside water, and he handed us a list of Scriptures about water and blessing. A few years later, at a ridiculously low price, Elijah House obtained our present property—and 1,350 feet of it front the Spokane River! Hundreds of other people have been similarly blessed by Dick Mills' prophecies. And I suppose most of us have heard of countless other instances of modern-day prophets foretelling great blessings that came to pass. What a joy these instances are to us prophets! We love to share in people's joy and celebration and to see how God fulfills His words through us.

What a joy it must have been to the prophets who foretold the great blessings of the coming of our Lord Jesus Christ! So many times they had to pronounce warnings of doom and gloom. How refreshing it must have been to prophesy the other side!

Imagine the joy of prophets like Isaiah when, in heaven centuries later, they were told how wondrously their prophecies were fulfilled! Or imagine their delight at actually watching from the portals of heaven as their prophecies came true! I think God would have allowed them to watch, as Hebrews 12:1 seems to me to indicate. Some think not, for various theological and other reasons. But whichever the case, imagine their joy when the Messiah proved to be so much more than anyone had understood, and when He fulfilled all that their words had intimated with such glory and beauty.

Today's prophets rejoice when we are allowed to share with our fellow humans that God is about to do something wonderfully loving for them. But we rejoice even more because each time we give such words of coming blessings, we know our loving Father is taking the initiative to come and bless His children. Prophets share our Father's joy in blessing those He loves. We seldom, if ever, know if what we predict is eternally determined or if it is conditional, but we rejoice each time in the Father's intent.

Conditional and Unconditional Prophecies of Blessing

Many times I have seen the new house God will provide or the buildings of the college a person will attend or the one who will become the friend a person needs—whatever blessing God wants to bring into someone's life. Dangers, of course, are inherent in such gifting. We who give such words often worry about raising false hopes. We think, *What if it does not happen?* There are always contingencies.

The prophecy may be unconditional. Sometimes what God speaks through prophets is utterly determined. Those prophecies do not depend on *our* faith or behavior at all. God has said He will do it, and that's that. The best examples of these predetermined blessings are the prophecies of the coming of Christ. Once God spoke His promises of blessing in the coming Messiah, history would go no other way. *Such prophecies depend solely on God's faithfulness.*

Other words are conditional, such as Jonah's prediction that Nineveh would be destroyed. *Conditional prophecies depend much more upon our repentance and prayers.* God is always faithful, but it is as simple as when

58

our children do something wrong: We tell them we will punish them if they are disobedient. So we predict a dire future. But we do not want to have to punish them. Their sincerity in repentance gladly enables us to mitigate or rescind the discipline altogether. Neither does our loving heavenly Father want to have to fulfill dire words given through His prophets: "Perhaps they will listen and everyone will turn from his evil way, that I may repent of the calamity which I am planning to do to them because of the evil of their deeds" (Jeremiah 26:3).

Sometimes people think that once a prophecy is said, it is determined and *will* happen. So, they think, why pray? But that is not always true for dire predictions, nor for blessings. Few are unconditional. Most are conditional upon our responses. Unfortunately, *many times what God intends when He speaks through His prophets is aborted because His people do not respond in faith and obedience*. I am sure the urgency in my heart as I write is more than shared in the hearts of God's prophets throughout the Body of Christ. We grieve when the good things God prophesies through us do not happen or happen in lesser degree than God intended. And we grieve when the bad things still happen because people do not repent.

A person's sins, or unfaith, may block a blessing God wants to give him or her. For example, someone may impetuously marry the wrong person before the spouse of the vision could arrive, or a couple might buy a house different from the one God designed as their blessing. I can still see in my mind's eye the vision the Lord gave me of the wonderful house He wanted some dear friends of ours to have—but before they found it, they purchased and moved into another, and then saw the wonderful house God would have given them! Sometimes God's first and best will is not done because we interfere. If His will were always done, our Lord would not have commanded us to pray, "Thy will be done on earth as it is in heaven."

Perhaps the Old Testament prophets did not know that their messianic prophecies were absolutely unconditional. Certainly they did not know how much more than a Messiah they were predicting. Though their prophecies intimated it, no one knew Jesus would be the very Son of God for the salvation of the whole world. They must have sensed something of the eternal greater consequences of what they were predicting. But none could or did grasp the fullness of their prophecies. Nevertheless, what a joy it must have been to proclaim the wonderful words of love and blessing they knew their God would do! Prophets today feel that same joy whenever God allows us to foretell blessings He wants to bring to His children.

Prophecies of Blessing in Marriage

Many times single people have come to Paula and me wanting prayer, and by vision God has shown us their spouses. Actress Anita Bryant came to us for help. Not by choice, she had become embroiled in warfare against allowing homosexuals to teach in the Dade County school system in Florida. She was undergoing immense persecution. Her husband divorced her. Hurting, she came to us. The Lord brought some healing to her as we prayed. Then, I am sure He wanted to give her hope, so He gave me a vision of the man whom He would bring to be her husband. Because it would not have been wise, I did not tell her what he looked like, but I did tell her that I had seen him and God would bring the two together. After she left, I described him to Paula. About a year following our prayer, Anita reacquainted with Charlie Dry, a childhood sweetheart, and married him. Paula and I went to Branson, Missouri, where at that time Anita had her own theater and show. Charlie appeared exactly as I had seen him!

It has been our joy to do this many times. I saw our son Loren's wife, Beth, five years before he did. I saw Mark's wife, Maureen, ten years before. And God gave me a vision of our Andrea's Randy two years before she met him. Not only was it a joy eventually to see that our children's spouses were exactly as I had seen, but it was an immense blessing to have been praying for them during those years before our children met them. All three marriages have been greatly blessed.

Think what a blessing it would be if God were to place prophets gifted in this way in local churches. What if they could see and, without revealing descriptions, call the members of the church to pray that God's will be done in marriages? How many truly blessed marriages might result? Anyone can, of course, and should pray for his or her children's prospective spouses without prophetic visions. But what a witness and encouragement to faith if such visions were recorded and kept confidential until the wedding ceremony was complete! How encouraging it would be if the prophet's words pronounced long before were read at the wedding reception! Exactly that happened in New Zealand. I saw a young man's bride-to-be and gave a prophecy concerning the two, which the family wrote down. At their wedding reception the father of the groom read the prophecy, and all were blessed as they saw all that had been prophesied unfolding before their eyes.

Prophecies of Blessing with Fertility

The first instance of the mention of a prophet as a prophet concerns interceding on behalf of a couple for the blessing of children. "Abraham prayed to God, and God healed Abimelech and his wife and his maids, so that they bore children" (Genesis 20:17).

Paula and I also have been gifted to pray blessings of fertility upon couples unable to conceive. I remember when the daughter of one of our dearest friends plopped herself down beside me in a house where a group was meeting. She had heard that sometimes God miraculously opens wombs when we pray. "Now, John," she said, "let's do it. Pray for me." I felt the power of her faith. In a couple of months she was pregnant. I could have said, "Go in peace. Your faith has made you whole." What a blessing it is when faith meets faith: "If two of you agree on earth about anything that they may ask, it shall be done for them by My Father who is in heaven" (Matthew 18:19). In this instance, I did not have a prophecy for this woman and her husband, but God had me stand in the office of prophet and intercede for this couple. It is just as much a joy every time we see her and her child as it would have been had I given a word of prophecy for them.

Phyllis, a member of our staff at Elijah House, had the same problem. After four years of futilely trying to conceive, she asked us to pray. She was soon pregnant. Another staff member, Vickie Freligh, and I both had premonitions of trouble at delivery time. We did not want to worry Phyllis, as anxiety itself might have added to whatever the problem was, so we did not tell her. Instead, we told a few prayer warriors who could keep confidentiality. Sure enough, when she went into labor, trouble started. The baby's heart began to fail, but the doctors were alert and quickly solved the problem. The baby was safely delivered. What a joy it was to us to be part of God's desire to bless Phyllis and her husband!

We had a neighbor whose sperm count was supposedly very low. That did not bother God. He told us to pray. Now this man and his wife have two beautiful children. How thankful we are to be able to function in that part of a prophet's task, to pronounce and pray for the blessings God wants to bring!

Prophets and the Church

The Church needs to know how to receive prophets' words of blessing.

Receiving Words of Blessing

Where do we begin?

First, an individual who is given a word of blessing should receive the word in faith: "Lord, I hope this is true. I choose to believe and accept it. Thank You, Lord."

Second, prepare the heart. That means to say as David did, "Search me, O God, and know my heart; try me and know my anxious thoughts; and see if there be any hurtful way in me, and lead me in the everlasting way" (Psalm 139:23–24). We could add: "God, search out any blocking attitude or any sinful condition." You may have heard it said, "Whenever God promises something good is coming, *duck!*" God is most likely going to humble and prepare your heart first. If you humble yourself, the preparation for blessing will be much easier and less hurtful.

Third, tell a few trusted friends who can help pray until the blessing unfolds. Tell *only* a few. A wise old saying admonishes, "Do not talk away your good fortune." Sometimes the unbelief in people to whom you talk can block blessings. Jesus, when He raised the official's daughter from the dead, did not allow anyone to enter with Him except Peter, John and James and the girl's father and mother (see Luke 8:51). He knew the people's unbelief could block healing, for "they began laughing at Him, knowing that she had died" (verse 53). Furthermore, unwise sharing can inform demonic hosts that can block blessings, since Satan certainly wants to do all he can to prevent us from receiving good things from our Lord.

Sometimes prophetic blessings do not come because we fail to pray consistently until the blessing comes to pass. Daniel prayed, seemingly fruitlessly, for many days. Finally, an angel told him that he had been unable to come because "the prince of the kingdom of Persia was withstanding me for twenty-one days" (Daniel 10:13). Daniel's consistent prayers enabled the archangel Michael to come and help Gabriel move past the devil's blocking spirit. *Don't leave your "angel" stuck halfway. Pray your prophesied blessings all the way to fruition.*

Hospitality for Prophets

People in Bible times knew God would bless through His prophets. The people may not have wanted to be around when God spoke warnings and scolded through His prophets publicly, but they always wanted His prophets to be with them privately, in their homes. There were two major reasons for this. First, they knew this: "He who receives a prophet in the name of a prophet shall receive a prophet's reward" (Matthew 10:41). They knew if they did anything good for a prophet, the prophet became duty-bound to bless them. Second, Galatians 6:7 says what all had known for centuries: "Whatever a man sows, this he will also reap." The people knew if they did a good deed they would reap good from it. Thus, they fully understood what Jesus meant when He said, "Do not store up for yourselves treasures on earth, where moth and rust destroy, and where thieves break in and steal. But store up for yourselves treasures in heaven, where neither moth nor rust destroys, and where thieves do not break in or steal" (Matthew 6:19–20). They knew the only way to lay up treasures that would not perish was to do good deeds. God's laws are incorruptible and infallible. If they helped a man of God, they knew they would receive their reward (Matthew 10:42).

For this reason, it was especially important in biblical countries to practice hospitality. The people believed that anytime they gave hospitality to a guest they were procuring blessings from God. Therefore, they would not allow a stranger to remain unhoused in the streets. Job protested that he never allowed a stranger to remain in the streets (see Job 31:32), and for that reason he was doubly disturbed. He was suffering terribly, which was bad enough, but where was the reward God promised? Of course, the Lord proved faithful, and in the end all was restored to Job.

The Israelites constrained people to stay with them in order to heap up reward. After Cleopas and the other disciple walked to Emmaus with Jesus, He "acted as though He were going farther. But they urged Him [KJV says they "constrained him"], saying, 'Stay with us, for it is getting toward evening'" (Luke 24:28–29). Not yet knowing who He was, they were following the usual custom. They invited, even urged, Him to be their guest so as to heap up reward.

This is what is also behind this advice: "Do not neglect to show hospitality to strangers, for by this some have entertained angels without knowing it" (Hebrews 13:2). Abraham did this in the truest sense; he entertained the Lord and two of His angels (see Genesis 18), though he rather quickly realized it was the Lord and the angels. The word *angel* means "messenger." The writer of Hebrews probably meant not only heavenly angels, but also those human messengers who are men of God.

Receiving the Prophet's Reward

In the biblical countries there were three kinds of beggars. The first was a real beggar. He came in rags, begging a handout. One gave to him to find reward with God.

The second kind of beggar was not a beggar at all. He might even have been wealthy, as blind Bartimaeus most likely was (see Mark 10:46), since he was honored in Mark's story by his name and his father's name, something Mark would not have done if Bartimaeus had been a lowly beggar. In that country, if people contracted a crippling disease or had an affliction that doctors could not heal, they became beggars. If someone gave something to one of these beggars, he probably would give it to a real beggar or put it into the collection plate. Such beggars were only there to humiliate themselves so that God would regard their lowly estate and their humble hearts and send someone to heal them.

This is why Bartimaeus would not be silent and cried out all the more loudly, "Jesus, Son of David, have mercy on me!" (verses 47–48). He had waited there no telling how long for a holy man to come by. No one was going to be allowed to deny him! Likewise, if we want a blessing from God or from His prophets, we have to charge past human concerns, undeterred by what other people think of us.

The third kind of beggar was also not a beggar at all. He was a holy man, or a prophet. One hoped beyond hope that such a man would grace his home with his presence, because the holy man, or prophet, was bound by duty to place blessings upon him and his house. Abraham's hospitality to the Lord and His two angels resulted in the birth of a son to infertile Sarah. It was not a holy man but the Ark of God that resided for a while in the house of Obed-Edom, but the principle is the same: "And the LORD blessed Obed-Edom and all his household" (2 Samuel 6:11). Giving hospitality brought God's blessings. The people knew this principle and prayed that a holy man might come and stay with them. Again, this may have been one of the meanings of the advice not to neglect hospitality because one might entertain an "angel," a human messenger of God, unawares. This is also why Jesus sent His disciples out without provisions and extra clothing.

The Shunammite woman, though not a Hebrew, also knew this about God's prophets. For this reason, she said to her husband that she perceived the man who often came by was a prophet. "Please, let us make a little walled upper chamber and let us set a bed for him there, and a table and a chair and a lampstand; and it shall be, when he comes to us, that he can turn in there" (2 Kings 4:10). They did, and Elisha stayed there. That meant he should bless her, so he asked his servant Gehazi what this woman needed, and Gehazi answered, "Truly, she has no son, and her husband is old" (verse 14). Gehazi called her and when she came, Elisha told her, "At this season next year you will embrace a son" (verse 16). Sure enough, she did! The Shunammite woman had entertained a messenger of God, and she received a prophet's reward.

Let's see how this works today as we explore the prophet's right response to overtures from the Body.

Jesus' Instructions on Hospitality

This habit of practicing hospitality in hopes of receiving reward was what lay behind Jesus' instructions when He sent His disciples out into the towns and villages:

> "Do not acquire gold, or silver, or copper for your money belts, or a bag for your journey, or even two coats, or sandals, or a staff; for the worker is worthy of his support."
>
> MATTHEW 10:9–10

Be Dependent upon the People

Jesus was making His disciples totally dependent on the people. As people gave to the disciples, God would reward the people with blessings. The Lord still wants His servants to operate this same way. We are not, of course, to travel without proper changes of clothing—today, that would appear to be presumptive and manipulative. But the principle is still true that

65

God's servants are to make themselves dependent upon the generosity of His people so that they may receive a reward. If a modern prophet demands money, especially exorbitant sums, before he will come to speak or prophesy, that man or woman is not a true prophet of God. In our Elijah House ministry our staff only asks that travel, room and board be covered. We have never stipulated a fee. We must charge for our schools when people come to us to learn, but when we go out to teach we serve freely and receive whatever our hosts want to give. This is God's way. The people are blessed as they give to God's servants. They cannot lose their reward.

On the other hand, there are those church leaders who take up offerings and declare, "All the money will be given to our speaker." And then, they withhold much of it for their church, or worse, for themselves! Paula and I have talked with many traveling teachers and prophets who have struggled to forgive leaders like these. We grieve for such leaders, as they do not know that they have forfeited the blessings God would have provided. Nor do they understand that they have just committed the same sins that Ananias and Sapphira did in Acts 5. They have lied to the Holy Spirit and have withheld funds promised to God for His servants. It is only by the grace of God that they do not suffer the same fate as Ananias and Sapphira. This is another excellent example of how sin can prevent God from giving blessings through His prophets.

Bless the Giver of Hospitality

Later on, when Jesus sent out the seventy disciples, He said:

> "Whatever house you enter, first say, 'Peace be to this house.'
> And if a man of peace is there, your peace will rest upon him; but if not, it will return to you. *Stay in that house*, eating and drinking what they give you; for the laborer is worthy of his wages. *Do not keep moving from house to house."*
>
> LUKE 10:5–7, EMPHASES MINE

It is interesting to note that Jesus expected His disciples to have sufficient discernment to know if their blessing was being received or rejected, even without words! Most of us who are prophets understand this by experience. We feel when the flow of God's Spirit comes onto a person. We likewise sense when God's Spirit runs up against blocks in a

66

person's heart, even if he cordially greets us and extends smiles and a hand of friendship. The Lord wanted to honor those servants in each village who He knew were worthy of His blessing. He still does today.

Do Not Stay Where God Is No Longer Calling

What follows in Jesus' admonishments has a rather comical, though very practical, base. "Do not keep moving from house to house." Remember that people wanted to give hospitality in order to heap up rewards. They would constrain guests to stay with them. If Jesus had not commanded this, the disciples could have succumbed to the urging of people to move from house to house within one village in order to honor and bless each one. If that had happened, God's work would have been waylaid. For example, the disciple might stay a few days with his first host until he accomplished the Lord's purposes in the village. Then, as he prepares to leave, his host might ask, "Which way do you plan to go?"

"I thought I'd go south."

"I hear there are robbers in the pass. You'd better stay another day."

So the disciple stays another day. The next morning as he is preparing to leave, his host says, "You're still planning to go south?"

"Yes."

"There's a major storm coming. Storms always hit worst at the pass. You'd better wait another day."

So he stays another day. Finally he struggles free from his host. Now the nextdoor neighbor comes and says, "You gave my neighbor opportunity to reap rewards from God. It's not fair if you don't stay with me, too."

So he stays for a while with the second host. And when he is ready to leave, the second host comes up with reasons for him to stay. So the disciple stays longer. And then the third man comes, and the fourth, and so on. The disciples would never have been able to leave the first village! Jesus did not want them to fall into that cycle. God's Kingdom business was too urgent for that.

The lesson for us today is that we must not let fleshly urgency or importunity sway us to minister or to stay where God is no longer calling. How hard this is, especially when those who pull on us are longtime friends! How easy it is to return where we know we are honored and the anointing is great! So often in a prophet's ministry he meets skepticism and scoffing. How comforting it is to return to the warm embrace and faith of friends!

67

You will recall how often Paul talked about wanting to return to see his friends. But remember also how he said, "We night and day keep praying most earnestly that we may see your face" (1 Thessalonians 3:10). Paul would not return just because he and they wanted him to come. He prayed fervently because he would only go where God called him.

Today's prophets wrestle with the same feelings Paul did. The welcome and importunity of our friends can become a powerful temptation to us who find the prophetic walk so lonely at times. For this reason, our staff at Elijah House carefully prays over every invitation for our teachers. We want to go only where the Lord sends. It is especially sorely tempting when those who invite have proved to be generous givers, and funds are running low in the organization! Serving Him requires daily death to our own desires and wishes.

But what joys follow obedience! Many prophets could testify to wonders of blessing that happened when we obeyed against our will and did not stay where God was no longer calling, but went instead where we thought nothing good could happen.

Abide Where God Does Call

The other side of Jesus' command was to "stay in the house" that receives us. Sometimes we do not want to remain, slugging it out in seemingly fruitless ministry. But the Lord wants us to bloom where we are planted. He did not call us to succeed but to obey. We never know when He is planting seeds that will remain and bear great fruit later. Often when I was in the pastorate, I would feel that some in the congregation had received nothing of the Gospel I tried to bring, only to discover years later that those seeds had burrowed deeply and grew to bear much fruit. Out of such seed came a man who I thought would never amount to anything, and yet he became a great pastor and evangelist! And there was another who became the leader of a powerful prayer group. How thankful I am that I stayed where God called me!

Bestowing Blessings Can Bring Persecution

Bestowing God's blessings is not always fun and easy. In fact, probably more times than not it is fraught with grief and persecution. The Book of

Ecclesiasticus in the Apocrypha is not canonical Scripture, but sometimes it offers wisdom. Sirach (Ecclesiasticus) 2:1–6 says:

> My child, when you come to serve the Lord, prepare yourself for testing. Set your heart right and be steadfast, and do not be impetuous in time of calamity. Cling to Him and do not depart, so that *your last days may be prosperous* [another version says *"you will be honored only at the end of your life"*]. Accept whatever befalls you, and in times of humiliation be patient. For gold is tested in the fire, and those found acceptable, in the furnace of humiliation. Trust in Him, and he will help you; make your ways straight, and hope in Him.

EMPHASIS MINE

Prophets are tested in the fire both when they bring warnings of judgment and when they try to bring God's blessings. As He said to Ezekiel, God has sent us to a rebellious people (Ezekiel 2:3). Prophets must remember that it is not the receipt of blessings that they are called to enjoy, but the giving of them. And by following God's calling in our lives, we will ourselves be blessed. It remains one of the greatest joys of a prophet's life to be one through whom God brings blessings to His people.

Be Careful What You Prophesy

I cannot leave the subject of blessings without relating something that still tickles my funny bone whenever I think of it. Paula and I were teaching in California. We stayed in the home of some friends. They had a daughter, sixteen, and a son, eleven, and did not want any more children. The husband was planning to retire as soon as the nest was empty. The morning we were leaving I said to the wife, "You've done a Shunammite's ministry; therefore you get a Shunammite's reward." I knew the Lord would reward her, but not necessarily with an actual baby, as He gave the Shunammite woman. She said, "What's that?"

So I explained it and said, "This time next year you shall embrace a son." I was only joking. I did not really mean it as a prophecy of exactly that. I had no idea God, or anybody, would take that seriously. A few months later I received an irate letter from her husband. I wrote back and said, "Hey, buddy, I did not do it. You did it!" Sure enough, the next spring she did embrace a son! Strange thing, we have never been invited to visit there again.

FIVE

HEALING

HEALING IS ANOTHER FUNCTION prophets enjoy performing. It is one of a prophet's greatest joys to be the Lord's servant when He acts to heal His children.

In February of 2001, one of the men in our Wednesday morning prayer group announced he had cancer and that the prognosis was not good. The doctors planned to operate on a massive tumor and gave him little hope. As the nine of us prayed over him, the Lord told me this was not purposed unto death but was an attack of the enemy on this man, trying to prevent his precious puppet ministry to children. I commanded the powers of darkness to cease and desist, and we all commanded that the tumor be gone. I left for Korea and, two weeks later, found out that my friend had been trying to contact me because when he prevailed upon the doctors to take another x-ray before doing the surgery, nothing was there!

In another instance, our dear daughter-in law, who sings alongside our son on his worship team, had uterine cancer. God gave me permission and authority to cast it away as an attack of the enemy. Afterward, it was simply gone. The same happened with our granddaughter. Paula and I interceded for both of these loved ones, but we did not speak of our prayers until healing was confirmed and the disease long gone. What a blessing and a joy it is to be part of the Lord's gift of healing for His children!

Early Prophets and Healing

As we noted earlier, the first mention in Scripture regarding prophets had to do with the gift of healing. Abraham prayed for Abimelech, who was healed, and the wombs of his wife and maids were opened so that they bore children (see Genesis 20:17).

Another example of an early Old Testament prophet praying for healing was Elijah. During the famine that followed Elijah's prayers for drought, God sent Elijah to a widow in Zarephath, and the Lord miraculously provided for the widow, her son and Elijah (see 1 Kings 17:9–16). But then the widow's son became ill and died. The widow cried out to Elijah, who took the boy to his own upper chamber and laid him on his own bed. Elijah "stretched himself upon the child three times, and called to the LORD and said, 'O LORD my God, I pray You, let this child's life return to him.' The LORD heard the voice of Elijah, and the life of the child returned to him and he revived" (verses 21–22).

Later Elisha followed this example set for him by Elijah. In the last chapter we discussed how Elisha stayed with the Shunammite woman and blessed her with healing—God opened her womb and gave her a son late in life. But there is more to the story. When the child was grown, he went out to be with his father in the field. With today's medical knowledge, we understand that most likely he suffered a sunstroke. The boy cried out, "My head, my head" (2 Kings 4:19). Servants carried the lad to his mother, where "he sat on her lap until noon, and then died" (verse 20). His mother refused to utter a negative word. She would not acknowledge death; she would not invite finality. She laid her son on the prophet's bed, shut the door and went out. She called to her husband to send a donkey, and when he asked why, she answered only, "It will be well" (verse 23). Ordering her servant to make all possible haste, she went to find Elisha.

When Elisha saw her coming, he sent Gehazi running to ask her what was the matter. The Shunammite woman would not say her son was dead. To Gehazi, she answered as she had to her husband: "It is well" (verse 26).

71

When she came near and caught hold of Elisha's feet, Gehazi tried to push her away, but Elisha said, "Let her alone, for her soul is troubled within her; and *the LORD has hidden it from me and has not told me*" (verse 27, emphasis mine).

Even when she came to Elisha, she would not utter the words of death. Rather, she asked, "Did I ask for a son from my lord? Did I not say, 'Do not deceive me'?" (verse 28). Elisha sent Gehazi running to lay his staff on the lad's face, under instructions to say nothing to anyone along the way. Gehazi did so, but he returned to Elisha saying, "The lad has not awakened" (verse 31).

Elisha, then, went to the lad. "He entered and *shut the door behind them both* and prayed to the LORD" (verse 33, emphasis mine). In the same way Elijah had done, he stretched himself upon the boy, eyes to eyes, hands to hands, and mouth to mouth. Then he got up, walked back and forth, stretched himself upon him again, and the boy sneezed seven times and came back to life! What a beautiful example of a prophet bringing God's healing to His people!

If You Believe, You Will See God's Glory

Observe that in the stories of both Elijah and Elisha, the healing was performed in private. Both Elijah and the Shunammite woman shut the door. We have already learned that unfaith can block healing. In these instances, they did not want anyone who did not have faith to insert streams of doubt. For the same reason, Elisha gave instructions to Gehazi not to speak to anyone. Elisha gave him such a stringent command not solely to make haste but also to prevent the entrance of doubt. Courtesy was important in their culture; it would have been considered extremely rude for Gehazi not to answer when addressed by friends along the way. But he followed Elisha's directions, which were given in order to prevent the unfaith of others from interfering with the healing God wanted to do—the fewer people who knew of the problem, the better. Jesus addressed this principle in the New Testament as well. Remember how He said to Martha, "Did I not say to you that *if you believe*, you will see the glory of God?" (John 11:40, emphasis mine).

Paula and I have learned this principle by experience. Remember that when we prayed for our daughter and granddaughter to be healed of uterine cancer, we told no one of our prayers until healing was confirmed and the disease long gone. We did not want others' lack of faith to prevent the healing that God intended.

Another experience that taught us about how unfaith can block healing—and even reverse healing—happened while I was serving as a pastor in the early seventies. A woman in my church, Gladys, was diagnosed with lung cancer and was dying. Her husband responded to her pleas and provided money for Gladys and me to fly to Los Angeles to attend one of Kathryn Kuhlman's meetings. We stayed in the home of my friend, Margaret Sedenquist, who took us to the coliseum. Kathryn, a woman used by God during her lifetime to bring healing to thousands, could not complete her sermon. She suddenly announced, "There's a triple anointing for healing here today!" And she began to call out where God was moving and what He was doing. "There's a woman down here on my left, who is dying of lung cancer. God is healing her right now!" She was talking about Gladys! Gladys had been praying and had not heard. I jabbed her with my elbow and commanded, "Breathe! Gladys, breathe! She just called out your healing!"

We were the first called up on stage. Kathryn prayed first for Gladys. A man had been assigned to stand behind Gladys to catch her in case she fell "slain in the Spirit."

For those not familiar with this phenomenon, it is what happens when God's power falls on a person so intensely that he or she can no longer stand and falls to the ground. There, the person rests in a peaceful sense of being inundated with God's love, and often God performs a healing while the person rests in His presence. Normally, one does not lose consciousness or enter into a sort of trance or altered state, though that does infrequently happen to some. After a while, the anointing wanes and the person stands and continues to worship.

Gladys was so determined not to allow anything ungenuine to happen that she stood—until her catcher fell! And then she fell on top of him. Kathryn then began praying for me, and the same thing happened. Each of us was slain twice, each time falling on top of our catchers, while everybody laughed.

Thus began the miracle. For two days following, Margaret and I prayed for Gladys while she vomited noxious stuff from her lungs. In the end not only was she healed, she was radiant—and ready to go home. Margaret pled with Gladys to stay a while longer, explaining that the healing needed to have time to seat itself—like piston rings after an overhaul. I agreed and joined in with my advice and reasons to stay. But Gladys felt great and would do nothing but return home to her family and friends.

On the way home, again and again I instructed Gladys, "Do not go out and tell everyone, or anyone, that you've been healed. You need time to regain strength. The unfaith of others can affect you." The town where she lived was a rough mining town. Six miles away was another small mountain town with five open houses of prostitution and numerous bars. The entire valley was riddled with sin, scoffing and unbelief.

Gladys would not hear. Her doctor was amazed and said bewilderingly, "She must be in remission." How could anything bad happen? She was healed. She felt great. Indeed, the bloom of life was in her cheeks, her complexion was ruddy and she walked with a teenager's spring.

But the people were not glad she had been healed! This would mean that God was real and that all of their sins were upon them. These people did not believe in the grace of God for forgiveness. They hated Gladys, and told her it was only a momentary remission: "You just wait. It will come back. It always does." None but a few prayer group people who had prayed for the miracle rejoiced. All the rest in the valley scoffed and jeered at "that silly religious woman." Streams of hate and rejection poured over her. Hate murders (see 1 John 3:15).

The cancer did return. Hour after hour, day after day, I labored over her in prayer with laying on of hands—to no avail. A couple of months later, she died. How indelibly that wrote onto my heart and mind to "shut the door" when praying for a miracle! When faith meets faith miracles happen, but when unbelief and scoffing are allowed into the mix, God's blessings can be horribly prevented.

Instructions to Prophets

Other people, who are not at all prophetic, administer the gift of healing—far more and better than I and some other prophets. Many in other offices, or in no office at all, are endowed with the gift of healing. I wish there were more who were so gifted. Why speak of healing as a function of the prophetic office? What is the difference between prophets and others? The fact that God often uses prophets to give words of healing. Here are some instructions.

Know Your Own Gifting

It is not as though the gift of healing were in any way exclusive or special to the prophetic office. Healing is just one of the functions into which the Lord calls His prophets. But I do notice one significant difference: I am just no good at all at praying routinely for healing. Early on, a wise teacher said to us beginners, "Start out with something easy, like for someone with a cold." Oh, sure! If I pray for someone with a cold, not only do they not get better, they are likely to fall right into pneumonia! Not really, I am exaggerating—but you get the point. I just do not have the gift of healing, though I wish I did. But there are some times when the situation is connected with a prophetic word the Lord gives me. Then I have the faith and know I have the authority. I *know*. It *will* be done! That's the difference. A prophet's authority, especially if the people have faith and/or the recipient has blessed the prophet in some way, allows God to give a prophet's reward. Joyous numbers of times the Lord has called me prophetically, and miracles of deliverance and healing have resulted.

The message? Know your own gifts, especially those pertaining to your office.

Do Not Measure Yourself Against Others

Refrain from jealousy over anyone else's gifts. Yours are special to you—and needed by others. We work as teams in the Lord. Do not measure yourself or your gifts against what anyone else can do.

My friend John Paul Jackson has fantastic gifts. I have seen him tell a man whom he has never met what the man's struggles are, how God is going to change him, what a blessing that will be and so on, giving details none but God, the man and me as his counselor could know. I am a prophet, too, but I do not begin to have that gift, though I have seen it bring healing to many needy lives. Should I be jealous and covet that gift? Should I strain to have that gift? Why? God has given us varied gifts for His purposes. Learn to be content with what God has called and equipped you to do. Yours is neither inferior nor superior. Nor is it superfluous. That kind of measuring has no place in God's Kingdom.

If you have been given one talent, and someone like John Paul has eight or ten, serve with all your might with that one. I know a lot of people who do not begin to have the many gifts God has given some of us, but who are going to be far more blessed in heaven. Of him to whom much is given, much will be required. I wish I could be as diligent as some with far fewer gifts—though perhaps I just measured myself against another and should quit that, too! The paradox is that though we are all called to become more and more corporate, realizing we are to work together with each joint supplying (see Ephesians 4:16), God still works with each of us individually and measures each of us by no other standard than our own.

I say all this because I have seen so many young prophets attaching themselves to others, as though they sought to become clones of their gifting, especially in regard to the bringing of healing through prophetic words. Rather, young prophets should learn from others as much as possible, even imitate them while learning; I will expound more fully about mentoring in chapter 16. But do not forsake your own calling and gifting. Do not fall into idolatry. Not one prophet, nor anyone who serves in one of the five offices, has it all, and not one is worthy of our abandoning who we are to become what someone else is.

Beware of Presumption

A prophet may also have the gift of healing. I have known several who do. If you do not, know that there will be times when your authority as a prophet may be the very ingredient the Lord wants to use in particular instances of healing.

But beware of presumption. A great need or the urgency of friends or any number of unhealed aspects of your own character can push you to think you are hearing a prophetic word of healing. There is no way to know the difference except through the school of hard knocks. Practice is necessary in every field, and the same is true for the office of prophet: "The mature . . . because of practice have their senses trained to discern good and evil" (Hebrews 5:14). Keep a humble mind and heart, cherish the corrections of others, and you will learn.

Do Not Fall into Supposed Methodologies

It is an unparalleled joy to serve alongside the Lord as He heals His own. But be careful not to fall into supposed methodologies that will always work, like some magic incantation. How silly it would be if we thought that because Elijah and Elisha did it that way, we ought to stretch ourselves out on people to heal them! Given today's concerns about sexual harassment, such a technique could land a prophet in court or in some other place of shame and disapproval! God is the God of variety, and each situation is unique. We saw this in the life of Jesus. One He healed with a spitball of mud in the eyes and another just by a word of command. One He healed by saying, "Your sins are forgiven," and with another just as sinful there is no mention of forgiveness. The point? We are called to listen to Him, specifically, in each situation. When we think we know by experience and neglect to ask the Lord what is needed in a situation, we are relying on ourselves rather than Him. In such instances, nothing good ever happens!

Recognize that Both Faith and Knowledge Are Necessary

Two elements are necessary for healing. Sometimes if one just has enough faith, healing happens. But sometimes we can have all the faith in the world, and nothing happens! Sometimes the second aspect is needed, which is the right key of knowledge. Sometimes if we just get the right insight, the requisite key of knowledge, miracles follow. But sometimes if we have all knowledge, as in 1 Corinthians 13:2, we gain nothing. *We need both—faith and knowledge.* Here is where the Lord's teamwork is so vital. The nine of us men praying for our cancer-infested friend needed the prophetic key of knowledge the Lord gave to me, but what virtue would there have been had that not been joined by the faith of the eight others? In another small group that meets in our home, we often tackle a project in prayer for the Lord, and though the power and anointing of the Lord are there, it seems nothing happens until the Holy Spirit presents a key of knowledge to someone in the group. Here is where the prophetic gifting can be most valuable. *Prophets are the servants most specifically designed to present keys of revelation for the faith of all to employ.*

Whatever key is required will not always come through the prophetic one. Such insights can come through anyone, but I have found that such revelations come more readily and accurately when there is a prophet in the group. The prophet's anointing is supposed to be shared, as Moses was able to impart his anointing to the seventy in Exodus 18:24–27. *This enabling of others to receive revelations that bring healing is an important function of today's prophets.*

A little warning: It is tempting to gain influence and power by always being the one through whom key revelations come. Watch out for

77

immature prophets who do this. Years ago, traveling caused me to be absent from our small group for several weeks. When I returned, I was stunned and ashamed when I happened to overhear some of them rejoicing because they had discovered that they, too, could have revelations when I was not there to preempt them! I repented and said, "Lord, put a check on my lips, so that others may have their chance to shine in your gifts." Work on yourself as a prophet to die to self so that others in the group also may have the joy and confidence-building experiences of receiving helpful revelations.

But how joyous it is when God calls you as His prophet and gives you just that key or that needful authority so that the blessing of healing that God wants arrives as He intends. It has been my joy to see this happen many times. Paula often is given a comical vision, and it becomes teamwork as the rest of us ponder her vision and discover the insights God desires for us to have. We laugh and have fun, as God reveals. And I could swear there are times I have seen Him chuckling behind His hand—He was having fun, too.

Be Willing to Admit When You Do Not Know

Brother Winston Nunes of Canada said to me, after we had been ministering together and answering questions, "Brother John, do you know how I knew you were a true prophet of God?" I said, "No, how?" He replied, "When that woman asked you a question and you said you did not know how to answer that. If you had been a false prophet you would have made up an answer. The Lord's true prophets do not always know the answers, and they aren't afraid to admit it."

In the story of the Shunammite woman, when he saw her from far off, Elisha did not know why she was coming toward him. He sent Gehazi to ask her what was the matter (see 2 Kings 4:25–26). God had not told Elisha, who used simple common sense to send Gehazi to find out. Beware of prophets who always know. And as a prophet, do not assume that God will always tell you. Be willing to admit when you do not know.

Keep a Humble Heart

No matter how expert or successful in prayer we become, there are always mysteries and unanswered questions. For example, upon learning that a friend, Phillip, was filled with cancer, a group of us prayed fervently for over a year for this valuable servant of the Lord. Finally, we won. Tests showed the cancer was totally gone. He was completely healed, and the physicians even said any recurrence was not likely. But two weeks later, Phillip dropped dead from a heart attack! Why? What was all that healing for, if it was to end like that? Who knows? Only the Lord. Always, we need to keep humble hearts before the Lord. His ways are not our ways, and His thoughts are high above ours.

Who Knows the Mind of God?

In *The Elijah Task* I told a remarkable story of a plane crash—with me in it. But there is a sequel I have never shared in writing before. I will retell the story as briefly as I can.

I was scheduled to attend a meeting in Chicago on a Thursday. We lived about a hundred miles away, on the Santa Fe Railroad line. I did not have enough money for a round-trip ticket, and there were no credit cards in those days. So on Wednesday I said to the Lord in our morning prayers, "Lord, if You want me to go that meeting, You're going to have to provide a ride, or the money." The Lord said to me, *I'll get you up there, but you'll have to pay your own way back.* I thought, *That's strange. What does He mean by that?*

Later that day, when I came back from making pastoral calls, Paula said, "Call Don Perisho." He was a local jeweler who was active in the Boy Scout program. He said, "John, could you speak for me at the Cub Scout banquet tomorrow night?"

"I don't know, Don. I have to be in Chicago for a meeting tomorrow, and I don't know if I'll be back in time."

He said, "Oh? When's your meeting over? I have to be in Chicago, too. I'm flying up. If your meeting's done soon enough, you can fly with us and be back in time to speak at the banquet."

The next morning as they were rolling Don's beautiful blue and white Piper Cub out of the hangar, the thought hit my head, *My, what a shame to ruin such a beautiful little plane.* I shook my head and thought, *Where did that come from?*

As we took off, Don's wife, Mary, looked back at me and shouted something I could not hear. Sid Krotzer, a sturdy truck driver sitting beside me, yelled in my ear, "Mary wants to know if you've asked the ol' Man upstairs about this flight." I nodded, and she looked greatly relieved, but frightened. I thought, *That was strange. She has flown all over the country with Don. She should not be afraid of flying.*

As we flew toward Chicago I had an unusually clear vision, like watching a movie. I saw our plane go across Chicago, out around the Adler Planetarium and then south to land on Meigs field. There are dozens of fields near Chicago. I had no idea which one we would use. But as we landed I saw us crash! The plane was totally demolished.

I said to the Lord, "Are we going to crash?"

Yes.

"Can't I prevent it?"

No. But if you'll pray, the plane will crash but no one will be hurt. There will not be a piece of torn clothing or a scratch or a bruise. No one will be hurt.

So I sat back to pray! You bet! Fervently. And then tried to relax.

Sure enough, we flew out around the planetarium and turned south to land on Meigs field. As we touched down, a sudden gust of wind lifted us and turned the plane sideways. We hit on the sides of the wheels, buckling the struts, and the plane crashed down onto its belly. We wiggled and waggled one hundred yards down the runway, demolishing the prop and wings, to say nothing of ripping up the belly. It was a miracle we did not flip over or burst into flames.

There was not one piece of torn clothing or a bruise or a scratch!

We climbed out and Mary said, "Reverend Sandford, did you have a premonition about this flight?"

"Yes, I did, Mary," I replied, "I think the Lord told me we were going to crash."

"I did, too," she replied, and walked off to join Don.

That evening, I bought my ticket home. Remember, the Lord told me, *I'll get you up there, but you'll have to pay your own way back.* On the train, I saw Don and Mary in the diner having supper. We were too late for the banquet.

Once in my seat I prayed, *Lord, I know the devil wants to destroy me. Did I endanger them and cause their plane to be destroyed by being on that flight?*

The Lord said, *On the contrary. Look at your watch. Remember when Don called you several years ago and said, "No pastor ought to be without a watch," and gave that to you? John, that was the crumb cast on the waters that saved his life. Remember, if you give to a servant of the Lord, you can-*

not lose your reward. Don is not a praying man. I knew the accident was about to happen. I wanted to save his life. I knew you would pray. Therefore, I moved you onto his plane. I found out later Don bumped someone else off to put me on the plane.

Thus, I thought the entire incident was for Don. But here is the sequel.

Time passed, and Mary came down with cancer. The affliction was so bad she was confined to a wheelchair. She nearly died. God miraculously healed her, and for many years she traveled around to speak and pray for sick people.

Don had purchased another plane. Twenty years later to the day, Don and Mary flew again to Chicago. Their plane flew across Chicago, out around the Adler Planetarium, and headed south to land on Meigs field. They landed safely and came to a stop at the very spot where we had climbed out of the wreckage. Mary stepped out and dropped dead of a heart attack, exactly where twenty years before her life had been miraculously spared!

Who can understand these things? Did God give Mary those years? Was it as though He said, "I'll give you twenty years, Mary. I'll try you nearly to the point of death and see what you'll do with your life." I am confident God had it all planned, but who knows the mind of God?

Prophets need to know that we do not know everything. In fact, we know very little. Like the saying of many old-time military men, "Ours is not to question why; ours is but to do and die"—on the cross, daily, so that His will, and only His, is accomplished.

SIX

PRONOUNCING JUDGMENT

PRONOUNCING JUDGMENT is not something that prophets
ever want to do. If a prophet does enjoy this, there is something wrong
with his heart.

In *Prophets: Pitfalls and Principles* Bishop Bill Hamon speaks of this
problem and how it can be avoided:

> The line between pronouncing God's genuine prophetic judgments and
> ministering out of a wounded heart or spirit of rejection is a thin one. That
> is why all prophets need to be related and accountable to someone they can
> trust enough to allow that person to be the spiritual surgeon who operates
> on their spirit and attitude. The spiritually diseased area must be surgically
> removed, the wound must be cleansed and closed properly, and time must
> be given for healing and restoration in those areas of the person's life.

For this reason, I do not believe that God normally calls a novice
prophet to present His words of judgment. When giving or receiving
prophetic words of judgment, one needs to apply caution, common sense
and wisdom. Circumspection is especially called for when a new Christian or fledgling prophet thinks he or she has a word of God's judgment
regarding one's life, ministry or anything else. This is an area most sus-
ceptible to presumption and carnal judgments rather than the purity of
the Holy Spirit.

Warning of Judgment vs. Pronouncing Judgment

Pronouncing judgment is not the same as giving warnings that judgment is imminent. The latter carries with it grace and hope. God speaks warnings through His prophets in hopes that the people will repent and God can then "repent of the calamity which I am planning to do to them because of the evil of their deeds" (Jeremiah 26:3). Warnings are almost always conditional, given for the precise reason that repentance can still heal and set straight.

On the other hand, when judgment is pronounced there is little hope of redemption. Pronounced judgments are usually unconditional. Normally, it is too late for all but the most fervent cries of repentance. Here are some examples.

Elisha Pronounced Judgment on the Royal Officer

An early example of pronounced judgment occurred in the days of Elisha. King Ben-hadad of Aram, or Syria, besieged Samaria, whose people suffered from famine because of it. But Elisha prophesied a brief turn of events: "Tomorrow about this time a measure of fine flour will be sold for a shekel, and two measures of barley for a shekel, in the gate of Samaria" (2 Kings 7:1). A royal officer scoffed and said, "Behold, if the LORD should make windows in heaven, could this thing be?" (verse 2). As we said earlier, unfaith is harmful and can actually prevent God's blessings. When men sin in this way, a prophet is duty bound to rebuke (see Ezekiel 33:6). Elisha pronounced judgment: "Behold, you will see it with your own eyes, but you will not eat of it" (verse 2). The next day Ben-hadad's army fled in haste, leaving great stores of food. The royal officer had been placed in charge of the gate, "but the people trampled on him at the gate, and he died just as the man of God had said" (verse 17).

Jeremiah Pronounced Judgment on Pashhur

God also instructed Jeremiah to give warning of judgment to the people of Jerusalem. Jeremiah told them that because of their sins God would bring calamity upon Jerusalem. To many this was treasonous, since they reckoned in the flesh, not by the Spirit. They had been given ample chances to repent, but they did not. Pashhur, the priest, had Jeremiah beaten and put in stocks by the upper Benjamin Gate (see Jeremiah 20:1–2). Jeremiah had no choice; he had to bring the judgment of rebuke upon Pashhur and the people of Jerusalem.

Jeremiah knew judgment had to be pronounced, but the questions that remained were "What, how and when?" Having been in similar circumstances—not so severe but certainly made to look like a fool—I know a bit of the wrestling Jeremiah must have gone through during the night to forgive, and to maintain a pure heart and mind so as to hear God clearly. In the morning, Jeremiah pronounced God's judgment: "Pashhur is not the name the LORD has called you, but rather Magor-missabib" (verse 3). *Pashhur* meant "peace," but from now on his name would mean "terror all around." Now, every time the people looked upon Magor-missabib, they would see another witness reminding them to quit sinning or they would reap terror all around. And Jeremiah's pronouncement continued:

> "For thus says the LORD, 'Behold, I am going to make you a terror to yourself and to all your friends; and while your eyes look on, they will fall by the sword of their enemies. So I will give over all Judah to the hand of the king of Babylon, and he will carry them away as exiles to Babylon and will slay them with the sword.'"

VERSE 4

Do you think Jeremiah felt satisfaction and triumph when what he pronounced in judgment happened exactly as he had said? Having been in such a position, I can testify to the almost overwhelming grief that ensues. True prophets do not need vindication. Their security is in God. Their hearts are filled with grief because they are filled with God's love and grief for His people who suffer so needlessly. A true prophet grieves *with* God, sharing *His* sorrow. Oh, how deeply it hurts to have to pronounce judgment—and how much more when the judgment comes to pass! Other modern prophets may have borne this weight in far more drastic circumstances than I, but from the little I have known, I can tell you that no prophet in his right mind wants to be a prophet! The cost is just too great!

We also learn from Jeremiah how very carefully we must treat the Lord's prophets. It is one thing to question humbly. It is another to judge God's messenger and act as though you are absolutely right and the prophet is so wrong as to deserve punishment. Such a judgment is equivalent to judging and reproaching God Himself. Remember when Jesus said, "To the extent that you did it to one of these brothers of Mine, even the least of them, you did it to Me" (Matthew 25:40)? And when Paul had been persecuting Christians and God knocked him down on the road to Damascus, the Lord said to him, "Saul, Saul, why are you persecuting Me?" (Acts 9:4, emphasis mine). Even if a prophet is palpably wrong, we must approach him with humility and respect. He is still God's servant, and God will move on his behalf.

Jeremiah Pronounced Judgment on Hananiah

The prophet Hananiah falsely prophesied that within two years all the vessels taken from the house of God would be returned, as would all those who had been exiled to Babylon (see Jeremiah 28:1–10). This led the people into deception, causing them to trust in a lie. Jeremiah had to respond. He spoke God's true word that destruction, not peace, would be their lot. Hananiah then took off the ox yoke Jeremiah was wearing as a sign the people would go into the slavery of captivity. He broke it and told the people that within two years God would break the yoke of the king of Babylon. Jeremiah "went his way" (verse 11).

How well we who are His prophets today understand those few simple words, "went his way"! We know how Jeremiah had to be alone with the Lord—no matter how well surrounded by supporters and intercessors. He had to process his own needs to forgive so that he could hear God accurately. We know the weight of responsibility that rested solely on Jeremiah's shoulders. Could Hananiah be right? What if I *am* preaching treason, as Magor-missabib and many of the people think? And if I am right, and God assures me that I am, what then? What does He want me to do about it?

Jeremiah did not want to hurt Hananiah, nor did he want to have to pronounce God's judgment on the people for their sins. But he had to obey. Therefore, he pronounced that whereas Hananiah had broken off a wooden yoke, God would put a yoke of iron on all the nations, and they would serve Nebuchadnezzar because God had given them and even the beasts of the field into his hands. Because Hananiah had made the people trust in a lie, "'Behold, I am about to remove you from the face of the earth. This year you are going to die, because you have counseled rebellion against the LORD.' So Hananiah the prophet died in the same year in the seventh month" (verses 16–17).

Moses Pronounced Judgment on Three Rebellious Men

When the three men named Korah, Dathan and Abiram, along with their families and followers, rebelled against Moses' leadership, at Moses' word, "the ground that was under them split open; and the earth opened its mouth and swallowed them up, and their households, and all the men who belonged to Korah with their possessions" (Numbers 16:31–32). "Fire also came forth from the LORD and consumed the two hundred and fifty men who were offering the incense" (verse 35). But before pronouncing this judgment of the Lord, Moses had gone to Korah and his followers to plead with them to repent, and twice he had fallen on his face in intercession to plead with the Lord not to destroy all of Israel for the sins of the few (verse 22). No genuine prophet enjoys calling down God's judgment. Moses did all he could to save the people from destruction.

The List Continues

We could list many more times God's prophets have had to call down God's judgment. In the New Testament, Peter pronounced death upon Ananias and Sapphira for lying to the Holy Spirit and for stealing (see Acts 5:1–11). And Paul called for blindness upon the false prophet Bar-Jesus (see Acts 13:11). God's severe judgment pronounced through His prophets is not simply an Old Testament phenomenon. It is very much applicable in our New Testament times. In fact, let me give you a personal, modern-day example.

Paula and I were returning from a teaching tour when God spoke to us. He said that when we arrived home, we would hear a man saying libelous things about us and our ministry, scoffing and ridiculing what God was doing through us. He explained that this man had slanderously and vituperatively attacked many other ministries. He had been warned by a number of servants not to continue to act so divisively and harmfully in the Body of Christ. But he had not heard and had not stopped, even becoming worse in his denunciations. God instructed us to tell the man that His judgment was being leveled upon him, and that God would soon remove his anointing. Note: There is a difference between gifts and anointing. The man had many gifts and retained them afterward. God did not remove his gifts. But when anointing is removed, our gifts begin more and more to be operated by our flesh, and if we do not repent, they can be controlled demonically.

86

We did not want to have to pronounce that judgment. Upon arriving home, we heard a taped message recently delivered by a pastor in a nearby city. We were astounded that any man could get his "facts" so confused and be so sure of himself without checking with those he was accusing. Many had slandered us, but this was by far the worst.

We fell on our faces before the Lord on his behalf (see Numbers 16:4, 22). But there comes a time when God says, "Do not pray for this people, and do not lift up cry or prayer for them, and do not intercede with Me; for I do not hear you" (Jeremiah 7:16). The Lord gave us that Scripture, which simply meant it was too late and His judgment would fall. This word of the removal of the man's anointing was not conditional; it *would* happen. Remembering how Abraham kept pleading, even though God already had pronounced judgment on Sodom and Gomorrah (see Genesis 18:20–23), we kept on praying. But all the while we felt the finality, as Abraham did when the number of righteous men required to save the cities was set at ten and Abraham knew that was as far as the Lord would go.

We tried to make an appointment to go directly to our brother, as Jesus instructed in Matthew 18:15, but he kept putting us off. Finally, we prepared a letter, explaining what God had said to us and pronouncing that if he did not repent God would remove His Anointing. We hoped he would still repent and stave off the judgment. In the off chance that we might see him, we took the letter by hand to his office. Whether he was indeed gone or had told his secretary to say so, we do not know, but we did not see him. So we left the letter with his secretary, instructing strictly that no one was to read the letter other than the pastor.

Subsequently and very soon after that, God did remove His anointing from the man. His thriving church began to struggle. Controversies and quarrels broke out. I understand that almost half of his church split away.

Rather than repent, the pastor spread it far and wide that Paula and I had put a curse on him! But we were continuing to grieve for him and his people, blessing them continuously in our prayers.

Judgment Can Be God's Best Mercy

When God orders His prophets to pronounce judgments, it is because He has waited full term. The Lord has spoken but not been heard—or if heard, not obeyed. The Lord has remonstrated, called others to pray that the person(s) repent and change, and perhaps even given prophetic warnings—but to no avail. At this point, judgment is God's best mercy.

One might ask, "Wait a minute, isn't that the very definition of judgment, when God acts and mercy is no longer possible?" In a sense, yes, judgment falls when every other recourse has failed. But no action by our loving heavenly Father can be made outside of love. He is love. "God is Light, and in Him there is no darkness at all" (1 John 1:5). Therefore, just as an earthly father has to spank because he loves his children, Father God must let His judgments fall because He loves us.

Judgment Is Part of God's Blessing

Many are confused about judgment. First, they believe judgment is always something dire and hurtful. This is not necessarily so. Scripture says, "It is appointed for men to die once and after this comes judgment" (Hebrews 9:27). The writer said this in the context of teaching about the end times, so it is apparent that he was speaking of our usual interpretation, that when we die physically, we will stand before the Lord's judgment seat.

But when did we die? When we received Jesus as Lord and Savior. Before we were born anew, our Father God could not treat us as sons. "It is for discipline that you endure; God deals with you as with sons; for what son is there whom his father does not discipline? *But if you are without discipline,* of which all have become partakers, *then you are illegitimate children and not sons*" (Hebrews 12:7–8, emphasis mine). The moment we were born anew, living under His discipline became part of our blessing, our birthright in Him: "You only have I chosen among all the families of the earth; therefore I will punish you for all your iniquities" (Amos 3:2). Jews and Christians, therefore, live under the mighty, personal and direct hand of God. He moves to set us and our world straight, in kindness and sensitivity.

We live, moment by moment, under His discipline, which is the first level of judgment—but that judgment is enacted in love. Whenever we are instantly repentant, God's judgment just as quickly becomes healing. Oh, how we need His constant and gentle discipline! Understanding it this way, we ought to pray continually, "Judge me, O God. Let me not wander out from under Your judgments."

Unfortunately, many misinformed Christians pray, "O God, keep Your hand of judgment far from me." Listen to what judgment actually is! Judgment is God's Holy Spirit, brooding over His creation, finding out what is null and void because of darkness. Seeing need, God moves to set it straight. That is judgment, and His purpose in it is to heal and restore. Judgment is a supreme act of love. If God's people will hear and respond, judgment becomes mercy. Repentance, forgiveness and Jesus' death on the cross can then redeem.

Reaping What We Sow

The second level of judgment is tougher. If His people will not or do not hear and respond, the Lord allows us to reap the evil we have sown, mitigated by however much our posture before Him allows. This reaping of the law is impersonal on God's part and is certainly not His first choice. He does not want us to have to suffer what we merit. It is as simple as when my brother and I as youngsters wanted to go swimming in the old swimming hole too early in the spring. Mom would say, "Wait a while. It's too cold. You'll catch your death of cold." But we were impatient. Winter had seemed so very long. We would disobey and jump in. Mom knew we would, but what could she do, chain us to the bedpost? It was as if she said, "Okay, you will not listen, so learn the hard way." We would reap heavy colds—and miss out on the first part of summer's glorious swimming. The law of sowing and reaping taught us what we could have learned the easy way if we had listened and obeyed. The impersonal law of sowing and reaping is spoken of scripturally as God's law, because all the laws of the Bible are His, but harmful reaping is not what He wants to happen.

Bishop Hamon speaks of times when God gives us what we want, even when He knows it will not be good for us:

> We should note . . . a more general principle in the Bible whether or not prophetic ministry is involved; God sometimes gives us what we want, even when it is not best for us. This reality is evident in the parable of the prodigal son, where the father—who represents God the Father—gives his son his heritage prematurely, even though the father knew it would cause the son's downfall (Luke 15:11–31).

When God in His foreknowledge comprehends that we will not repent, the most merciful thing He can do is to speed up the process of reaping. How is that merciful? If God were to allow the law of sowing and reaping to operate in its own slow but inexorable way, our reaping might not come until the harvest was its heaviest and hardest to bear!

When we will not repent, His mercy allows us to reap before the harvest has grown to its worst amount. For example, if you are sitting under a tree that is appointed to fall in your direction and you will not move, would you rather that the tree fall on you as a sapling or when it has grown massive? Quicker judgment under the law is an act of God's mercy.

Sometimes I have been called upon by the Lord to pray that a man's reaping come quickly. I cannot do this successfully if my heart is not right and I want him to "get what's coming to him." My heart must be full of God's forgiveness and mercy, so that I do not want him to suffer the fullness of what he is due. In commanding me to pray that a man reap quickly, our Father is trusting that my heart is indeed right—else He could not and would not give me such a command.

God Can Send Personal and Direct Judgment

The third level of judgment occurs when God acts personally and directly to send upon His erring child, or children, whatever punishment is most appropriate. The law of reaping is still in effect, but in this instance God steps in personally to activate it.

A simple parallel would be my father stepping in to spank us children when we kept being disobedient. Throughout the Bible the prophets spoke of how "the LORD raises against them adversaries" (Isaiah 9:11), withholds the rain (see 1 Kings 17:1), sends "scorching wind and mildew; and the caterpillar was devouring your many gardens and vineyards, fig trees and olive trees. . . . I sent a plague among you after the manner of Egypt; I slew your young men by the sword. . . . I overthrew you, as God overthrew Sodom and Gomorrah" (Amos 4:9–11).

Unfortunately, the same lack of intimacy with God that precludes gentler corrections often causes men and women not to understand when disasters arrive at the hand of God. Worse yet, their lack of wisdom causes them to react in anger and rebellion. Therefore, after he listed each action God had taken, the constant refrain of Amos was, "'Yet you have not returned to Me,' declares the LORD" (verses 8, 10–11).

Mother Basilea Schlink has described how many recent natural disasters have happened exactly where sin was most rampant. She reported, for example, how the epicenter of a major earthquake in California was in the very valley in which pornographic movies and other materials are produced. Revelation 16:11 says that when the fifth angel poured out his bowl and mankind suffered great pains, "they did not repent of their deeds," and after the sixth and seventh angels poured out their bowls, "men blasphemed God" (verse 21). All the buildings and materials of the porno producers were greatly damaged or destroyed in that earthquake. But when these people were made aware that their losses were likely at the hand of God, they replied that they did not care. They vowed that their buildings would be rebuilt, and their production of smut would be running full tilt again within a few weeks! This is a perfect example of people reacting to God's hand of judgment in anger and rebellion. "'Yet you have not returned to Me,' declares the Lord."

Another such instance occurred in 1910, when a great firestorm engulfed northern Idaho. All the forests except for a few stands of cedar trees were burned to the ground. Despite the ferocity of the fire, two towns, Wallace and Harrison, escaped destruction—all except one section of each. The very areas where the brothels stood were totally destroyed by fire! But both towns quickly rebuilt the brothels.

A Pastor's Heart, a Prophet's Burden

God sends destructive judgments in the hope that, as Amos said, His children will turn back to Him. Even His harsh judgments are acts of love and mercy, especially because we deserved total rejection rather than the continuing, longsuffering love He holds for us.

I thank God I have not had to pronounce God's judgments more than a few times. I think it would be best if every prophet were required to be a pastor for a number of years before transition to the prophetic office. He or she would then have a greater sensitivity to what the pastor must live with once the prophet has spoken. Having a pastor's heart helps to temper prophetic utterances. Nowhere is this truer than in the function of having to pronounce God's imminent judgment.

There is a flip side to that benefit. Having a pastor's heart immeasurably increases the pain the prophet endures when he knows that what he must pronounce will bring fear and pain to the sheep he has been trained to love and protect! But, oh, what a pleasure it is when the pliant and repentant hearts of God's people allow His prophets to bring only that first level of judgment—His mercy and healing grace.

May God grant His people soft hearts and limber necks, so that His prophets do not have to pronounce the heavy weights of God's hand.

SEVEN

WARNINGS
BEFORE TRAGEDIES HAPPEN

GOD IS OMNISCIENT. He knows what will happen before any tragedy occurs—whether it be natural disaster, illness, accident, death, war, separation and divorce, molestation or rape. Because He loves and cares more than any earthly father, He does not want harm to come to any of His children. When harm is imminent and threatens one of His children, He tries to warn us.

All, born anew or not, are His children. Some believe that no one is a child of God until he is born anew, but if we were not once His children, there would be nothing to have fallen from! Our Father God is the Father of spirits (see Hebrews 12:9), which means He is the Father of all of us. God so loved *the world* that He not only sent His one begotten Son to save our souls for eternity (see John 3:16), but he is still sending Him to rescue His children from every conceivable kind of harm. But because of our sin, all of us have turned from our position as children of God and only some of us are reborn in Christ. So we ourselves make it more difficult for God to save us from trouble.

Children who walk in harmony with their parents are most easily protected. Children who are sometimes disobedient make it harder for their parents to protect them. But children who rebel and disown their parents, acting continually against their counsel and will, remove themselves from their parents' ability to protect—and suffer the consequences. The first two types of children are like Christians, children who are imperfect but do provide their parents opportunity to protect. The third type is like unbelievers. They were born children of God but have rejected their heritage. Therefore, God has little opportunity to protect them from their own bad choices. Their own stance affords God no opportunity, but others may pray for them, which grants God a chance to express His loving will for them.

Most of the time, being rescued from harm depends upon our hearing Him. It is like when an earthly father sees a truck heading down the road toward his children and shouts, "Look out! Get out of the way!" If they are deaf or do not listen, the father becomes frantic, trying to get their attention. God does the same thing. If His children are not born anew, they are deaf to His words of warning. If they are born anew but do not listen, the sorrow in His heart is much more poignant. He grieves because they should have heard His warnings.

Unfortunately, not all of God's children practice the prayerful discipline that could enable them to hear His warnings before trouble comes. Sometimes He steps in to act sovereignly to prevent or ameliorate harm, without human help. But He has given us free will. The law of sowing and reaping is immutable. If we sow harm, we *will* reap it. Law is law. God does not want us to have to reap harm, but unless we repent or someone else cries out in repentance for mercy for us, we will suffer retribution for our sin. And that, as we will see in the ensuing chapters, is why intercession is a major call upon prophets.

It is a dangerous world. The enemy wants to destroy us (see John 10:10). Sadly, the majority of Christians do not even know that it is possible to hear Him moment by moment, day by day. Many who do know they should be alert and attuned to His Spirit have become lax and inattentive. Consequently, the need is great for prophets whose practiced discipline is to hear God's warnings before tragedies occur and call people into prayer. God wants to turn potential disaster into blessing.

How God Seeks Opportunities for Blessing

King Hezekiah was mortally ill. God sent Isaiah to tell him, "Set your house in order, for you shall die and not live" (2 Kings 20:1). The Lord did not say this to Hezekiah out of ill will. He did not want him to die. He wanted him to live, to continue to reign as a good king. He spoke the warning through Isaiah to prevent Hezekiah's death.

Hezekiah turned his face to the wall, and prayed to the Lord. He reminded God that he had served Him faithfully, and Hezekiah wept. Before Isaiah had even left the palace, the Lord spoke to him, telling him to go back and tell Hezekiah He had heard his prayers and that he would not die but live fifteen more years, and He would deliver his people from the king of Assyria. God wants our hearts to be like Hezekiah's, so that He can have the opportunity to turn disaster into blessing. But in order to give Him this opportunity, we must hear Him, repent and return to walk in His ways.

I served as a pastor in a silver, lead and zinc mining community. Work in the mines, thousands of feet under the ground, was always dangerous. The Holy Spirit spoke to me, warning, *In the next two weeks, men in your church are going to be killed in the mines, unless you pray.* Paula and I prayed earnestly each day in repentance for our own sins and the sins of the church and community, crying out to God for the protection of our people. In this case we did not tell others, lest fear and tension increase the likelihood of accidents. Within two weeks huge boulders crashed down, narrowly missing our head deacon, a devout and faithful man. He received a scratch on his thumb. A man who attended church infrequently was hit by falling rocks and sustained a gash in his right calf that required several stitches. Another member of the church, who never attended, was hurled by a speeding ore car against a wall, breaking several ribs and bruising his hip badly so that he spent time in the hospital.

None was killed and the experience underscored how vitally important it is to stay close to God's heart. The man closest to the Shepherd was greatly protected, and those farthest away were protected from severe harm. Because of our prayers, God was given opportunity to avert what could have been disaster.

Heeding the Warning

The message that our response to God's warning affects the outcome of our experiences was driven home early one March. God commanded me to warn a local pastor that if he and his congregation did not repent, by June a great split would occur in his church and half his people would leave. Unknown to me, our son Tim gave him an identical warning, carrying out God's tradition of sending two witnesses before the event. The pastor did nothing. He should have called his people into discussion and prayer. He should have used the warnings to uncover whatever unrest was fermenting in his church. In June, his church split in half! The people who had known about the warnings asked the pastor, "Why didn't you do something about the Sandfords' warnings?" He said, "I thought I'd wait to see if it was a true word!" Talk about foolish! Even if he questioned whether or not they were true prophetic words, what would it have hurt to have called a few trusted believers into prayer, just in case?

God's people must learn how to respond to prophets' warnings. God gives warnings through His prophets, and others who may not be prophets, because He does not want trouble to happen. But we must respond.

It was a different story with my own beloved pastor. I kept hearing a word from the Lord and waited for confirmation. Finally, it was clear that I should present the warning to the pastor, and only to him. One day I dropped by the church and, by God's providence, caught my pastor with a few minutes' free time. I told him the Lord warned me that "one will arise in the church who is trusted by the people, but he will lead the church into division." Immediately, Pastor Bruce bowed his head and prayed that if there was any sin in our Body giving access to division and trouble that it be revealed, and he asked God to protect his flock from harm.

In the months following this meeting, the church expanded rapidly and outgrew its facilities. Though its sanctuary held nine hundred, the church had to conduct five worship services each weekend and still was too crowded. Bruce decided to build another building and split the church into two churches, placing his associate over one and himself over the other. I became concerned and invited Bruce and his associate to lunch. I said, "Bruce, many of these new Christians have never known any pastor but you. Many will feel abandoned and rejected if you split them off and assign them to the other church. They don't want to be shuffled off to another pastor. Besides that, I do not think it's wise to set up Pastor Terry in competition with you." Bruce sat back and thought for a while. Then his face lit up, and he said, "I know what we'll do. We'll have one church in two locations. Terry and I will rotate preaching. That way, we'll have two reaping machines for the Lord, but only one church, and one pastoral staff." Terry and I chorused agreement.

95

Then the Lord reminded me of the word and Pastor Bruce's prayer. I said, "Bruce, the Lord just reminded me of that word we prayed about a few months ago. *You* are the one who has arisen in the church! You are the one who is greatly trusted. You were about to lead the church into division. The Lord has answered our prayers!" Because Pastor Bruce heard God's warning and responded in prayer and repentance, God was able to change the outcome.

To me, this story illustrates how we may not understand God's words of warning. Never in a million years would I have thought of Pastor Bruce as the one who would create division in the church! But God knew what Pastor Bruce was thinking. Bruce had not meant to create division and was grateful that the Lord had preserved their unity as one church in two locations. We do not have to know the exact problem, or the outcome. If we pray humbly and sincerely, God will use our prayers, and trouble can be prevented.

A few weeks following this revelation, the Lord gave me a warning that one would arise in a church in our community who would become involved in sexual sins, and great scandal would rock the church. This time He led me to warn only two associate pastors in that church who could be relied upon to pray and to handle the warning with quiet discretion. Staff was made alert, without being told of the prophecy. Shortly, it was discovered that a man helping in the children's department was trying to involve preschoolers in sexual activities. The matter was handled discreetly and appropriately, without publicity or a breath of scandal. Again, because the Lord's prophet acted and leaders went to Him in prayer and supplication, God prevented harm—to the children and the church.

Receiving Only Partial Protection

Sometimes words of warning bring only partial protection, though copious amounts of prayer have assailed heaven. Often we do not know why. Our son John built a barn for the stabling business he and his wife, Diana, share. He decided to build another much larger barn to serve as an exercise arena. As the building started to go up, the Holy Spirit gave me a vision of John falling off the high roof and being seriously injured or killed. I warned John and Diana, cautioning him to be careful. Paula and I enlisted our prayer group and others in praying for his protection. John fell off anyway! The miracle was that he was not killed. His right heel was badly shattered and took many months to heal. At the time he was head of the ski patrol on Silver Mountain. All winter he had to be on the ski slopes, supervising but unable to ski! This event caused him to realize that when a sheep does not walk closely enough, the Shepherd breaks his leg. John increased his devotional life and church attendance.

But was that enough to explain why our prayers were only partially answered? For me it was not enough. Could the Lord have prevented it altogether? With God nothing is impossible, so why did He not? Probably we will never know, this side of heaven. Nevertheless, thoughts of guilt assailed me. Should I have prayed more? Was there more I could have done?

At the same time, I had another vision. In it Diana was thrown by a horse who turned, rose on his hind feet, crashed down on her back with his front hooves and killed her. I told Paula but not Diana, as I did not want to cause her anxiety that might then be sensed by a horse. We prayed for her protection. We were away, traveling and teaching. When we returned, I discovered that much of what I had seen happened! The horse's hooves missed her spine by a scant inch! She had to go to the hospital for a checkup and still bears the marks of his hooves on her back, but she is okay today. Would she have been killed without God's warning? I think so, but who knows? Why was harm not prevented altogether? Why did our prayers not bring fullness of protection? Who knows?

Many times I have warned about imminent natural disasters, calling for prayers of repentance and protection. In 2001, for example, God gave me a warning before the great earthquake in India. Our teaching team was with me in Japan. I became heavily grieved, knowing a major earthquake was coming that would kill millions. I was thankful as our team gathered around me, helping to carry the burden, and joined in praying for God to save as many as possible. Thousands were killed, rather than millions. Did I hear wrongly, or did our prayers enable God to save many? Was it mere imagination, or did our prayers actually help? Who knows, other than God? Prophets just have to obey God and serve.

Prophets must learn to live with unanswered questions. We must not take ourselves too seriously or load ourselves with presumptive guilt. In the end we just have to say, "Forgive me, Lord, if I should have done something more." Then we must forgive ourselves and know that the Lord is the one in control. Prophets need to be humble before God, giving thanks for whatever measure of protection His warnings and our

97

responses accomplish. Then we must say, "Teach me better next time, Lord," and move on.

I grieved both before the earthquake and after it for those who were killed. The grief was not my own but our Lord's for His children. I asked the Lord about this grief: "Lord, natural disasters happen all the time, killing many, and accidents maim and kill, as do diseases. You know before any one of these happen. Why do You grieve so? It seems to me if I were You, I would grow rather callous after a while." He replied, *John, I grieve over the untimely death of any one of My children, but especially when an earthquake like this kills so many who do not know Me, and now will never have that chance.* I knew He was also telling me of His gratitude for His many children who stand in the gap and pray in response to His warnings, by their prayers enabling Him to rescue many.

Historical seismological statistics show that the frequency of great earthquakes around the world is increasing exponentially. The earth is fairly writhing. The Lord needs an army of prayer warriors to stand in response to prophetic warnings as the cataclysms of the end time descend upon us more and more.

When Prayers Do Not Seem to Affect the Outcome

Judah, before the time of good King Josiah, had fallen so far away from the Lord that they even lost the Torah, His book of commandments! Hilkiah, the high priest, found it while they were cleaning out the Temple. King Josiah commanded the high priest and several others to inquire of Huldah the prophetess about the book of the law. She informed them that because they had burned incense to many false gods in the sacred places of the Lord, His wrath was against the people and "it shall not be quenched" (2 Kings 22:17). But she went on to give God's words to Josiah: "Because your heart was tender and you humbled yourself before the LORD . . . I will gather you to your fathers, and you will be gathered to your grave in peace, and your eyes will not see all the evil which I will bring on this place" (verses 19–20). He would not see the wrath that would come down on his people.

Josiah knew this was a warning from the Lord's compassionate heart. He knew God did not want to have to maintain His wrath for the people's sins. Josiah, therefore, did not rest in selfish satisfaction that he had been spared. He was not comforted to know that he would be spared but evil would come upon his people! Josiah instituted a number of reforms, destroying the false idols and altars of the Baalim, bringing down the houses of prostitution, defiling the high places of spiritual adultery, doing away with the horses given to the sun, etc. (see 2 Kings 23:1–14). Chapter 23 contains a long list of evils Josiah stopped, ending with his removing the spiritists and mediums and the teraphim and idols of abomination. Nevertheless, "the LORD did not turn from the fierceness of His great wrath with which His anger burned against Judah, because of all the provocations with which Manasseh had provoked Him" (verse 26).

Sometimes we can respond with repentances and changes galore, and they may not be enough. We may do all we know to do, and more, and it may yet not be enough to ward off disaster. Prophets must be prepared to know this and to love and adore God anyway, without complaint or cavil. It is not that God is churlish and waits with malicious glee while His servants strive futilely to please Him enough to appease His anger. He is never capricious or willful—as Greek mythology sometimes portrayed its gods. Rather, His thoughts and ways are far above ours. "The LORD longs to be gracious to you, and therefore He waits on high to have compassion on you" (Isaiah 30:18). God is faithful.

King Josiah performed all those many reforms, but the Bible says nothing about how much the people repented of their sins. Perhaps the people's lack of repentance was why the Lord's anger continued without relenting.

A Warning for Us Today!

I mentioned earlier that Dutch Sheets warned of the supreme importance for Americans to elect God's choice for our president in the 2000 election. Immediately after the balloting, our son Loren and I received an identical warning that men would try to steal the election. We gave that warning to whoever would listen, and called for fervent prayers for God's will to be done. It was on our hearts to pray that President Bush be elected. Needless to say, other Christians may well have disagreed with our conclusion about which candidate was being cheated. They may have thought the election was being stolen from Al Gore and prayed just as fervently in that direction. But the point does not concern political parties or allegiances. The point is that God calls and warns concerning national and political issues, and we need to respond. What concerns the Lord is that if His children respond in prayer, He is given the opportunity to accomplish His purposes.

The United States of America has been filling up the cup of her sins at a rapacious rate. The abominations of homosexuality and abortion alone are so enormous in the sight of God that I think it is only by amazing grace that we have not yet suffered the fate of Sodom and Gomorrah. Sexual immorality, divorce, greed for mammon, murders, violence and so many other sins increasingly defile our land. It is not enough that a godly leader pray on our behalf. Yes, this is important, and I believe that God gave us a leader who is a Josiah-type president. But we, the people, must repent and pray for God's redemption.

I wanted to end this chapter on a positive note—of hope for what is coming. But this chapter is about warnings before tragedies strike. *So, because God has put it so heavily on my heart, I must warn that disasters of unimaginable horror loom on the horizon for our country! Like Judah, we may be about to cross a threshold beyond which all the massive reforms of a Josiah-type leader are fruitless. Godly leaders may be unable to stem the tide of reaping that must follow such vast sinning.* There is an urgency. Will enough of God's people respond in prayer and supplication, falling on our faces before Him? Oh, that we would pray fervently for God's mercy, repenting of our country's sin, so that our God may turn tragedy into blessing!

While this book was undergoing the editing process, the unimaginable horror of the terrorist attack upon the two towers of the World Trade Center and the Pentagon happened on September 11, 2001. More terrorist attacks are expected, and the United States and its allies find themselves engaged in a war to destroy terrorism wherever it may be found. Our nation has responded with unparalleled unity, patriotism and prayers of repentance. It remains to be seen whether or not our repentances will "bear fruit in keeping with repentance" (Matthew 3:8). That is, will we reform our ungodly behaviors, or will returning to normalcy mean returning to spiritual apathy and moral dalliance?

EIGHT

PROTECTION THROUGH DISCERNMENT AND WORDS OF KNOWLEDGE

NEARLY EVERYTHING A PROPHET DOES is a gift from God for the protection of His people. Prophetic teachings are protection from error. Prophetic blessings protect us from missing out on God's best for us. In this chapter, we will look at how the prophet uses discernment and words of knowledge to help keep God's people safe.

Most of the anecdotes told in the previous chapters, especially those in the last chapter on "Warnings Before Tragedies Happen," could have been included in this section on protection. And the incidents related in this chapter could have been in the last. The difference is that the earlier stories reveal how our reactions to warnings can affect our Lord's actions. My goal was to teach and call Christians to respond appropriately. The focus here is more on the prophet's role to protect and two key functions he uses.

Discernment: The Abiding Equipment

God wants to protect His people through gifts of discernment that He gives to His prophets and others. Many who are not prophetic receive keen discernment, which ought to be heeded. But such discernment happens only sporadically. Discernment ought to be the abiding equipment of prophets, who should always be on the alert, ready to receive and act on discernment given by our Lord.

I was with a pastor friend in his church when God gave me discernment about his worship leader. I knew, without knowing how I knew, that the man was a usurper. Privately, I warned my friend that when he would go on a mission trip, this worship leader would try to wrest control from him. He would try to usurp his position and oust him as pastor.

My friend heard me but, unfortunately, did not know what to do with a prophet's warning. He should have at least prayed, and at best talked with his staff and the young man. In fact, while the pastor was on a teaching tour, the worship leader did try to take over the church and oust the pastor. He failed, perhaps due to the warning and the Lord's protection. But the event caused unnecessary division and hurt in the church that could have been alleviated had my friend known what to do.

God gave me a similar discernment while I was teaching on Wednesday evenings in a local pastor's church. The pastor and I were prayer buddies, sharing lunch together each week at a favorite soup and sandwich place. We talked often of prophetic matters, so I thought he would know what to do with a prophet's warning. One Wednesday evening, a strange man attended the service. He had come from a church in Alaska to plant a church in Coeur D'Alene, though I did not know that at the time. The first time I saw him, I knew what he would do. I warned my friend that this man would take a third of his people out to start a new church. Surprisingly, my friend also did not know what to do with a prophet's warning. I would have checked with him and coached him, but I left immediately on a teaching tour. Within a few weeks the man took away a third of my friend's church members!

Scriptural Warning for the Church

These examples bear witness to the fact that the Church simply must learn how to respond to the discernment and warnings of the Lord's prophets. I have learned the hard way not to take it for granted that anyone knows what to do.

Bishop Bill Hamon testifies of an instance in which a prophet should have known how to respond but did not:

> The Bishop and the Board of Governors came to the conclusion that [a particular] prophet had a spiritually contagious disease that needed to be "surgically" removed. In fact, we told him he had a "blind spot" in his life that prevented him from seeing the gravity of his situation.
>
> All thirty ministers present at the meeting agreed that the root problem was serious enough to require the prophet to withdraw from public ministry for a season. We offered to bring him to our ministry's campus for an extended time of ministry until he was delivered, healed, transformed and reinstated to public ministry.
>
> Sad to say, this prophet allowed us to cut the "Johnson grass" of the problem during our meeting with him—but as it turned out, he would not let us walk with him through a "winter season" withdrawn from public ministry so that God could destroy the deep weed roots in his heart.
>
> The prophet finally talked himself into believing that all the other thirty ministers were wrong, and he alone was right. His conclusion was a classic statement of self-deception: "You say I have a blind spot concerning my problems, but 'I do not see it.'" In the end, he resorted to the typical excuse of all those who are more "spiritual" than others, and who want to do their own thing; "**God told me**," he said, "that I am not to submit to your discipline but to continue my great ministry to the church." This minister had the potential to become a great pillar of truth and a father of the faith during his lifetime—if he had only submitted to the counsel of his bishop and the board of elders.

I was involved with a group of pastors called the Northwest Christian Fellowship. Among them was a pastor with whom I had a relationship of love and support like that between David and Jonathan. I loved him dearly. The Lord was elevating my friend into places of high service. The group discerned several areas of pride and possible error in him. They wanted to bless and protect him, and they offered to pray with him. The brother dutifully sat down, and the fellowship gathered around him. Since I knew him so well, I knew that their prayers were right on target; they could not have been praying more accurately and effectively. Their prayers could have saved him untold grief. But to my horror and chagrin, my friend arose from the chair and said, "I thank you brothers for trying. Your intentions were good. But I have to be the arbiter of my own soul. I have to judge that you are wrong, and I have to reject what you have prayed for me!" Eventually that man became mentally ill, basically from megalomania, and he fell from the ministry altogether. Sadly, this man did not know how to respond to discernment and, thus, God could no longer use him.

Scripture warns of this mistake:

Grievous punishment is for him who forsakes the way; *he who hates reproof will die.*

PROVERBS 15:10, EMPHASIS MINE

A fool rejects his father's discipline, but he who regards reproof is sensible.

PROVERBS 15:5

A wise son accepts his father's discipline, but a scoffer does not listen to rebuke.

PROVERBS 13:1

A rebuke goes deeper into one who has understanding than a hundred blows into a fool. A rebellious man seeks only evil, so a cruel messenger will be sent against him.

PROVERBS 17:10–11

Where there is no guidance the people fall, but in abundance of counselors there is victory.

PROVERBS 11:14; SEE ALSO 15:22; 20:18; AND 24:6

The sad experience of so many is that pride and individualism are endemic in the Church. Prophet after prophet, pastor after pastor, and leader after leader have fallen morally or in other ways because they have not cried out to God for a humble mind and spirit—or could not receive them. The man who can hear reproof and profit by it is all too rare. I plead with readers to look up in a concordance the many Scriptures about "understanding." Read them every day for a while. Burn them into the mind and heart. Be determined, and set your mind and heart to hear and cherish the warnings and reproofs of others in the faith. Your ministry—and your very soul—is at stake.

The violation of this principle is so epidemic and serious in the life of the Church that I must add a little more. Listen again to God's Word:

> He who neglects discipline despises himself, but he who listens to reproof acquires understanding.
>
> PROVERBS 15:32

> He who gets wisdom loves his own soul; he who keeps understanding will find good.
>
> PROVERBS 19:8

There is no way to overstress the importance of this teaching. God told Ezekiel He was sending him to a rebellious house. So many in God's house are rebellious, not willing to listen to God's word for their lives. Especially galling to God's prophets and other leaders is that most Christians pride themselves that they have humble minds. They believe they can easily listen to words of advice and hear corrections well. But the sad truth is that when we offer advice or give reproof Christians almost invariably react in anger and reject us and what we say! Oh, how much God's people would be protected from harm if only they, especially His leaders, would learn this most simple of lessons—the humility to love and cherish rebuke! Seek it, friends. Ask brothers for rebuke and counsel. Hear what they say—even when it seems all wrong. Ask God, "What truths would You have me hear in what they tell me?" and then ask brothers and sisters to tell you what you should hear. The enemy covets our souls. As I have said before, it is a dangerous world. Proverbs 24:6 states that "in abundance of counselors there is victory." Other versions translate, "there is safety."

I experienced another instance where the leadership in a church was not willing to listen to God's word and, thus, neglected the protection the Lord was offering them. I came home from a teaching trip and found a new man sitting at the soundboard in the church we were attending at the time. The Lord instantly gave discernment. I knew this man was not sexually clean. I warned the leadership, in confidence, that he would be sexually seductive to women in the congregation. But no one took heed. He was allowed to mingle freely among the members. In a few weeks he ran off with an elder's wife. She would not repent and return. The elder finally had to divorce her for infidelity—the one allowable ground for divorce as outlined in Matthew 5:32. She chose not even to be present in court.

How grievous it is when the Body does not respond to discernment and receive God's protection!

The Shield of Protection

It was a different story in a large ecumenical community in Sydney, Australia. This group is about 70 percent Catholic and 30 percent Protestant, working to build unity in the Body of Christ. Fortunately, they knew how to respond to prophets' discernment and warnings. Paula and I had been among them several times. This time I felt something wrong— a general, vague discernment, not focused on any one person. The Lord revealed to Paula and me that an Absalom would arise who would attract the love of many in the Body to himself and create division, trying to usurp leadership. I spoke privately to Joe Chircop, the leader of the group. He called his intercessors into praying for repentance and protection for the group. I think he also talked with the core leadership so that they would be alert. A few months later, an Absalom did arise and try to lead many astray. At first it seemed he might lead away as many as fifty people. But prayer had prepared the Body. In the end, only five people left. The community was protected, thanks to this leader's humility of heart.

This is one important reason God gives prophets as gifts to the Church, so that He may have opportunity to defeat the devil's schemes before they take root and grow to cause harm.

Paula and I were invited to teach in a large church connected to a Christian university. When we arrived, we discovered that several young men, sons of professors and leaders in the church, had been killed in accidents. The Lord gave us discernment that these were not mere accidents. He reminded us of the story in the Book of Joshua, when Achan stole the devoted things and hid them in his tent (see Joshua 7). The next day Israel was defeated in battle, and the young men were killed. God told Paula and me that hidden sin also dwelt in the camp of this church community. He commanded us to warn the pastor that these young men had died because hidden sin in the camp had broken the shield of God's protection, and if the people did not repent and turn from their sinning, more young men would die.

We did not want to risk giving that word. All week we delayed, hoping not to have to present it. At last, on the final evening, we took the pastor aside and told him what we discerned and what God had said to us. He received the word humbly and promised to think about it. Within half an hour, an elderly woman who always gave him positive, encouraging words presented the same message to him.

The pastor went on his knees before the Lord, saying, as David did, "Acquit me of hidden faults. Also keep back Your servant from presumptuous sins; let them not rule over me; then I will be blameless, and I shall be acquitted of great transgression" (Psalm 19:12–13). The Lord revealed to this pastor levels of pride for his successes, especially in ministering to leaders in Christ. The following Sunday he stood before his congregation, many of whom were professors at the university, and confessed his sins of pride and partiality. He made them aware of the word that had been given and of the disaster that had befallen Israel when hidden sin broke their shield. He called for all the people to examine their own hearts and lives. They were directed to write letters of confession to him and his wife, who would keep them utterly confidential, pray forgiveness for them and write to each one a letter pronouncing absolution.

The pastor told us later that 850 letters came! He and his wife went on retreat, and for three weeks they read and prayed and wrote replies. He said, "I was absolutely stunned! I was astounded at the number and magnitude of sins in the camp! I had no idea." The tragic deaths stopped.

I discerned blockage over another large church whose senior pastor was my friend. This was a new church formed by several churches uniting. While I was checking the word with my team, one of the pastors overheard our quiet conversation and immediately said, "That word needs to be heard by the entire leadership team." He called together all the leadership.

Our team revealed what we had seen. In this case, they were trying to be super spiritual but had not taken the time to get to know one another humanly. First Corinthians 15:46 says, "The spiritual is not first, but the natural; then the spiritual." The leadership of this church could not safely scale the spiritual heights because they had not taken requisite human time together, as Jesus and His disciples did when they walked and talked, got to know and trust one another. Jesus, in His mercy, was throwing a damper over them until they could meet and grow together in communication and

107

understanding. The leadership heard and obeyed the Holy Spirit. They held a retreat for no other purpose than just to be together, to build acquaintanceship and become friends. As that happened, the Holy Spirit fell on their meeting with great power and joy, and the church was protected from spiritual stagnation. Our team rejoiced that here was a church whose leadership heard and obeyed the Lord's words through His prophet.

Words of Knowledge

As with the other functions of the prophetic office, God gives gifts of knowledge to His prophets because He wants to deliver His children from harm. Often it works. But we are at best faulty vessels. Our knowledge is imperfect and incomplete. At no time have I been more keenly aware of how "My people are destroyed for lack of knowledge" (Hosea 4:6) than in this matter of the Church's often weak or faulty responses to prophets' warnings. And the weakness can be not only on the part of the people but also on the part of the prophet. We prophets are faulty vessels as well, using our prophetic hearing and seeing only partially or in less than effective ways to deliver people successfully from harm.

Many times we have been more grateful than we can express for the way God gave us revelation and used us to spare lives. But so often, we have a word of knowledge and make it known, the Church responds well, and yet fullness of freedom and safety do not follow as we hope they will. These are mysteries beyond our comprehension.

We can testify to examples of both failure and success in heeding God's words of knowledge.

When Safety Proves Elusive

After the previously mentioned pastor responded so well and stopped the succession of tragic deaths in his church, I became aware of a sense of death over him. The pastor was already beyond retirement age and still working long hours. I spoke *only* to his wife, telling her what I had seen and advising her to try to get her husband to slow down. She said she knew he could not slow down as long as he remained the senior pastor. I said he needed to be kept in much prayer, and that it would be best if she could convince him to retire. She did manage to talk him into retiring, watched over his diet, and made him get enough exercise and sleep. But several months later, while he was out jogging, he dropped over dead from a heart attack! She had responded to my warning and many people had prayed. But he died anyway. We do not know why. Perhaps my gift of knowledge in that instance was unconditional, or perhaps we did not pray enough.

This experience, along with many things, remains wrapped in mystery. Of course I asked God, "Why did he die, when You gave the warning and as far as I could see everyone responded rightly and did all the things that should have spared his life?" There comes a time when God does not answer, when we just have to let go and trust and honor His arcane wisdom. Continuing to pester God for answers may have more to do with unfaith and pride than trust in His wisdom and goodness. Habakkuk 2:4 says, "Behold, as for the proud one, his soul is not right within him; but the righteous will live by his faith." Through years of trying to advise prideful prophets and leaders who were cocksure of their own insights and opinions, I could aptly paraphrase Habakkuk 2:4 to say, "He who is proud of his own knowledge and insights is not upright, for the just are willing to walk humbly and blindly, trusting God." Or, "He who *has* to know all the answers is not upright, for the just shall walk by faith."

In a similar instance, I recognized death over my older brother, Hal. I wrote to him, telling him I was not ready to lose my brother. He also was past retirement age, working long hours as an accountant, chain smoking all the while. I pleaded with him to retire and to stop smoking, knowing his wife would read the letter. Martha got him to retire and stop smoking. But by then he had ruined his lungs and had to be on an oxygen tank 24 hours a day. He lived only one more year. At Christmastime, he and Martha went to visit their daughter who lived quite a bit north of their home in Georgia. Hal came down with a cold, which turned into pneumonia. He did not have the lung power to survive. He died in January. Granted, neither Hal nor Martha was strong in faith. But again, I could not help wondering why he was not given more years, when Martha had acted wisely and Paula's and my faith and prayers were applied as best we knew how. Why, when God warned and we acted, did my brother still pass away? It remains another unanswered question.

I recognized death over our beloved Pastor Bruce. I did not feel that he or the staff could hear and respond rightly to such a word of knowledge. They were not used to prophetic words of that magnitude and might take it too negatively—so I told Associate Pastor Bob Fetveit, who meets with us regularly in a small group. We began to pray. Soon thereafter, doctors discovered a melanoma on Bruce's back. It was removed, and many thought all danger had passed. I did not think so, because when I thought about it my spirit did not leap in celebration but, rather, sank in grief. The cancer returned. Despite hundreds of prayers and every medical treatment available, it soon metastasized. Bruce maintained faith. I have never seen such a glorious witness of faith in the midst of adversity—but after a prolonged season of prayer and warfare, we lost him.

His death remains one of the questions high on my list when I go to see our Lord face to face in heaven. Why could we not save him? Why did God warn me, even before the cancer entered his body, if He did not intend to heal him? Or did He intend to save him but we somehow missed whatever would have allowed God to do so? Some deaths hurt more than others. That one still touches my heart when I think about it.

I have said earlier that no one in his right mind wants to be a prophet. How painful it is to know things in advance and be powerless sometimes to prevent! A wise old adage says, "Knowledge increases sorrow." How true that is! Many proverbs in Scripture laud how knowledge increases gain, is a protection, is a fruit of wisdom, etc. But a prophet's knowledge before events happen not only carries the possibility of prevention of harm and the obtaining of blessing, but it also loads his heart with grief when people do not respond and tragedy happens so unnecessarily. Even worse is when Christians do respond with everything we know to do, but tragedy happens anyway. Sometimes, like Jeremiah in the stocks complaining before the Lord (see Jeremiah 20:7–18), the prophet almost wishes not to know or to have the gifts God has given to him.

When Protection Ensues

As difficult as it is for a prophet to see his word of knowledge not protect God's people, what a blessing it is when it allows protection and safety for many! I want to share a number of instances when warnings did bring blessing. Most of these are from our own family experiences. I suppose it is easier for the Lord to get through to us about those closest to us.

My sister also was a smoker. I was given a word of knowledge about death over her, as well, and warned her. She knew what to do. She prayed and stopped smoking. Today she is still with us and healthier than ever.

I saw death over our daughter-in-law Beth, and warned Loren and her. They and we called others into prayer. Cancer of the uterus was quickly discovered. I saw that the cancer was an attack of Satan, and I rebuked it from her body. Others discerned and prayed the same way. The cancer disappeared, and she is still serving alongside Loren today.

Another instance where God's word of knowledge brought protection to our loved one involved Loren himself. He worked between semesters in the silver, lead and zinc mines that I referred to earlier. At the time, he was working 7,500 feet below the ground. One day, I had a sense of danger and said, "What is it, Lord?" He gave me knowledge through a mental picture of Loren in a stope, which *Webster's* defines as a steplike excavation formed by the removal of ore from around a mineshaft. A huge boulder was tumbling down from high above. I knew if it hit him, it would kill him. I cried out, "Lord, get him out of the way!" That night I told Loren what I had seen. He said, "Yeah, Dad, that's exactly what happened today. I don't know how it missed me, but it did." God gave me this vision of danger because He wanted to save my son and knew I would pray.

Another day I had a very similar premonition. The Lord showed me Loren riding on the back of an ore car. A runaway ore train was speeding down the track behind him. I knew if it hit him, it would cut him in two. I cried out, "Lord, cause him to jump. Get him out of the way!" In the vision I saw Loren jump onto the ore car in front. That night when I told him what I had seen, he said, "Dad, you did it again. At the last second I jumped onto the ore car in front. The train hit with a big crash, but I wasn't hurt."

God gave me a word of knowledge for our son John, too. Paula and I were teaching in a retreat center in Illinois. On Thursday I finished praying with people before Paula did and returned to our room. The Lord said, *I'm glad you're here. I've been waiting to talk with you. John is going to get into a car with another boy. The young man will drive too fast. They are going to have an accident and both will be killed, unless you pray.* As soon as Paula returned, we entered into fervent prayer together.

When we arrived home, Johnny had a long scratch on his neck. We asked him what had happened. A young man had offered to take him out for a drive. John did not know at the time that the boy had stolen the car and this was an illicit "joy ride." They drove 100 miles an hour down a country road and crashed into a pickup that pulled out in front of them! The pickup and their car were totaled. But the farmer in the pickup and the boys were spared serious harm. The man's back was sore, John's neck was scratched, and that was it. We praised and thanked God. The young man and his family were held responsible. John was excused, as he was ignorant of the crime and held no prior record.

A short time later the Lord said to me, *You'd better pray again. John is getting into another car.* John's friend who lived across the street invited him for a ride around Hayden Lake. The first rendition of the story given to us was that they were traveling 40 miles per hour. Later, they admitted to 60—and finally, we discovered the speed was 80! They failed to negotiate a curve, slammed into a low bank and flew through the air, flipping twice before crashing into a tree. The car bounced back, turned twice more, and wound up back on the road, upside down! The car was accordioned on both ends, with only the passenger compartment remaining intact. John had seen the crash coming and had slid down onto the seat with his feet touching the ceiling. The impact tore his boot off and sprained his ankle, which was the only harm he suffered. His friend was not harmed at all—a sheer miracle for both of them.

Many young people are tragically maimed or killed on our highways every year. What if several prophets were in every church to give God's words of knowledge and call people into prayer? How many injuries and deaths might God be able to prevent? It is my heart's desire and my prayer that God will raise up and train His prophets—quickly!

John is an expert skier. He flashes down the hill like a bullet. Loren is a very good skier as well. He and John went down a long ski run together. But that was too boring for John, so when they went to the top again on the lift, he left Loren there and shot down the hill, caught the lift, rode back up, and beat Loren down! On the way back up again, he showed Loren his tracks—right across the tops of the moguls!

One day, as I let John out of the car at the ski lodge, I had a strong premonition. I knew John would have an accident and prayed for his protection. Have you seen the cartoon that shows ski tracks that go on *both* sides of a tree? John did that—at full speed. He hit the tree so hard he knocked all the snow off and buried himself! Miraculously, he suffered not even a bruise, not a scratch or a piece of torn clothing. Johnny was only angry because it took him the better part of an hour to dig himself out from under the snow! Again, God gave me a word of knowledge, and then He used my prayers to protect my son.

Another incident of protection occurred when two pregnant women, both in late term, planned to take a trip by auto. A prophetic person in their prayer group had a vision of their being in a bad accident. He warned the two and the prayer group. The women felt God was calling them to take the trip and that it would be an act of unfaith not to go. The group redoubled its prayers. A huge eighteen-wheeler lost control and side-swiped their car. Every window was shattered into bits. The car was demolished. But neither woman sustained even a cut from all that flying glass! God kept them and their babies perfectly safe.

God also kept one of our deacons safe by giving me a word of knowledge for him. As I came out of a deaconate meeting one day, I saw the deacon's car parked by the sidewalk in front of the church. I knew, without knowing how, that there was something wrong with the right front wheel. I said to the deacon, "You know my premonitions. There's something wrong with your right front wheel. Do not drive fast. Go very slowly down to the service station, and let them check it. Okay?" Normally he was a fast driver and would have peeled rubber halfway down the block. Instead, he drove at a snail's pace, and when he turned left at the corner, the right front wheel fell off! God did not want him hurt—or his car to hurt someone else. The man heeded the warning and was protected.

God gave me a word of knowledge for Ken Campbell, who was one of the trustees of our church and is my best friend. In north Idaho one cannot wade the streams to fly-fish during spring runoff, as the water is too deep, fast and dangerous. I had a dream of Ken falling into a whirlpool, being sucked under and drowned. I prayed for his protection but had no time to warn Ken because he and his son Greg went out to fish early the next morning.

Ken was standing on a big boulder above the river, fishing in an eddy by the bank. In front of him was a mammoth whirlpool. He thought, *Man, if anybody got caught in that, he'd never get out!* Just then Greg floated by, headed for the whirlpool—he had fallen in upstream from Ken. There was nothing to do but to throw down his pole and jump in after Greg! Somehow the current carried Greg off to the side and he climbed out safely. But Ken was sucked into the whirlpool. To this day, he does not know how he got out, but he did.

I think I may have told that story somewhere in our writings. I retell it here to relate the sequel. Subsequently, Ken developed two successful real estate offices, becoming both a broker and an appraiser. He was becoming quite well-off. But the Bunker Hill Mine closed, and with it the only smelter for all the mines in the Silver Valley. Twenty-seven hundred men lost their jobs overnight. Most moved out, looking for work. No one wanted to move in. Hundreds of houses stood empty, and nobody wanted to buy. For example, the worth of the parsonage, owned by the church, fell from $65,000 to $8,000! Ken's own house, appraised at $80,000 (probably $150,000 in today's market), fell to $18,000 and even then had no takers! Ken was being sucked down in a financial whirlpool. He lost everything.

The loss drove him to drink and to even heavier smoking. His health was sinking into another whirlpool. Under the strain, the health of his wife, Donna, deteriorated into crippling arthritis—another seemingly inescapable whirlpool.

Our prayer group kept on praying for Ken and his family. He suffered a heart attack and wound up in the hospital. The Lord so miraculously healed his heart there was almost no trace of any problem. His doctors even said if he applied for health insurance he would have no trouble getting it. During his short stay in the hospital, the Lord took away his lifelong smoking habit and his desire for alcohol so completely that he has never touched, or wanted, a cigarette since and no longer has a drinking problem. He began doing some business consulting for Elijah House, and shortly thereafter he became our CEO!

God miraculously healed Donna, and she became our telephone receptionist, who assigns callers to appointments with our prayer ministers. Though that is one of the most responsible and, thus, most stressful jobs at Elijah House, her arthritis did not return.

What a parable God used in Ken's life! He not only wanted to rescue Ken from the physical whirlpool, but He wanted to save Ken and his family from every other kind of whirlpool. And God used the process to mature him so that he could become the one who would lead Elijah House into its present property and sound financial practices.

How many men and women, teenagers and others are there who have been sucked under various kinds of powerful whirlpools because there were no prophetic people to see the hand of God and pray them through? How many needless accidental deaths have claimed the lives of God's soldiers and servants? How many tragedies could have been averted had there been established prophets on the job, alert to the Holy Spirit's summons?

I suggest every reader study Cindy Jacobs' *The Voice of God* and Dutch Sheets' *Intercessory Prayer* and develop a habit of listening to God in order to intercede. It is true that not all are prophets to whom God speaks His words of warning. However, all can hear, and should. But listen especially when prophets warn.

Even Prophets Must Heed Words of Knowledge

I cannot leave the subject of protection without confessing something humbling—maybe it will be a lesson and, therefore, a protection. Throughout this chapter, I have been pleading with all to hear and pray when prophets warn. In early May 2001, Paula and I were in Olathe, Kansas, teaching about inner healing. A prophetic type of person came to me at the close of one of the services. He said, "John, I see a small artery at the top of your heart that is going to cause you trouble." Every EKG, blood pressure test and cholesterol rating has shown my heart to be in perfect condition. I thanked the brother for his word and said I did not know what it meant but would pray about it—*which I promptly forgot to do!* On Friday, May 25, I suffered a heart attack because a small artery at the top of my heart had become blocked! A 9–1–1 call resulted in an ambulance ride to the Coeur D'Alene hospital, followed by a helicopter lift to Sacred Heart Hospital in Spokane, Washington, and then immediate surgery. The cardiologist did an angioplasty and inserted a stent. I am now at home again and recovering slowly. Every scheduled trip for that summer was cancelled. I could do nothing but rest—and write this book.

Have you heard the warning? *At the very time I was pleading with the Body of Christ to heed prophets' warnings, I failed to do so myself and am paying the price for it!* I did not share this just to be humble and honest— I am not that much of either. But I hope it helps to make us all keenly aware that even when we know and are properly trained about the blessing of prophetic warnings, we can get so busy and preoccupied that they float right on by! It is so easy to overlook the still, small voice of God, both inwardly and when spoken by others.

God had been telling me He would give me a time of rest—but I kept on working. Now, by the grace and providence of God I will have nothing but rest—and the time to write, which had been eroding more and more into busyness. For the less stubborn and the more obedient, there

115

are easier ways to receive God's best for us! I wonder if I myself have heard my own words. Have you? I pray it may be so.

Please join with me in praying for the Lord of hosts to raise up an army of intercessors and a cadre of prophets who can give concrete direction to their prayers. *Receive them when they arise. Listen to their warnings, and respond.* God gives His prophets as gifts of love and protection to His Church.

NINE

PERSONAL WORDS AND
THE PROPHET'S CHARACTER

GIVING PERSONAL WORDS—that is, a personal prophecy for an individual—is the most well-known of all the prophetic functions. It is perhaps the one that can most easily be wrong and cause damage to the Church! Do not misunderstand, I am all for the giving of personal words. This function is one of God's best gifts to the Body of Christ.

But whatever God gives to us for great blessing can be misused to the same degree of harm. For example, He gave us the Holy Spirit, the very God of unity, the Giver of great gifts, the very expression of His love among us and the Prophet of the Father's intended blessings. And yet, we have managed to fight over who has the Spirit, who does not, whether or not the gifts of the Holy Spirit exist for today, what they are, and how or if they are to be employed. Similarly, He gave us the sacrament of Communion as the uniting, healing bond of our hearts. We have fought continuously over the Lord's Supper—who ought to serve it, to whom and not to whom, when and how—and even if it is really His body and blood or just a memorial. The gift of tongues was given to us for blessing, and who does not know how we have argued and divided over that gift? How

117

about the wondrous gift of marital sex? Of all His blessed and holy human gifts to us, have we not defiled this gift more than any other? We have turned it into a scourge of immorality and amorality, and a carrier of deadly diseases. *In short, precisely to the degree of blessing of any gift God has given, to that degree we can and have turned that gift to harm.*

This is supremely the case with the prophetic movement and the giving and receiving of personal words. Bishop Bill Hamon speaks of this with great insight and clarity:

> Every movement since the beginning of the great restoration period, which began in A.D. 1500, has become more powerful with greater potential for salvation or self-destruction. The process is like the progressive inventions of warfare weapons, from gunpowder to single-shot rifles to the multi-firing. From the Gatling gun to our modern rapid-fire assault weapons; from dynamite and nitroglycerine to atomic and hydrogen bombs and now to space warfare.
>
> If atomic and laser power were to fall into the hands of unprincipled, self-centered terrorists, they would have no scruples about using this power to destroy many lives to further their own selfish ends. They would use these weapons to intimidate, manipulate and control people to build their own dictatorial kingdom.
>
> The ministry of prophets and prophecy is much the same way. As the latest and most powerful force and spiritual weapon of warfare being brought forth in the Church, it has the most potential for blessing or destruction of any restoration movement during the last five hundred years. Prophets and prophecy have great power to influence and affect the lives of people. If a prophet does not have a right spirit and motivation, Christ's character and biblical principles, he or she has the potential to control and manipulate people with supernatural knowledge, visions, revelations and miracles. But if a prophet does have the right spirit and motivation, he or she has great power to influence people for God toward unity, obedience, humility and Christ-likeness.

In chapters 10 and 11, we will discuss how the Church needs to mature in order to rightly receive and employ personal words, but I regard it as imperative that we first examine the role of the prophet in this function. The demand for Christlike character in those of us who are His prophets is perhaps never greater than when giving personal words of prophecy to others.

A Task of Great Responsibility

A prophet is called to speak as the very mouthpiece of God. But God does not simply "use" any person like a channel. Because we are all imperfect, God takes a risk in speaking through human vessels. We have already looked at how people's sin can interfere with the blessings God wants to give. In similar ways, the faults of a prophet, if not dealt with, can affect the message God wants to give. For this reason Paul wrote to Timothy,

> Now in a large house there are not only gold and silver vessels, but also vessels of wood and of earthenware, and some to honor and some to dishonor. Therefore, if anyone cleanses himself from these things, he will be a vessel for honor, sanctified, useful to the Master, prepared for every good work. Now flee from youthful lusts and pursue righteousness, faith, love and peace, with those who call on the Lord from a pure heart.
>
> 2 TIMOTHY 2:20–22

Such advice is good for any person in any office or function. But how is it unique when applied specifically to prophets in the function of giving personal words?

Preachers know that however much they are inspired by the Holy Spirit, it is their own words they are speaking—not direct words from God. It is the same for teachers. And healers do not normally say, "Thus saith the Lord." Prophets are different. They speak for God—it is hoped not with their own words but with His. Prophets may say, "Thus saith the Lord" and mean their words to be taken as His even if they do not actually say words He gave them. That is, although they may be sure of the meaning God wants them to convey, they may have to express it in their own words. Even so, they are still speaking as the mouthpiece of the Lord. This requires far greater death of self and fuller intimacy with God than other offices. The prophet must maintain a pure heart so that he does not mislead the people with intentions and words that are not God's but his own.

No one is used as a pipeline. God does not simply lift one end up and pour His water down through it so that it remains unchanged and unsoiled in the process. To use another descriptive picture, God does not speak through a telephone line that has no life of its own. He speaks through the person of the prophet. The messenger is also the message.

119

Therefore, a prophet ought not to say, as some have, "Brother, that was from God, not me." Even though God speaks His words through the prophet, those words come through the prophet and, thus, bear his stamp. The prophet, then, is responsible for those words. This is a mystery of partnership, for which reason Paul said, "I labored even more than all of them, yet not I, but the grace of God with me" (1 Corinthians 15:10). *I, yet not I, but God.* The mystery of our walk and all our service as prophets is contained in these words. He uses us as His vessels, so it is we who do His work because His message comes through what we are; yet if we are in Christ it is actually not we but God in us.

How the Cross Changed the Prophetic Role

In Old Testament days, until the great change in Ezekiel 4, it could seem as though God wanted nothing of His prophet's flesh involved and simply used the prophet as a pipeline. I say "it could *seem*." Many people hold an idealized view of Old Testament prophets, as though somehow they were perfect transmitters. To use another metaphor, some believers think prophets were like tape recorders. They think that God could record His message on a cassette in the prophet's mind, punch the replay button and out would come God's message, unchanged in the transmission.

In fact, I think perhaps *most* Christians hold that faulty notion—that prophecies of Old Testament prophets were always accurate and true. But few concepts could be further from the truth. The major and minor prophetical books, the Neviim Rishonim and the Neviim Aharonim (the historical books called by the Jews "The Earlier and Later Prophets") do record the many accurate and powerful words of God's prophets. But those actually may have been glorious exceptions rather than the rule! Even a casual reading of the Old Testament reveals so many false prophets and erring words that Jeremiah (chapter 23) and Ezekiel (chapter 13) thundered against their erring ways! Hundreds of Zedekiahs, Pashhurs, Hananiahs and Balaams dot the historical landscape, and those are only the instances we know about! God had to work on His prophets drastically in order to speak an accurate word through them.

Actually, each prophet's entire being was involved, and the character and personal development of the prophet had an impact on God's message. The point I am making is the difference between the Old and New Testaments. In the Old, the way in Christ had not yet been opened for fullness of death and sanctification through the blood and cross of Christ.

The writer of Hebrews contrasted Old Testament prophets and their prophesying to those in the New, extolling the greatness of Jesus as the difference. Hebrews 1:1–2 says: "God, after He spoke long ago to the fathers in the prophets in many portions and in many ways, in these last days has spoken to us in His Son, whom He appointed heir of all things, through whom also He made the world." Some students of the Word have foolishly lifted this Scripture out of context to say that since the Son has come, God speaks only through Him, and there is no longer need or use for prophets. This is incorrect theology, because the Word of God never contradicts itself, and throughout the New Testament God spoke in many ways and places through His prophets. So what does this Scripture mean? As indicated above, in Old Testament times when God spoke through a prophet, He risked the misrepresentation of His message by whatever degree of character and personality had not yet been broken and transformed in that prophet. Since the coming of Christ, this is not so to the same degree. *Now, God speaks through His Son in and through His prophets.* This means and calls for degrees of death of self and purging of heart and mind through the cross of Christ that were unavailable in Old Testament times.

This is so important for us to understand that I will repeat it, and add another dimension.

Hebrews 1:1–2 means that because we are sons and daughters, God speaks through us through the purification of Jesus' blood and cross. This purification was, of course, unavailable in Old Testament times. Therefore, we experience a more fulsome death of self and resurrection into new life than those prophets of the Old Testament. This means that something different now transpires within our character.

To be sure, today we have all too many false and immature prophets, but the grace of the Lord Jesus Christ to purify our hearts is available today as it never was under the old covenant. That is why God can so much more trustingly and, therefore, restfully today speak through His sons and daughters than He could before Christ came. There is to be "no sweat" in the house of God (see Ezekiel 44:18). Sweat is a sign of straining. Jesus' death is to become our death so fully (see Galatians 2:20; 5:24) that we enter into His rest (see Hebrews 4:9–10). Restfully abiding in our Lord

121

is what enables us to hear God clearly. That depth of rest in holy death and resurrection was not available to Old Testament prophets.

I recognize this is a startling statement to make to those of us who have been conditioned to think of Old Testament prophets as nearly perfect, but knowing so many of today's faithful prophets as I do, as well as some of the weak and false, I daresay the percentage of today's true prophets far exceeds that of Old Testament times!

For those who still believe such a statement is shocking, remember that the Kingdom does not go backward. Scripture tells us, "Do not say, 'Why is it that the former days were better than these?' For it is not from wisdom" (Ecclesiastes 7:10). Modern prophets are not a poor reflection of what was. Things get better, not worse. God has saved the best wine until the last. The prophets of today are not inferior to those of the Old Testament. Perhaps some Christians have not yet seen such miracles as the calling down of fire on bullocks and arrogant soldiers, the raising of the dead or changing poisoned waters to fresh. This is partly because the climate of belief in our society has not allowed many miracles, even as Jesus could work few miracles in Nazareth because of their unbelief (see Matthew 13:58). But some stupendous miracles are happening in our time, even better than in the Old. God's anointing rests on today's prophets as it never rested on those in the Old Testament, because the Holy Spirit dwells *within* them.

We read of how Peter raised Tabitha from death (Acts 9:36–41), and Paul raised Eutychus (Acts 20:9–12). These were single, startling evidences of the Lord's reality and power. But today, miracles are happening more frequently and in greater numbers than even New Testament times! For example, most of us have heard of the hundreds of miracles that have happened in meetings conducted by Reinhold Bonnke. No Old Testament prophet, nor even any prophet in New Testament days, did anything of that magnitude! The same happened in the ministry of Kathryn Kuhlman. And I know of modern prophets, who remain nameless here at their request, who have many times raised the dead! Jesus said, "Truly, truly, I say to you, he who believes in Me, the works that I do, he will do also; and greater works than these he will do; because I go to the Father" (John 14:12). Jesus was saying that because He was going to the Father, His power would increase among His disciples so that they could work even greater miracles than He had. To me, that is a statement of progressively greater power as the centuries go by. Can anyone suppose that as Jesus has continued to sit at the right hand of the Father, His power has declined or stopped increasing? Truly, the best wine does come last.

Notice that when the anointing was full upon Elijah he could perform far beyond the limits of his flesh, but when the anointing waned, he fled from an unbelieving woman (see 1 Kings 19:1–3). Under God's anointing, Jeremiah could stand against his entire nation, but read Jeremiah 20:7 to see how he reacted when the anointing of God no longer graced his heart and mind! Under anointing, Jonah converted all of Nineveh, but read chapter 4 to see how his flesh reared its ugly head when the anointing left. Balaam did well under anointing, but what a mess he made when left to himself. At first glance Moses might seem to be an exception, because he became more meek and humble than any man (see Numbers 12:3). But remember, it was because of a character flaw that he could not enter into the Promised Land. I wonder if that fact itself is meant to be a parable to us, by which God reminds us that none will be allowed to cross over into the promised land of Christlike character without drastic changes through the blood and cross of our Lord Jesus Christ.

Who knows how we might react today under circumstances such as these prophets endured? But it is to be hoped that because of Christlike transformation in modern prophets' character, the subsequent Christlike righteousness and ability to stand might persist long after anointing ebbs. Do you understand? *In each of these Old Testament prophets, God's anointing had to overcome, like a flood pouring over the top of a dam. But under the new covenant, God wants that anointing to flow in and through His Son, in and through the character of His sons and daughters—and when anointing wanes, Christlike character remains. What a dramatic difference between the Old and the New!*

The Prophet Must Be Willing

This drastic difference between Old and New Testament prophets depends upon the willingness of prophets to let God transform their character. And it depends upon *how much* they are willing to undergo His transforming work. A prophet's death to self and resurrection into the new covenant must be full.

To give a minor example, when dealing with me in preparation for the office of the prophet, and specifically about giving personal words, the Lord said, *John, if I gave you power to change anything, what would you change?* I thought a long time before answering, and finally replied, "Nothing, Lord." He said, *You have answered rightly.*

Why was that right? God was testing me. The unspoken question had to do with trust. It is God who orders His universe. Would I presume to "fix things" for God? Would I think I could make them better than He has? Or could I trust His grace to order and reorder whatever and whenever He so chooses?

The Lord continued, *If I gave you power to change anyone, whom would you change?* Again I thought awhile—there were and still are a lot of people I would like to get hold of and change! I used to say, "I'd like to grab hold of some people by the tongue, jerk them wrong side out, scrub them up and put them back in again!" But then I pondered, as Mary did, and at last I answered, "No one, Lord." Again He said, *You have answered rightly.* It took a lot of being slain by the Lord and dying with Him on the cross (see Galatians 2:20; 5:24) before I could make that kind of answer.

This principle is crucial for every prophet to learn if he is to be used by God to safely present personal words—or do anything else. *Jesus went to the cross and died for us rather than use His power to coerce any of us to change for the better.* He paid the price for our free will so that we may learn, develop and grow within ourselves freely and not by manipulation, intimidation, power or anything else. God will not force anyone to choose rightly or to do the right thing. He pays the price in painful reaping of what we sow in error and rebellion, so that we may have the requisite freedom to grow in grace and to become mature sons and daughters with whom He can have fellowship throughout eternity.

Every prophet, therefore, must be careful that his words not intimidate or coerce his hearers to choose what the prophet thinks is right. If under that duress the persons choose rightly, the result would not be good because their hearts would not have owned what God desires. God wants to raise sons and daughters who freely choose Him and His ways, not conformers who perform out of fear rather than adoration and respect in love.

This must be learned not simply theologically and biblically, but it must be written onto the heart of God's prophets through suffering. Scripture says Jesus never sinned, and He said of Himself, "I always do the things that are pleasing to Him" (John 8:29). So if Jesus always obeyed and always pleased His Father, how did He learn obedience?

A beginning pianist may perform in a recital after only a few months' training. Suppose he makes no mistakes and does only what pleases his teacher? That is well and good—he has not "sinned" against the "Ten Commandments" of piano playing. Now suppose ten or fifteen years later he performs at another recital, and again he makes no mistakes and pleases his teacher in all he does. He has never "sinned." But how much more accomplished an artist he has become! How much suffering in long hours of practice did that perfection require?

Picture a mother saying to her daughter, "Wash the dishes." The daughter obeys but grumbles all the while, "I don't see why I have to do all the work around here all the time." How different it would be if the daughter were to reply, "Oh, thank you, Mother. It's a delight to be allowed to serve the family," and meant what she said while she did the work with a joyful heart, grateful to be allowed to serve! Wow! I think we would faint dead away if one of our children responded that way! But Jesus responded like that.

"Although He was a Son, He learned obedience from the things which He suffered" (Hebrews 5:8). I believe this Scripture means that Jesus learned to delight in obedience through His suffering. In the same way, prophets must learn to delight in obedience through suffering, continuing to die to self in order that the Lord's will may be done through them.

This is why I say always to look for a prophet whose "spiritual body" bears a mass of scars from learning through suffering. It is the suffering that teaches obedience, and obedience is vital, for God looks for servants whom He can trust.

God is writing a book. It is entitled *The Slow Die-ers*. You and I are the pages! Look for a thick chapter.

Determining If a Prophet's Word Is True

Considering all of the above, let me summarize a list of conclusions or advice:

1. Beware of fledgling prophets who love to go around presenting personal words. God may speak through the young and immature, but test and wait more circumspectly for confirmation. Listen with respect to the older and more experienced prophets, though not without caution.

2. If possible, know something of the history and character of those whom God (or presumption) sends to give you a word. While you are waiting for confirmation, ask around about the prophet. Any genuine prophet will welcome and not be offended by that kind of inquiry.

3. Look for a prophet's humility and willingness to be proven wrong. Look for defensiveness or the lack of it. Look for openness and security of heart when questioned.

4. If the prophet stands on his office and demands that you hear him, turn away. Genuine prophets will respect your free will and will not use their position to intimidate you into accepting them or their words. A true prophet will only grieve and pray for you if you will not hear what he says.

5. If the prophet says, "Thus saith the Lord," with a finality and sense that you are in rebellion if you take time to ponder, most likely it is not something that the Lord really "saith." Or if it is, the prophet is so full of himself that his arrogance turns you away. Actually, I almost never say, "Thus saith the Lord," and would prefer that other prophets not do so. Once a prophet says, "Thus saith the Lord," how can the hearer be free to ponder what is said without fear of being in rebellion? I would rather say, and often do, "I think this is what I hear the Lord saying. How does it witness to you?" If it is a true word, God will vindicate and confirm. The prophet does not have to validate himself. The Lord will.

6. In addition to testing a prophet against the Word and sound doctrine, test by the nature of our Lord Jesus Christ. Demand, control, manipulation, threats, flattery, cajoling and the giving of false comfort are never of the Lord. Since the coming of our Lord Jesus, truth is not simply mere objective fact—truth is a Person. A prophet may say many things by revelation that can convince you this really is something supernatural, but does God's Holy Spirit also witness? Is the presentation given within Christ's loving nature?

A prophetess with what is known as a Jezebel, or controlling, spirit came into a church we knew of. She thought she had a gift like a Nathanic prophet to accost people with their sins so they would repent. But there was nothing of Nathan's gentle way in what she said and how she acted. Actually, she had a demonic quality of suspicion and accusation, and she would accuse people of things that were long ago laid at the foot of the cross and forgiven. If the people demurred, her voice rose to a shout and labeling ensued: "You're in rebellion!" Her facts were often accurate. Accuracy by itself is an insufficient test. Test all by the loving nature of Jesus.

7. Wait. Satan hurries and demands. Jesus allows plenty of time for confirmation. Act on nothing until it is confirmed out of the mouths of two or three witnesses. Since Satan copies and will also try to confirm, remember that nothing is done in isolation and other tests may invalidate false confirmations. For example, ask: Is it scriptural? If the principle is not directly in Scripture, as many modern things are not covered specifically in Scripture itself, is it consonant with the flow of Scripture's purposes? Does it follow? Is it in Christ's nature?

The Body Must Test All Personal Words

God is not pleased by slavish obedience to personal words. He wants us to test each one. "Beloved, do not believe every spirit, but test the spirits to see whether they are from God, because many false prophets have gone out into the world" (1 John 4:1).

But just as He wants His words to be presented within His own nature so also He wants testing to be done within the same Holy Spirit. There is a fine line between proper testing and rebellious resistance. Let the Body pray to have a humble but not a compliant spirit.

Great blessings await those who learn how to hear God's words—directly and/or through His prophets. Be among them.

TEN

PERSONAL WORDS
AND DARK SPEECH

WE HAVE OBSERVED the changed nature of purification for New Testament prophets, and we have looked at some of the tests we ought to employ when presented with personal words. Now, let us look at the nature of the words themselves.

The Nature of Personal Words

In Numbers 12:6–8, the Lord said:

> "Hear now My words:
> If there is a prophet among you,
> I, the LORD, shall make Myself known to him in a vision.
> I shall speak with him in a dream.
> Not so, with My servant Moses,
> He is faithful in all My household;
> With him I speak mouth to mouth,
> Even openly, *and not in dark sayings,*
> And he beholds the form of the LORD."

EMPHASIS MINE

Though the term *dark speech* sounds ominous, it simply refers to times when the Lord speaks in figures or parables. Remember when the disciples said, with evident relief, "Lo, now You are speaking plainly and are not using a figure of speech" (John 16:29). Psalm 78:2 prophesied that the Lord would speak to us in dark speech: "I will open my mouth in a parable; I will utter dark sayings of old."

Sometimes God speaks directly, as He did to Moses, Aaron and Miriam in Numbers 12 and to the disciples in John 16. But much of the time, even when we may think He is speaking directly, He is actually communicating in dark speech.

The Nature of Communication

Why does God use this form of communication? There are a number of reasons. First, because of the polite, indirect nature of the Eastern culture. Speaking too directly can insult another's intelligence, force decisions and control others. If you read John 3–4 with this in mind, you will see how much of the discussions with Nicodemus and the woman at the well hardly seem to follow consecutively. In fact, to our Western ears, trained as we are to value and honor directness, much in those conversations hardly seems to make sense. Little follown upon what the other said. Frankly, we would probably feel like saying, "Hey! What's going on here? Are they really talking to each other?"

For example, Nicodemus said, "Rabbi, we know that You have come from God as a teacher; for no one can do these signs that You do unless God is with him" (John 3:2). We Westerners would expect Jesus to say something like, "Thank you. I'm glad you see that." But Jesus leaped way beyond to say, "Truly, truly, I say to you, unless one is born again he cannot see the kingdom of God" (verse 3). Jesus read Nicodemus' heart and mind and spirit, and He offered Nicodemus a polite invitation to ponder and keep asking questions. We moderns might have sensed, "Hey, this guy is beginning to open up," and then we would have blurted out, "Have you been born anew? Let me share the Four Spiritual Laws with you!" Eastern courtesy will not override the other's necessity to ponder and think for himself. Therefore, Jesus often spoke in parables and figures.

We see the same thing in John 4. Jesus commanded the woman to give Him a drink. She answered rather directly for a person of her culture:

"How is it that You, being a Jew, ask me for a drink since I am a Samaritan woman?" (verse 9). Jesus did not answer her question at all. Rather, He read her spirit and saw that here was a woman who could come alive in Him. So He said, "If you knew the gift of God, and who it is who says to you, 'Give Me a drink,' you would have asked Him, and He would have given you living water" (verse 10). Not only did His reply not answer her question, but He also did not blurt out, "Listen up, woman, I'm the very Son of God." Instead, He politely invited her into discussion and revelation, careful not to override or cut short her own enterprise of discovery. He spoke in dark speech, inviting her to think about what He could mean by figuratively speaking of Himself as "living water." It was only when she was deep into her process of discovery, when He knew it was time and that what He said would confirm to her mind what her heart and spirit were sensing, that He spoke directly. He then told her, as modern prophets do, what was happening in her life, "You have correctly said, 'I have no husband'; for you have had five husbands, and the one whom you now have is not your husband; this you have said truly" (verses 17–18).

They talked some more, and revelation dawned upon her. She saw with great excitement that He was the Messiah. But note the indirect, polite way of the East; she does not blurt out, "Oh, my gosh, You're the Messiah!" Rather, she offers, "I know that Messiah is coming" (verse 25). This left it up to Jesus to confirm or deny, and He responded with clear and direct speech, "I who speak to you am He" (verse 26).

See again the polite Eastern way when she ran to her village. We would most likely have shouted, "The Messiah's here! I've seen Him!" Instead, she said, "Come, see a Man who told me all things that I ever did. *Could this be the Christ?*" (verse 29, NKJV, emphasis mine). She would not abrogate her villagers' rights to make their own decisions. She asked rather than told, thus inviting the people into the enterprise of making their own discovery. In the end, when many had come to believe, they said, "*It is no longer because of what you said that we believe, for we have heard for ourselves and know that this One is indeed the Savior of the world*" (verse 42, emphasis mine). Not only did she not forestall their own path to discovery, she opened the door of revelation so that by themselves in the Holy Spirit, they saw not only that He is the promised Messiah, but that He is "the Savior of the world"! This was a revelation no one else had yet seen, a truth that even the disciples would have trouble accepting long after His resurrection!

Prophets Must Emulate Jesus' Polite Way

Here is a lesson I fervently hope today's prophets will not only hear but ponder by the hour. *When we as prophets present personal words as if they are fait accompli, something finalized, and give the hearer the impression that all he or she has to do is to submit or be in rebellion, we are not acting in Jesus' wise and gracious way!* Jesus speaks so often in dark speech in order to invite us into the process of discovery. He does not want to violate our enterprise in that process. If revelation is simply handed to people as a finished product, they have had no part in it. Even if the word is believed and accepted, it may not yet have become theirs because they have not been invited to own it.

As a prophet of the Lord, you may receive a true word that He wants you to impart to a person or group. But please ponder, think and rethink, *How does God want me to present it?* Ask the Holy Spirit for His wisdom, His tact and graciousness, so that you present the word not only in His kindness and graciousness, but in such a way that your hearer(s) is invited into the enterprise of discovery. Do not squelch people's initiative by your polish and finality.

This may be a small part of what Paul meant when he said, "I was with you in weakness and in fear and in much trembling, and my message and my preaching were not in persuasive words of wisdom, but in demonstration of the Spirit and of power, so that your faith would not rest on the wisdom of men, but on the power of God" (1 Corinthians 2:3–5).

While God was drilling this into my recalcitrant heart, a young man came to me after I had just spoken and prayed rather eloquently. He said, "John, you're a spellbinder." At first I felt complimented and rather proud—and then I began to feel the Holy Spirit's gentle nudging. That was no compliment. It was a warning. The cross was being emptied of its power by my behavior. I was reaching out, through the power of eloquence, to control audiences, "spellbinding" them into receiving. *Prophets, above all others, have that kind of power to influence.*

Bring it to death, dear ones. Flesh seems to produce results, but in the end it profits nothing. Do not be afraid of stumbling and sounding foolish. It is by the foolishness of the Gospel that we are saved.

Do you "lay words on people," or do you lay out options that invite pondering and the slow process of making decisions? Do you love to tell people what to do? Have you noticed that whenever you ask the Holy Spirit if you should do this or that thing, He seldom answers directly? Most of the time He just gives you more information for your decision-making process rather than make up your mind for you.

Many times I have seen a person's prospective spouse. Never would I describe the spouse and command the person by saying, "God says you are to marry this one." In such instances, as I have mentioned, I do not even give a hint as to what the person looks like. The Holy Spirit does not want my prophetic gift to rob the other of the enterprise of his own life, even if that means running the risk that the other may not choose God's highest and best for his life.

Friends, may I plead with you to die a thousand deaths to self rather than to control another life? Always, always respect the heuristic (seeking) spirit of the other and the leading of the Holy Spirit. He is the guide for others' lives, not you. Therefore, following the example of our Lord Jesus, prefer to speak in parables and figures.

Dark Speech Is for Our Own Good

Sandy DeLoach, a prophetess in Dallas, Texas, did it rightly. I had previously laid down my Indian heritage, cutting free from the negative and harmful aspects of it. But God wanted me to pick it up again and embrace the godly aspects of that heritage so that He could use it for His purposes. Sandy did not come and say directly, "God says, 'Pick it up again, John.'" Instead she came one morning in between teaching sessions and said, "I have a word for you, John." Her presence was not demanding, nor did her words give the impression that I must hear this or be in rebellion. She was asking, "Do you want to hear it?" I said, knowing and trusting her, "Yes, I'll hear it."

Sandy said, "As I was listening to you teach, the Lord came and said to me, *Look at John. What do you see?* [Do you see how the Lord did not just lay a word on her, but invited her into a process of discovery?] I said, 'I see a strong man, a teacher in the Lord.'

"*Yes, and no, Sandy. What do you see?*

"'I see a father in Christ to many people.'

"And the Lord replied, *Yes, and no. What do you see?* The next second I saw an Indian lance flashing down out of heaven. It hit you in the top of your head and shot down through you, six feet into the ground."

As Sandy spoke, there was a great "whoosh" as that spiritual lance did in fact shoot down through me. Paula, standing six feet away, felt the power of it. Sandy went on to say that the Lord said to her that I am a father in Christ to the nations, called to minister reconciliation among natives and others around the world.

Acts 13:1–2 says:

> Now there were at Antioch, in the church that was there, prophets and teachers: Barnabas, and Simeon who was called Niger, and Lucius of Cyrene, and Manaen who had been brought up with Herod the Tetrarch, and Saul. While they were ministering to the Lord and fasting, the Holy Spirit said, "Set apart for Me Barnabas and Saul *for the work to which I have called them.*"

EMPHASIS MINE

When the Holy Spirit called Barnabas and Saul to be apostles and changed their ministry drastically from then on, He had already "called them." The personal prophetic words confirmed what they already knew. Most of the time, I am sure, when God presents a personal word, He would prefer that the word come as a confirmation of what He has already told the person or intimated it in his heart. In this way, though the message may bring fresh revelation, the recipient has a sense of "recognizing" what he already "knew."

When Sandy spoke God's word to me, it was a confirmation of what God had already told me. The Holy Spirit had been informing Paula and me that He would change our ministry. The first mandating Scripture of Elijah House is Malachi 4:5–6: "Behold, I am going to send you Elijah the prophet before the coming of the great and terrible day of the LORD. He will restore the hearts of the fathers to their children and the hearts of the children to their fathers, so that I will not come and smite the land with a curse." Therefore, ten of our twelve books were written to heal and restore hearts and family relationships, and we have ten prayer counselors on staff who minister every day to turn the hearts of family members to each other.

But remember that sometimes when we think God is speaking directly, He may also be speaking figuratively, and that one interpretation may not exhaust what a word means. The Lord had recently come to me to say, *You did not understand Malachi 4:5–6. He said, You thought it meant natural fathers and mothers, and of course it does. But John, it means far more. The Jewish people are the fathers of Christian faith; Christians are the children. The hearts of the fathers and the children need to be turned to each other. Pray for the peace of Jerusalem, knowing that this means far more than you think it does. For Protestants, Catholics are the fathers, Protestants are the children. Pray for reconciliation and unity in My Church. In any land colonists are the children, natives are the fathers. You are called to pray for reconciliation and healing between Native Americans and their fellow countrymen, as well as for the natives of other countries and their countrymen.*

Sandy's word came as confirmation.

But what about the image of the lance? As I said, God speaks in parables and figures because He wants us to ponder, as Mary did. That pondering gives Him opportunity to involve us in discovery, so that we "know" what we know as our own. I pondered about that lance. I knew that Cheyenne warriors would drive their lances into the ground, tie themselves to them with a sash and by that declare, "Here I stand and fight. I will not retreat. I will fight here until I die—or until the battle is won." I thought, *The Lord is calling me into reconciliation and spiritual warfare for native people around the world, and He does not want me to retreat from it. He has pinned me to it.* But then the Lord said, *You did not drive that lance, John, heaven did. That means heaven will fight for you and will not retreat from you!*

The powerful word from Sandy was confirmed immediately. Elijah Harper, a devout Christian and member of Parliament in Canada at the time, invited me to be part of the First Sacred Assembly. This was a gathering of two thousand native Canadians and many white officials and other people for the purpose of reconciliation and healing. Then, Monte Ohia and Richard Twiss invited me to attend the first World Christian Gathering of Indigenous People, held in Rotorua, New Zealand, in 1996. And Jean Steffenson invited me onto the board of the International Reconciliation Committee for Indigenous People. I subsequently have attended many meetings for reconciliation, and edited and written endorsements for many books of native brothers. Sandy's word not only brought me personal healing, but it changed the course of our ministry drastically.

I share this story as a prime example of how personal words should be given in ways that do not impose, throttle inquiry, control or manipulate. It also is an example of how the Lord, in His great wisdom, often prefers to give personal words in the context of dark speech because it is for our own good.

Dark Speech Plants Seeds in the Heart

Another reason for dark speech is to plant a seed into the heart when the mind is not yet ready for complete understanding. Ecclesiastes 3 says there is a time for everything, and everything has its season. There are times when we are not yet ready to receive and understand truth. But God wants to implant into our hearts seeds of remembrance that will spring up into revelation when our minds and spirits are ready.

Jesus Set the Example

Jesus said, "Therefore I speak to them in parables; because while seeing they do not see, and while hearing they do not hear, nor do they understand" (Matthew 13:13). He went on to say that the hearts of the people had become dull and that they had closed their eyes and ears. At first glance, this way of speaking "over people's heads" could seem cruel and uncaring, or at least insensitive. But remember that our God is love, and Jesus is the Father's heart in action on earth. Let's ask ourselves, "If everything Jesus does is love, how is this way of speaking in parables to unbelieving people an act of love?"

Why speak at all? The people deserved for Jesus simply to turn away in rejection. Speaking to them at all was an act of love. He spoke parables to them, knowing that if He spoke plainly and they rejected it, their sin would be far greater. He would have cast pearls before swine and enticed them into truly reprehensible reactions. They would most likely have rejected and blasphemed direct truths of revelation. But parables intrigued them, without necessarily enlisting rebellious reactions. By speaking in parables, He was seeding into their hearts words that would spring to life later when their hearts changed.

This is not something mystical or hard to understand. We know it is not good to tell our tiny children about a number of things—sex, for example. So we speak in parables and figures, knowing they will understand when they are old enough and we can explain more directly. Jesus used such common sense as this. He also cared that if He unwisely cast pearls of wisdom to them, the people's unbelieving and scoffing mentalities would reject Him outrightly. Recognizing all of this, it is easy to appreciate the wisdom of our Lord.

Personal Words Are Most Effective in Dark Speech

The same principle applies to the giving and receiving of personal words. Often we think God is speaking directly through His prophets—and miss what is really happening because He was actually speaking in dark speech!

In 1988, the Holy Spirit showcased the prophets in what was then a large Vineyard church in Denver. Paul Cain, perhaps the foremost and most well-known of the early modern prophets, was there. After his teaching, he called people to receive personal words. One was our son Loren. Paul spoke some details of Loren and Beth's family and ministry, validating that he had really heard the Lord concerning them. Then he said, "God is going to put together twelve marriages in your church." Loren thought, *Oh, no, I'm going to be stuck in the office doing marital counseling for hour and hours.* Instead, God killed his singles ministry by marrying them all! This was not dark speech. Loren simply misunderstood what God was saying, as the Lord had not been speaking of marital counseling at all.

Then Paul said, "There is going to be a breakthrough in your church." This seemed to be direct speech. Loren thought, *Hallelujah! We are going to break free from the things in our valley that are blocking us from the fullness of what God wants for our church, and we are going to grow in numbers and maturity.* But it was dark speech. No breakthrough came in that area. The church not only did not grow in numbers, but it diminished, and many reacted in infantile ways during the next year—the church did not grow or mature at all! But the Lord used that year of suffering to break Loren! Loren was in the church. That was the *breakthrough in the church!*

This is difficult for many to understand. We are so indoctrinated to think directly, rather than in the way of the Lord, who often uses puns as His dark speech. *Breakthrough* did not mean what Loren's heart leaped to believe. It was a pun of the Lord, signaling that Loren would be "broken through" by the Holy Spirit—in hopes that sometime in the process Loren would understand and be blessed by the crushing God was doing in his heart for his good. Few understood. But Paula and I and some intercessors understood it. God was speaking through Paul Cain in a symbolic pun, to prepare Loren's heart to withstand what the Lord knew was coming, and to call us into intercession.

Dark Speech Means Not Having to Understand

One of the blessed virtues of God's seeding through dark speech is that we do not have to understand fully mentally. We even may get a totally mistaken idea of what a word means—though, of course, it is best if we do understand it correctly. But God knows that the impact of the word will still bless our hearts, below the level of understanding. It will prepare us for what is coming.

The prophet Bob Jones was also at that meeting, and he called for Paula and me to come backstage to see him. He said, "For many years I have seen you two wearing the collar of a slave, and your ministry has borne the stamp of a slave. You have led many into servanthood to the Lord Jesus Christ. But now I see the Lord removing your collar. Now He says to you, 'Friend.'"

Both Paula and I burst into tears. God's word through Bob was confirming what the Lord had been saying to us. Bob Jones went on to say, "As your ministry has borne the stamp of a slave, now it will bear the mark of a friend of God, for the servant does not know what his Master is doing but the friend does." I thought, *Hallelujah! I'm going to get to "read people's mail," as Paul Cain does!*

"Read people's mail" is a current charismatic expression that means the Holy Spirit will reveal hidden details in a person's life, as if you are able to read their utterly private and confidential "mail." But knowing private details of people's lives did not happen. I have not noticed any appreciable gain in receiving words of knowledge. Instead, wherever Paula and I go, I have a much clearer understanding of what God is doing—in any meeting or church or region—and I like that much better.

I shared these stories to make clear that even when words are spoken in direct speech, we may not really understand them. And many times we think we know what God means because we think He has spoken directly, but His words were actually given in dark speech. Readers should take to heart the necessity to ponder words received, even when you think you know what they mean, and the wisdom to seek the counsel and advice of many. Others may have altogether different insights into God's purposes than you alone may consider.

God's Use of Symbols in Dark Speech

It behooves every Christian, but especially prophets, to study an anthology of symbols. I have included a very short list of double symbols in this chapter. But let us look at a few examples of symbols God uses when communicating with His people through dark speech.

God may send a prophet to say, "Drive carefully. You're going to have a car wreck." That seems direct enough, and you know a wreck does not have to happen if you just pray, enlist others to pray and drive carefully. Therefore, you do not have a wreck, or maybe you barely escape having one. So you give thanks and think the prophecy was fulfilled and, thus, is a past issue. But the way you think, your philosophy of life, the way you feel emotions, your confidence about yourself, even your job—these are all "cars" in which your life is riding. God may want a good wreck to happen, so that you die to something on the cross, or He may desire to protect you from a wounding wreck—such as friends betraying or deserting you. The word from the prophet calls you to ponder and pray—and to realize that the direct meaning may not be all God intends for you to hear.

Let's look at another example. You dream one night of being pregnant and miscarrying the baby, and then a prophet tells you that you are about to have a miscarriage. If you are indeed pregnant, that can be quite frightening. Or maybe there is no way you could actually be pregnant (especially if you are a man!), so you are tempted to blow that word off as a bad dream or someone's errant prophecy. What should you do?

If you are pregnant, the dream or the word may be direct speech calling you into repentance and prayer because God wants to protect your baby. But whether you are pregnant or not, the dream and the word may be dark speech. When change brews in our hearts, remember that it is from the heart that the issues of life come: "For out of the heart come evil thoughts, murders, adulteries, fornications, thefts, false witness, slanders" (Matthew 15:19). Something evil may be hatching in your heart, in which case you should pray for a right kind of miscarriage. Or maybe a revelation or an idea to do something good is forming in your heart.

In this case, the Holy Spirit probably is warning you, and others with you, to pray that the good thing not be aborted.

Some Christians, not understanding the double nature of symbols, are needlessly frightened by their dreams and visions. For instance, a man dreamed that a great black snake came and curled itself about him, looking deeply into his eyes. He was terrified that the Holy Spirit was warning him that Satan was about to entrap and control him hypnotically. While that is a possible interpretation, and it would not hurt anyone to repent of all possible areas that might be open to temptation and seduction, it is not wise to jump to conclusions. The snake could symbolize something else.

On the negative side, serpents stand for rebellion and cleverness against God. But on the positive, snakes stand for healing and wisdom. When the Israelites rebelled and complained against God in the wilderness, the Lord sent fiery serpents among them and many died. The people repented and asked Moses for help. "Then the LORD said to Moses, 'Make a fiery serpent, and set it on a pole: and it shall be that everyone who is bitten, when he looks at it, shall live'" (Numbers 21:8, NKJV). This image was a wondrous foretype of our Lord Jesus' death on the cross for us, hung as a "serpent" for all of us to see for our salvation: "But I am a worm and not a man, a reproach of men and despised by the people" (Psalm 22:6). Because of the way God used the symbol of the serpent in the lives of Moses and Jesus, serpents have been symbols of our Lord's healing. Thus, the caduceus, the symbol of the medical profession, is two serpents entwined about a cross.

Genesis 3:1 says, "Now the serpent was more crafty than any beast of the field which the LORD God had made." Craftiness, or cleverness, is the side of wisdom sometimes thought of as negative. So throughout history a serpent also has been a symbol of wisdom. In addition, a black snake did not necessarily mean something bad. In symbology, black is also the primordial color of creation, thus of creativity and new birth.

So how do we know what the Lord meant to tell the man who had the vision of the snake? Discussion, pondering and prayer revealed that the Holy Spirit was informing the man that He was asking him to heed His call to wisdom and healing. Why did he use the imagery of a snake? Because the process of his maturation would contain some risks of temptation. The man needed to prepare his heart for both the positive and negative possibilities. For this exact purpose, the Lord often employs symbols that can mean both sides, so that we may receive insight and wisdom in balanced perspective and prayer.

God's Use of Colors in Dark Speech

All colors are double symbols. We even speak of colors as symbols in our common daily language. Thus, in dreams, visions and personal words, colors are used as speech. If we walk close to the Lord, we are covered by the red blood and love of the Lord, but when we wander away it is not long before we experience anger—we "see red." Blue is the color of eternity and healing, but when we abandon God we have "blue" days and fall into depression—"Man, I feel blue today." Yellow is the color of gold, which stands for wisdom and the loving nature of God, but apart from Him "we have a yellow streak down our backs" because yellow is the color of cowardice. Green? New life. Or envy of those who have life while we suffer "the green monster of jealousy." Brown can refer to God's good earth, or we can use it negatively: "What a brown taste that left in my mouth!" Purple can mean rage, or it can be the color of royalty: "I saw purple (rage) when that undeserving person was elevated to wear the purple of reigning and royalty." Black can mean evil and the depressing lack of hope. But it is out of the primordial black that all good things were created. One can be "white as a sheet" when he or she is filled with fear, or white can stand for blessed purity and innocence.

God Uses the Seeds of Parables to Cause Us to Grow in Understanding

Does all this make the hearing of prophetic words sound confusing or too complex? God is not the God of confusion. Rather, He undergirds us with peace and courage to wait for clarity.

The Holy Spirit's delight is to hide things from the wise and reveal them to babes. Babies know to trust: "O LORD, my heart is not proud, nor my eyes haughty; nor do I involve myself in great matters, or in things too difficult for me. Surely I have composed and quieted my soul; like a weaned child rests against his mother, my soul is like a weaned child within me" (Psalm 131:1–2). In this instance the Hebrew word for *weaned* does not mean one who has grown too old to continue to suckle at the breast. Rather, it means a child who has so abundantly suckled at its mother's breast that it lies back in its mother's arms, totally relaxed and peaceful, utterly trusting. God wants us to be like the weaned child, trusting in our heavenly Father to give us solid food when we are ready.

Impatient Christians *have* to know answers. They jump to conclusions because they cannot stand to remain in the anxiety of not knowing. God speaks in double colors and other forms of dark speech to prevent us from leaping too soon. He wants us to ponder, trusting that in His own time and way He will reveal the true meaning of what He says. This is not meant to stifle questioning, but to harness it.

When instant or quick actions are needed, God speaks directly, sometimes imperiously. For example, one time He shouted to me audibly, "John, hit the brake!" and if I had not obeyed instantly I would have had a car wreck. But most of the time, the Lord begins in plenty of time, and He chooses to speak in parables and figures in order to cause us to grow in wisdom and understanding of His ways.

What Dark Speech Means for the Prophet

To prophets this means that we should not be too quick to offer what we think is a definitive interpretation of a word or dream or vision. We need to be careful not to cut short the other's needful time of pondering. In addition, the prophet himself may have caught only a part of God's intended meaning or missed it altogether.

Above all, seek the Lord. *Seek the Lord.* God puts things in dark speech to prevent us from thinking we can understand things and get along without Him. It makes us dependent upon Him. Dark speech forces us to wait upon Him rather than rely on our own experience and ideas.

God wants to build a corps of prophets who have learned above all simply to rely on Him. When they have died enough to self and learned to be "weaned," or to trust Him completely as in Psalm 131, then "each will be like a refuge from the wind, and a shelter from the storm, like streams of water in a dry country, like the shade of a huge rock in a parched land. Then the eyes of those who see will not be blinded, and the ears of those who hear will listen. *The mind of the hasty will discern the truth*" (Isaiah 32:2–4, emphasis mine).

Just as it is for the hearer, dark speech is intended to prevent prophets from being hasty. God wants to teach us to wait on Him patiently, until He is ready to reveal what He has hidden from our minds but seeded into our hearts. Remember how Jesus said, "I have many more things to say to you, but you cannot bear them now" (John 16:12). For that reason

God has hidden many things, to be revealed only at the right times. He said, "I will open My mouth in parables; I will utter things hidden since the foundation of the world" (Matthew 13:35), and "we speak God's wisdom in a mystery, the hidden wisdom which God predestined before the ages to our glory; the wisdom which none of the rulers of this age has understood" (1 Corinthians 2:7–8).

We are now approaching the eschatological moment in history that has lain hidden by God through all the ages. By speaking to and through them in dark speech, God is training His prophets in waiting upon Him for revelation in His own time and way. He is training them how to think in figurative, parabolic ways. Why? *So that when the time is fully upon us, prophets will be able to reveal what God is doing and what mysteries are unfolding before our eyes.*

A Warning to Those Who Prophesy About the End Times

I may anger or turn off many by what I say next, but I believe it needs to be said. Many students of prophecy believe they know how to decipher verses about the end times. They know what "seventy weeks" means, for example, and have charted history in clever timetables that seem to "fit." Some of these prophets hold "biblical prophecy seminars," proclaiming that they can chart out what is going to happen when, as history marches on and the Lord's Parousia, or Second Coming, draws nigh. They think this helps prepare the Body for His return. Regardless of whether or not their charts are right or wrong, I do not think such studies are truly prophetic, nor do I believe they help prepare God's people for His return. Obedience and trust are our only needful preparation. Someone asked St. Francis of Assisi what he would do if he were told that the Lord would return in the next hour. He said, "I would finish hoeing this row of peas."

More importantly, to me those studies walk close to divination because they try to see what God has kept hidden. It may be that God has kept these things hidden and may do so until the last moment, precisely to cause us to trust Him blindly.

A father came to his son and, taking him by the hand, said, "Let's go for a walk." The child said, "Where are we going, Dad?" to which the father replied, "Never mind, it's a surprise. You'll like it." But the son said, rather demandingly, "I want to know!" The father said, "Son, I'm the dad. Trust me." But the son yelled, "I'm not going anywhere unless you tell me where!" The father turned his son over his knee, spanked him and said, "Go to your room. We'll talk about this later." Our heavenly Father acts in a seemingly paradoxical way. If we so trust Him that we do not need to have answers, sometimes He will give them to us. But when we try to scheme and figure to know the future, based on a need to know in order to feel secure, we are not trusting God. In such an instance, we are behaving much like the child in this story who received nothing but discipline.

It may be that the many prophetic texts scholars examine and use to pronounce predictions are not what they think. That is, they are perhaps not direct speech but dark speech, meant not to be understood but to be sown into the heart in preparation.

The Lord said to me, *John, before I came the first time, all the biblical scholars thought they knew who I would be and what I would do, and they were all wrong.* He went on to say, *It's the same today. None of the eschatological scholars is right. They are all wrong. I have hidden these things. After I arose, I took Cleopas and the other disciple on a walk to Emmaus and opened to them what was there in the Scriptures all along. It will be the same when I return. Remember that I come like a thief in the night and no one, not even the Son, knows the hour and the day. Then I will take My Church on another "walk to Emmaus," and reveal what has been there all along.*

Dark speech is often precisely that—dark. Let us comprehend that God speaks in dark speech precisely because there are things He does not want us to know. Straining to understand what He has hidden may lead only to confusion—or discipline. Let us be content in trust, simply doing in obedience what He calls us to do, until He returns.

Common Double Symbols

Following are some symbols the Lord commonly uses in His dark speech. Some symbols are distinctly exterior—that is, directly referring to the person, animal or thing envisaged. And some are distinctly interior and must be interpreted by the context or story in which they appear. Many are both/and. In the last case, one meaning realized does not exhaust the range of possibilities. That is the Lord's economy in communication.

143

Negative Meanings	Colors	Positive Meanings
Anger, "I saw red"	Red	Love, the blood of forgiveness
Cowardice, "A yellow streak"	Yellow, gold	Wisdom, nature of God
Depression, "Singing the blues" "I'm blue today"	Blue	Eternity, healing, hope, sky and uplifting feelings
Jealousy, "The green-eyed monster"	Green	Life, new beginnings, nature
Disgust and disappointment, "Brown taste in my mouth"	Brown	Acceptance, warmth, success, earth, foundations
Death, despair and defeat, "It was all black"	Black	Creation, creativity, rebirth, new possibilities, new life
Rage, "He turned purple"	Purple	Royalty, reigning in power
Fear, "He turned white"	White	Purity, innocence, unbrokenness
Brashness, "Clockwork Orange"	Orange	Humility and beauty
Sadness and confusion, "It's a gray day," "It's all gray to me"	Gray	Comfort, mystery, hope obscured in hiddenness
Illness, weakness, immaturity	Pink	Health and joy, "I'm in the pink of condition"

Negative Meanings	Animals	Positive Meanings
Rebelliousness, cleverness	Snake	Wisdom, healing, caduceus
Pride in fleshly strength, "riding" thoughts or emotions	Horse	Strength, a philosophy or emotion to ride on
Rage, something that attacks	Bear	Courage to stand and fight
Unbeliever, outsider who rips	Dog	Watchdog, conscience, friend
Slinking, treachery, ambush	Cat	Gracefulness, speed, strategy
Satan, demon, ravages, devours	Lion	Jesus, the Lion of Judah, regal, protection, courage, strength, "lion-hearted"

Negative Meanings	Objects	Positive Meanings
Death, being persecuted, pain	Cross	Redemption, life, God's love
Destruction, division, defeat	Sword	Truth, rightly dividing Word
Hiding place, wrongly shielded, flight from destiny	Roof or house	Protection, heart's home, family, destiny in the Lord
Something "carrying us away," thoughts, emotions, projects	Vehicle, car	Faith, belief structure to ride in, a good thought or emotion

144

Negative Meanings	Objects in Nature	Positive Meanings
Trouble coming, truth obscured	Clouds	Blessing coming, Lord comes
Wrath and judgment approach	Storms	Vindication, God's power
Multitudes in opposition, or sinfulness hidden in the heart	Oceans, seas	Multitudes in support, or plunging into depths for insight
Persistent evil sweeping in, corruption flowing through	Rivers	Blessing pouring in, faithful, continual supply, flowing from the throne, making glad the city of God (see Psalm 46:4)

Negative Meanings	People	Positive Meanings
Enemy approaching, on guard, over-logical left brain	Man	Friendship, company coming, faith, good logic in left brain
Seduction, weakness, overemotional right brain	Woman	Nurture, beautiful fulfillment, intuitive, feeling side of us
Fear of authority, overbearing control, domination, too logical	Father	Authority, protection, discipline, faith and belief structure, caring
Fear of criticism and control, emotional manipulation	Mother	Affection, sweetness, emotional nurture, intuitional side of us

(Father and mother dreams may be about our actual fathers and mothers, for our healing, for prophetic warning and blessing and calling to intercession; the same dream or vision may have little or nothing to do with our actual fathers and mothers, being merely and solely symbolic. As with all other symbolic language, careful and prayerful interpretation is required.)

Warning to abort, something bad is being started	A baby	Birthing of new thought, idea or development—call to prayer
		(Or a promise of a real baby or call to pray for blessing or protection.)
Warning that good is dying—a person, project, emotion, etc.	A death	Calling for good crucifixion—a person, project, emotion, etc.

Also note that some dreams and visions are for catharsis, balance or revelation:

Orgies may signify repressed sexual or other urges, impulses or even good desires. Avoid leaping to conclusions; in prayer, examine the image with care.

Flying may portend marvelous spiritual experiences, but this image also warns of flying too high and becoming deluded.

Accidents may warn of heading into a physical or psychological crash course, or even an inner need to lose; that is, a subconscious, self-destructive motive. This image seldom has a positive meaning.

ELEVEN

RECEIVING PERSONAL WORDS

WHAT A BLESSED SWORD of truth God has given to His servants the prophets through the prophecies of personal words! Oh, how God wants to raise up more and more prophets for the edification of His Church, especially in these last days!

The Blessings of Personal Words

Personal words of prophecy can be great blessings in life. Through them God gives us the security of knowing we are in the very center of His will, doing what He created us to do. They can change our direction from stagnation in eddies and doldrums to excitement as we begin to flow more and more effectively in the currents of history. They can dispel confusion and open up clear trails of obedience. They can elevate Christians from distant ineffectual followers to torch-bearing trailblazers. They can open the way for teaching and consolation:

> Pursue love, yet desire earnestly spiritual gifts, but especially that you may prophesy. For one who speaks in a tongue does not speak to men but to God; for no one understands, but in his spirit he speaks mysteries. But one who prophesies speaks to men for edification and exhortation and

consolation. One who speaks in a tongue edifies himself; but one who prophesies edifies the church.

1 CORINTHIANS 14:1–4

Personal words can open the door for evangelization:

Therefore if the whole church assembles together and all speak in tongues, and ungifted men or unbelievers enter, will they not say that you are mad? But if all prophesy, and an unbeliever or an ungifted man enters, he is convicted by all, he is called to account by all; the secrets of his heart are disclosed; and so he will fall on his face and worship God, declaring that God is certainly among you.

1 CORINTHIANS 14:23–25

Many of us have seen this very thing happen. Our friend, Claire Huck, had a marvelous gift of prophetic words of knowledge. She could call out from among a group of worshipers someone she had never met and tell him that at such-and-such an age he had suffered an accident or illness, which Claire would describe in detail. She even would describe how the incident had left certain physical handicaps or psychological wounds. She could even tell him why that bad thing happened and how the family around reacted, and how that reaction affected the wounded one. As she would speak, the Holy Spirit would move, and the person's healing would begin, often dramatically and instantly. Even spiritual klutzes could see chains of unbelief falling off the audiences who watched her operate in her gifting. After she had "disclosed the secrets" of several hearts, many other people would hasten to the altar, seeking the way to salvation. Her gift of prophesying personal words truly served to evangelize.

I have heard people gasp audibly as a prophet revealed that God knew and cared about the events in their lives. In such instances, the mists of confusion and unbelief being blown away can almost be seen physically. The hearers' faces reflect the assurance that "God loves me." "He really does know me and love me!" "He is real! He is here!" And following that, the realization creeping into the minds of those receiving prophetic personal words is evident: "I'd better confess some things and get right with God!"

Personal Words Also Can Engender Harm

But as we discussed earlier, gifts that bring great blessing can to that degree engender harm. For the best treatise on both the positive and negative aspects of giving personal words, I suggest reading Bishop Bill Hamon's book *Prophets' Personal Words.* Another is *Your Sons and Daughters Shall Prophesy* by Ernest B. Gentile.

Today, God is regiving His fivefold office gifts to the Church (see Ephesians 4:11). Consequently, He is pouring prophetic books out of His prophets' minds and hearts at an ever-increasing rate. When Paula and I wrote *The Elijah Task* in the years between 1973 and 1977, no books on the subject of prophets, much less on personal words, were available at all. No one knew much of anything about it. It was a spiritual wasteland. The Church was in the valley of dry bones, and the breath of God was just beginning to blow (see Ezekiel 37:1–10). Today, much is available. Look for what God is saying in such books, that you may "Be diligent to present yourself approved to God as a workman who does not need to be ashamed, accurately handling the word of truth" (2 Timothy 2:15).

However, none of these can replace the Lord's own school of hard knocks. The Lord used dark speech in a funny way with me just now as I was typing. When I looked up from the keys, I found that instead of "the Lord's *own* school of hard knocks," I had typed "the Lord's *ow* school of hard knocks." It surely is. I can remember a lot of "ows" and "ouches" along the way. The point is, learn from your mistakes. I have sometimes said that America is literally strewn with the wreckage of my mistakes, but praise God for His grace, He has turned all to best wine, for myself and those I served.

What the Church Needs to Know

We have spoken earlier of the deep death to self that prophets must endure if they are to be faithful presenters of God's words of prophecy, and of how to test words and those who present them. Now let's turn to what needs to happen in the Church so that His words can be heard and responded to rightly.

When the prophets were showcased in 1988, the Church was not prepared to know how to receive words or what to do with them. A lot of mistakes ensued.

Do Not Make Your Prophecies Happen

As we found in the last chapter, people do not always understand how God uses dark speech, or they misunderstand what is actually direct speech. Many misconstrue what God is saying and respond foolishly.

To give just one example, a prophet said to a man, "God is calling you forth into a new ministry. What you are doing now is not what He created you to be. You will minister to the poor and downtrodden." The man, already disgruntled with his secular job, thought God was confirming his desire to enter into full-time ministry. He did not check with his pastor or the elders or his friends. Nor did he wait for confirmations, consult with his wife or ponder whether or not there might be meanings he had not seen.

Impulsively, he quit his job that paid quite well and supported his family, believing that God was going to open a new full-time ministry for him. Nothing of the kind happened and he was soon in financial straits, which truly disillusioned his wife and children. Had he remained in his position, the Lord could have opened to him a wonderful ministry to the poor—his job would have been his "tent making," while the new ministry would have fulfilled what God created him to be. As it turned out, he had to accept a lesser paying job and had little time or financial resources for the true calling that God wanted for him. He and many he influenced became soured on prophets and prophetic words. The fault lay not in the prophetic word, however, but in the man's immaturity and rashness in receiving it.

I do not think we need to relate other examples. Most charismatic Christians could share several similar stories. We have heard of brothers divorcing their wives or deserting their families or leaving their good jobs as this man did. Please hear these words of caution: If a prophet gives you a word that would drastically affect your livelihood and relationships, do not act quickly! Wait for unequivocal confirmations. Get the best advice you can—from your pastor, elders, prayer group and especially your spouse. Wait for the Lord to engineer His own answers—do not try to make your prophecy come true!

Endure the Ways in Which the Lord Will Test You

We have already said that if the Lord gives you a prophetic word that you are going to be elevated to a position of high service, duck! The Lord will likely test you in an effort to bring to death many character flaws you had no idea you had. Many, not understanding this and seeing things "go in reverse" after receiving a mighty prophecy, conclude either that the prophecy was false and/or that all such prophetic utterances are demonically inspired. Again, be in counsel with many, endure whatever comes upon you and wait in faith.

> In this [your blessed inheritance in Christ] you greatly rejoice, even though now for a little while, if necessary, *you have been distressed by various trials*, so that the proof of your faith, being more precious than gold which is perishable, *even though tested by fire*, may be found to result in praise and glory and honor at the revelation of Jesus Christ; and though you have not seen Him, you love Him, and though you do not see Him now, but believe in Him, you greatly rejoice with joy inexpressible and full of glory, *obtaining as the outcome of your faith the salvation of your souls*.
>
> 1 Peter 1:6–9, emphases mine

Peter was not saying that as "the outcome of your faith" you will go to heaven. Of course, you will, but the word *salvation* means far more than being born anew and becoming a candidate for heaven. *Salvation* comes from a root word that means healing and wholeness. Peter is saying that the trials you endure produce character made whole. Paul said virtually the same thing in Romans 5:1–5:

> Therefore, having been justified by faith, we have peace with God through our Lord Jesus Christ, through whom also we have obtained our introduction by faith into this grace in which we stand; and we exult in hope of the glory of God. And not only this, but *we also exult in our tribulations, knowing that tribulation brings about perseverance; and perseverance, proven character; and proven character, hope*; and hope does not disappoint, because the love of God has been poured out within our hearts through the Holy Spirit who was given to us.
>
> emphasis mine

151

Unfortunately, in many times and ways and places, we church members have not yet been conformed to the good and acceptable and perfect will of God (see Romans 12:2). Instead of being transformed by God's Word, we too much of the time become conformed to the world's way of thinking. The result is an assumption that being born anew puts a person on Easy Street every day. If it does not, the person concludes something is wrong with the preacher or the church, and he decides to find someplace else that will make him feel good.

If we are to hear and respond rightly to God's prophetic words, we are going to have to mature into a theology of redemptive suffering. We are going to have to learn how to "embrace the fireball," as my son Loren puts it in his teachings. It is not that we should become happy masochists, foolishly seeking to suffer. Enough will happen by God's providence without our purposefully inviting it! But when trials happen, we need to stop automatically blaming the devil or anyone or anything else—and stop being discouraged. Rather we need to say, "Lord, through all that You are having me endure, write on my heart Your eternal lessons. Give me ears to hear and eyes to see, or at least give me faith to endure and learn." "For His anger is but for a moment, His favor is for a lifetime; weeping may last for the night, but a shout of joy comes in the morning" (Psalm 30:5).

Remember that God's Time Frame Is Not Ours

Prophets and their hearers often err by trying to state definite times and places in regard to a prophecy, when God may not want to be so specific or may be speaking figuratively. Jesus said, "Truly I say to you, there are some of those who are standing here who will not taste death until they see the Son of Man coming in His kingdom" (Matthew 16:28; see also Mark 9:1; Luke 9:27). Therefore, many early Church disciples thought Jesus would return before they died. Thus, Peter had to write that the Lord is not slow about His promise (see 2 Peter 3:9), and Paul wrote to the Thessalonians not to get excited in thinking the Lord had already come or would come quickly (see 2 Thessalonians 2:1–4). The early Church and Christians throughout history have tended to want to finalize dates and places when the Lord has left them purposefully obscure. Actually, the Kingdom was "close at hand" when the disciples were sent out and worked miracles (see Matthew 10:7). The Lord's Kingdom did begin to come when Jesus arose from the dead—and has been coming ever since.

If a prophet says something akin to what Elisha did when he prophesied "this time next year," do not jump to conclude that it is direct speech and assume that the prophecy must happen by then or it is a false word. And if the time passes and the prophesied event has not yet happened, do not disbelieve. A prophet can be correct in most of his prophecy but be presumptive or in error about its timing. Or the prophet himself may not know his word was actually dark speech.

There is that old joke about a man who asked God if a day in His sight is as a thousand years, and God answered, "Yes." The man continued, "And is a penny as a million dollars to You?" God answered, "Yes." So the man said, "Well, then, could I have a penny?" And the Lord answered, "Yes, tomorrow." Remember, heaven is outside of time, and heavenly references to time may not match our twenty-four-hour time frames at all. God has a different perspective on time.

The Lord's prophets, therefore, must be more circumspect about time references than most any other area of prophesying. And recipients of the prophecy must hold prophetic words about time very loosely. The remainder of the word may be true, even if the spoken time is wrong. Or, the Lord may be speaking in dark speech or His own way of thinking about time, which is not ours. Unless the Lord speaks clearly and confirms unequivocally, do not act rashly, trying to make the prophecy come true before the prophesied time expires.

God is also "the 11:59 God," who often comes at the last minute, or even belatedly, to test us. Remember that Saul's kingdom was torn from him because when Samuel came late to Gilgal, "I forced myself and offered the burnt offering" (1 Samuel 13:12). Saul tried to make God's prophecy happen on time, or at least before troubles could mount, not trusting God when Samuel was late. God sometimes seems to be late, or actually is late, precisely for the purpose of testing our ability to trust.

Usually, the Lord begins speaking to Paula and me approximately two years before prophesied events begin to unfold. He uses the time to prepare our hearts. It may seem to us that He is late in coming, but things always happen in His perfect timing.

Remember what has been said to you in prophecy. Record prophetic words in journals, and look back through them every once in a while. You may be astounded to discover that what He said has already come to pass. You just missed it, or missed what it really meant, and now in the 20/20 vision of hindsight you can see clearly what was not so obvious before—

"Hey, it did happen!" Or, "Now I see what He meant. Why didn't I see that before?"

Ponder, But Do Not Strain to Understand

Do not strain to understand words given to you. That is not what is meant by pondering, which is a restful meditating and recollecting, not a striving to grasp capricious breezes in your fists. Pray and rest in the Lord. He will give you signs or cause thoughts to float into your consciousness.

On the other hand, do not just sit down and do nothing, waiting for God to interpret a word for you. Go on about your business, doing what your hand finds to do. Ships are guided by small rudders, which can have no effect if the ship is standing still.

My testimony can be read in *The Elijah Task* and other places, but I will retell it briefly to teach how God may progressively reveal when our strivings no longer block His revelation. I, like Jeremiah, was called before my birth. Eight months before I was born, my mother did not know that she was pregnant. In a dream, she drove in the night to the old family homestead. As the car lights swept across the garage, they illumined a great figure sitting and waiting. Frightened, she ran to the back door. As she touched it, a powerful stream of light coursed through her from a touch upon her left shoulder. She said it felt like a thousand volts. A voice said, "Do not be afraid, for I am God. You are going to have a son, who will be My servant." The Lord went on to tell her that the son would do many things for Him and what they would be. In the morning, though she could recall the entire dream vividly, the Holy Spirit kept her from remembering what the son was to do. Can you see the Lord's wisdom? He would not let my mother remember, lest she inform me, for that would cut short my own questing and seeking.

When I was seventeen, spading the garden for planting in the spring, the clouds parted so that the sun shone through in the form of a cross. As I looked at that wondrous image, the Lord spoke: *You are to be a minister.*

That fall, I preached my first sermon before leaving the next day for university training. That afternoon my mother sat me down and told me the story of her dream. She had wisely kept it hidden all those years, knowing that if it were true, God would call me in His own time and way. Now that He had, she deemed it was time for me to know His call upon my life.

I did not react in wisdom and patience. I hurled myself into frantic searching, trying to find out what God wanted me to do. Having been raised in the liberal church I did not search in the Bible—as I would today. I poured over books and treatises about every kind of "ism" there is—Hinduism, Buddhism, American Indian mysticism, German mysticism, Quaker pietism, Rosicrucianism, theosophic writings, philosophies, etc.

My parents saw what was happening and called me home for a family conference. Dad said, "John, if God could give your mother that dream, and give us the wisdom not to say anything of it to you, and then He could sovereignly call you as He did, do you not think He can lead you into what you are to do without all this frantic searching and reading?" That was actually the best advice I could have received. But I was filled with the pride of youthful zeal and haste. I thought they just did not understand; they did not know the weights on my heart and mind. So I plunged right on. This continued all the way through university and seminary. In the meantime I married Paula, and much of our course was marked by black skid marks, especially as Paula's Baptist upbringing and common sense jammed the brake pedal down hard!

My quest had two defined objects. First, where was the power to work miracles that was in the early Church? I did not have the sense to look in the Bible or in the lives of the saints in church history—I had read the lives of the saints and martyrs, but again I did not have "the sense to look in." I did not yet know the Lord as Savior, and the Holy Spirit had little access to open my eyes. So I did not see the truth in what I read. The second search was for the power to live life as Jesus demonstrated it. I was asking, "Why do I not see Christians manifesting more of His lifestyle, rather than the world's?" That was actually the question that drove me into the discoveries that have now become known as inner healing.

But of course, my heritage being from the liberal and modernistic Church, I did not seek answers to my questions in the right ways and places. Along the way, I looked for answers in the world of the occult and, in so doing, opened myself to the demonic. What little faith I had and the strong moral virtue from my upbringing kept this demonic influence in check, so that it was not able to operate in my life. But there it was, in me.

In June 1958, I was graduated from seminary and ordained as a minister one month later. Then I prayed, "Lord, I've tried everything else and found nothing but mouthfuls of dry dust. Now, despite what my modernistic seminary has taught me, I am going to decide to believe that the Bible is true from cover to cover, the miracles did happen as written, Jesus is truly the Son of God and born of a virgin, He did die on the cross and was raised for our salvation, and we do have to be born anew." In October, the Holy Spirit fell on me in my sleep; I woke up speaking in tongues and did not know what it was. In those days, the Holy Spirit had not yet descended upon the "old-line churches," and so not in my own Congregational Church. Dennis Bennett and I were the first Congregational pastors to receive the Holy Spirit and the gifts. Dennis later became an Episcopal rector.

My first question had been partially answered. I knew then that the Holy Spirit is God's Messenger of power, even if too few today give Him access to do the stupendous works Jesus said we would do after Him. But the second question remained, "Who today manifests the purity of Jesus' nature and character?"

But now, God had written indelibly upon my heart, *You cannot find out the secrets of God's Kingdom by striving.* When I gave up looking for the answers on my own and said, "God, I can't find the answers," God moved upon me to save me and fill me with His Holy Spirit. I gave Him control of my life, rather than trying to make things happen myself. Immediately, the Holy Spirit caused me to recognize the demonic hold on my life that my occult involvement had allowed. I repented of my occult delvings, cast away all demonic influence and closed those doors.

I have shared this testimony hopefully to speak to many hearts that receive heavenly promises and high callings. My simple but powerful advice is, "Give up!" Do not seek frantically, as I did, to find out what God wants you to do or to make your prophecies come true.

Work Diligently

What should you do? Put one foot in front of the other. Do with diligence whatever the Lord assigns. Bloom where you are planted. Two things will happen. First, your ship of faith will be moving, its sails filled more and more with the wind of the Holy Spirit. And second, God will be able to bring about His God-incidences, which can tumble you into what He wants you to do. Scripture says, "The mind of man plans his way, but the LORD directs his steps" (Proverbs 16:9). After a while, you will look back upon your track and see that you are already firmly set on the path the prophet prophesied you would walk.

God gave me ability to interpret dreams and visions. I did so for many, as diligently as I knew how. Many dreams and visions are about interior things of the heart and subconscious mind. That tumbled me into seeing the need and ways of inner healing, which is the application of the blood, cross and resurrection life of Jesus to the deep, hidden parts of the heart. After I pioneered in this area for quite a while, I looked back and saw: (1) In the quest to transform hearts and lives into the nature of Jesus, God had led me into finding some of the answers. I saw that it was hidden unforgiveness and practices lodged in the heart that prevented Christians from living the lifestyle of Jesus. God had shown me how to set people free from such bondages to become all that God intended them to be. (2) I was doing that for which He created me. (3) This was the very work of the Elijah task outlined in Malachi 4:5–6. Paula and I, therefore, cofounded Elijah House and began to write the books He commanded.

But please hear this—it is for this reason I have shared all this—Paula and I knew absolutely none of this when we started out! I did not see a vision of the work as a child, nor as an adult, nor as a newly born Christian. Even after I began the work, I did not see the import of what I was doing—nor how the work was fulfilling the many prophecies that by then had been said over us—until years into the work. Only then did God open my eyes to look back over our track and understand.

Why did God speak to my mother and link His revelations to her and to me? Why did He speak through other prophets in my life, yet neither Paula nor I understood? . . . Right. By now you know the answer. He was seeding into our hearts knowledge that was not yet revealed so that as we served Him, those subliminal seeds would act as homing beacons. It was as though each succeeding key of knowledge He gave us for the transformation of hearts was something our spirits "recognized."

Many have asked us, "John and Paula, how did you find out all those secrets of human nature that have helped so many to be set free?" This is how. Not by desperately searching for hidden things. But by setting out to heal the people He sent, doing what He put in front of us. The Holy Spirit guided us through the subliminal promptings of the Lord's prophetic words spoken over us. Revelations were "radioed" up through the heart into the mind by the Holy Spirit. Setting out to heal someone's heart, we would get stumped, unable to see how to counsel and pray for that person. We would then say our usual, fervent and righteous prayer—"Help!" It was in that context of trying to help others that revelations came. Very seldom have I received any revelation from the Holy Spirit that was not connected to some immediate need while serving Him.

See Prophetic Words as Guideposts

The prophetic words spoken over us served as guideposts along a subliminal way. That is a primary reason God gives us personal words, and often gives them in dark speech. He does not want us to be tempted to think we fully understand—and miss the virtue of His signals along the way. Imagine the turmoil of heart and mind and spirit in Paul as the Lord drove him out of the legalisms of Pharisaism and the circumcision party. A study of Paul's life and ministry ought easily to convince us that though his initial revelation of Jesus was so stunning as to knock him to the ground and blind him, it took many prophecies, eleven years at Tarsus, and much suffering from persecution and misunderstanding to settle into his heart and mind the full glory of the revelations God was giving to him. And how glorious the work God did through him! Paul's revelations of Jesus' purposes opened the door for us Gentiles to be grafted into God's Kingdom.

The fullness of revelation did not come to Paul, or to us, instantly through a few prophetic words, but by seeding, stumbling (see 1 Corinthians 2), pondering, praying and walking through the doors of service God opened.

Die to Self and Enter into the Joy of Your Master

Dear people, let me summarize all this for you. After receiving a prophetic word of direction, do not strive to find out all it means, or how you are supposed to do whatever. And do not sit back, doing nothing, waiting for God to clarify. Do what He puts in front of you. You will grow, almost unwittingly, into the fulfillment of what God has prophesied over you.

If you simply do what the Lord lays before you, eventually the Lord will come and say, "Well done, good and faithful slave. You were faithful with a few things, I will put you in charge of many things; enter into the joy of your master" (Matthew 25:21). There are no shortcuts in God's Kingdom. Do not seek elevation to high service. Seek with all your strength to do well whatever your hand finds to do. If a prophetic word promises you will be elevated, do not be a fool like young Joseph and go around puffed up about yourself. Joseph had to learn humility the hard way—in prison. Humble yourself. The Lord said to Paula and me, *The higher men and I elevate you, the more determinedly [we've learned this means "desperately"] you must humble yourself.* Again and again He speaks Romans 12:16 to our hearts: "Be of the same mind toward one another; *do not be haughty in mind,* but associate with the lowly. Do not be wise in your own estimation" (emphasis mine).

We have seen so many prophets disgruntled and unhappy because others do not recognize their gifting or themselves as prophets. Many are angry with the leadership of the Church and wish they would just be straightened out so prophets could have a proper forum for their ministry. Die to that, dear ones. Serve. Just serve. Recognition will come when God knows you are ready, when you "deserve" it because you have been humbly serving.

If anyone knew undeserved rejection and humiliation, Paul did. Listen to what he says about it:

> Not that I speak in regard to need, for I have learned in whatever state I am, to be content: I know how to be abased, and I know how to abound. Everywhere and in all things I have learned both to be full and to be hungry, both to abound and to suffer need. I can do all things through Christ who strengthens me.
>
> PHILIPPIANS 4:11–13, NKJV

The secret? He says it: "through Christ." You must have such a fullness of revelation of your depravity that you are grateful for any good thing—such a completeness of death to self and transformation into the nature of our Lord Jesus that you want nothing for yourself but only what will give glory to Him. One of the most important deaths is death to vain ambition and desire for glory among men. *The secret of abounding or suffering is found in losing your life for Him, until you literally do not care what people think about you. All your security is vested then in His love for you, and ambition withers and dies like a plant that no longer finds nurture.*

Listen to God on Your Own

Do not run to meetings where prophets will appear, hoping to receive "a word from God." Do your own listening. Be attentive to the still, small voice of God speaking quietly within your own mind and heart. Be grateful if it happens that a prophet calls you out and gives you a word, but do not manipulate events to try to get in position to be called out. After 1988, many Christians became downright discourteous, pushing and shoving to get seats on the front row, hoping to be seen by a prophet.

Be careful that your desire and importunity not so affect a prophet as to cause him to struggle against divination. If it is psychic readings you want, do not ask a prophet of God—just call one of those 900 numbers! I say this facetiously. I, of course, would never advise anyone to engage in such a sin. But be aware that your wrongful motives can affect a prophet's clarity to hear God accurately.

When Paula and I were in England a few years after 1988, Derek Brown, a pastor in Aldershot who is widely recognized as an apostle, said to us, "Do you know why the great Welsh revival of 1910 stopped?" We said, "No. Why?" Derek said, "Prophets arose and began to go around giving personal words. The people stopped listening to God for themselves and began to run after the prophets, seeking words from God. That killed the anointing and the revival died."

Both in *Healing the Nations* and in this book I have told stories of how personal words given to Paula and me drastically affected us for good. But understand: I have never, ever sought to be given a word. Each time, I was in the process of serving God, my mind and heart totally focused that way. Receiving a word was the farthest thing from my mind at the moment. Paula and I have developed and practiced a discipline of listening to God and keeping journals of His words to us—for more than forty years! No word that changed the direction of our ministry has ever come without being confirmation of something the Lord was already saying to us. For example, even before the prophecy just prior to my heart attack on May 25, God had been giving me warnings about a heart attack. I was just too thickheaded to grasp what His warnings meant. Now, looking back in our journals, we see it clearly.

Do your own listening. You may, like me, not understand at the moment what He is really saying, but what He seeds into you will make sense later. How many times did the Gospels record that the disciples did not understand what Jesus was saying until after His resurrection? Read John 10:6; 12:16; 13:7 and 20:9, for just a few. It was only then that hindsight made all things clear.

Summary

To sum up, though personal words can be a great blessing, do not seek them. Let God and His servants find you. When you receive words of great promise and high service, rejoice only a little, and set your heart right, because God is going to have to prove and crush you first (see Matthew 21:44). Do not be hasty or oversure that you know the meaning(s) of what God speaks to you. You may see only the tip of the iceberg, and God may be speaking in dark speech to seed into your heart for fruits that will later be revealed. Whether or not you have received words of promise, bloom where you are planted. Do what your hand finds to do. God's coincidences may follow, and looking back at your track, you may see what God has been telling you all along. Above all, wait for confirmation and check with those above and alongside you. Be corporate. God does nothing in isolation. When you find by serving and/or by confirming words that you are in the center of God's will for you, rejoice! Be at rest. Let God make His prophecies come true, not you. Serve. Serve faithfully, in small things. The day will come when He comes and says to you, "Well done, good and faithful servant. . . ."

TWELVE

DREAMS AND VISIONS

DREAMS AND VISIONS are not in themselves prophetic functions. Rather, dreams and visions are two tools prophets use to perform the function of hearing God. It follows that interpreting what visions and dreams mean is another tool prophets employ, both to understand what God may be saying to them and to interpret what He says to others. I say this at the outset because a fundamental error of many is to become too fascinated with dreams and visions and their interpretations. When people do that, interpreting dreams and visions can become an end in itself and invite spirits of divination. This then not only becomes sinful delusion, but it also distracts from other vital functions and from the Lord's purposes for dreams and visions.

Keep Dreams and Visions in Perspective

We must learn to keep exciting things such as dreams and visions in balance and proper perspective. It helps if we remember Paul's warning about those who take their stand on visions, not holding fast to the head, who is Christ (see Colossians 2:18–19). Paul said this in the context of false self-abasement, worship of angels and falling into false doctrines. We may not yet have fallen that far, but we can fall into seeking and being enamored of spiritual experiences *about* the Lord until they are no longer *in* Him.

Having and interpreting dreams and visions can be exciting and fun, exhilarating and spiritually intoxicating. I remember when a brother and I would become greatly excited each time we got together, sharing our dreams and visions and seeing double entendres and hidden meanings in everything. We loved to share these things with whoever would listen, gratified by their reactions. Another more spiritually mature brother, a sweet and gentle man who never curses, had seen us do this several times. One day he let loose with one of his own rather loudly, followed by "Not again!" That shocked us out of it, and we listened while he explained how offensive and distracting it was to others around us. That wrote onto our hearts a valuable lesson, never again to become carried away in the excitement of revelations. And we could understand Ecclesiastes 5:7, "For in many dreams and in many words there is emptiness. Rather, fear God."

On the other hand, we need not to quench the Spirit, and we should desire to have spiritual dreams and visions—but only to hear, serve and love the Lord. Along the way, He will give us whatever dreams and visions we need. To seek more plunges us into trouble.

Nevertheless, dreams and visions are tremendously important ways of listening to God, and so also is the skill of interpreting them. So much so that if you took dreams and visions out of the Bible, you would remove more than one third of its contents and nearly every major turning point in its history! Joseph and Daniel rose to power interpreting dreams. In a dream, Abraham was promised the land of Palestine and many descendants (Genesis 28). God spoke often to Jeremiah and Ezekiel through visions. In visions, the angel Gabriel visited both Zacharias and Mary to foretell of the coming of John the Baptist and the Lord Jesus. It was in a dream that Joseph was told to keep Mary because "the Child who has been conceived in her is of the Holy Spirit. She will bear a Son; and you shall call His name Jesus, for He will save His people from their sins" (Matthew 1:20–21). Through dreams, God warned the three wise men not to return to Herod, and He told Joseph to flee with Mary and Jesus to Egypt—and when to return.

The Language of Dreams and Visions

When the Lord spoke to Moses and to Aaron and Miriam at the door of the tent of meeting (Numbers 12), He declared that there are five primary ways He speaks to His servants the prophets: dreams, visions, dark speech, mouth to mouth directly, and aloud. These form a continuum, from the least clear and direct to the most. We turn now to the enigmatic speech of dreams and visions.

Dreams

Dreams given by the Holy Spirit are distinct from the other four ways He speaks by the simple fact that when they occur we are asleep. This means that the conscious mind is bypassed, and the Holy Spirit can convey messages with the least possibility of interference. Though the Lord can speak directly to us in dreams, as He did in telling Joseph about Mary's pregnancy, dreams by nature are most often dark speech. They are a figurative method of communication that calls for pondering and praying. Sometimes God communicates through dreams rather than directly because He does not want to give our carnal minds, which often oppose God (see Romans 8:5–6), access to block or warp what He wants to say. Or, He may communicate through a dream when He wants to speak a direct message and does not want fear or any other emotion to send the mind reeling into flights of interruptive fantasies.

Time is an important factor here. When there is plenty of time, God loves to give us dreams that require time to meditate on and seek communion with Him in order to gain interpretation. In this way, He matures us. But when urgent actions are vital, God chooses to speak directly. In these instances, He often uses dreams that require no interpretation, only obedience—like "Arise, . . . and flee to Egypt."

Visions

Visions are the next medium of communication, marked by the fact that we are awake but the Holy Spirit speaks to us through pictures. The conscious mind is again bypassed. Because we are awake, however, our minds and emotions are more likely to interfere and defile the picture-making process.

164

Visions occur on many levels. On the first level, our imagination seems to be all that is involved. We either make a picture or one pops unbidden into the mind with no discernible spiritual impulse. Normally we do not think of these occurrences as visions inspired by the Holy Spirit, but at times they are. They can come from an exterior source inspired by the Holy Spirit—such as a good movie we are watching or stimulation from something someone says—or they can come simply through the Holy Spirit living within us. As Christians we have given our minds to the Lord. He has permission and access. When He gives us visions, He may be using our imagination to help us, without our being aware that the Holy Spirit was behind it.

On the next level, we see a vision and know it comes through our imagination, but we are also aware that it is the Holy Spirit who is playing the movie screen of our minds. The pictures are coming solely by His impetus. Two things set this level apart from the first. One, we have an abiding restfulness. It is as though we are in a theater, sitting there watching, having nothing to do with turning the reel. Two, we have a sense of being caught up within the Holy Spirit. We feel the glory of God all around and do not want to embellish or think or interfere in any way. We want to bask in it, lest the glory vanish—like a bubble that bursts—and everything is lost.

It is easy to recognize these as visions. Some Christians, however, being overly afraid of the flesh, think that since the visions came through their own imagination, they could not be visions. They tend to think that a vision requires one to be so caught up in the Spirit that he or she is in a trance. They think the Lord would have overpowered and flooded the banks of their normal physicality. Such people do not understand incarnation. They do not realize that the Holy Spirit can work naturally and easily through them. They need to hear and ponder what we said earlier about God speaking in and through His Son, and thus in and through who we are (see Hebrews 1:1–2). Visions that come through our imagination by the Holy Spirit are not to be disregarded or thought of as something less than true visions.

The next level of visions is the one most people think of as visions. This is the type that occurs when our eyes are fully opened and we see spiritual reality as it is, as Stephen saw when he was dying. He literally and actually saw the Lord standing at the right hand of the Father in heaven (see

165

Acts 7:55)! Imagination is not involved at all. This type of vision is an actual seeing into the realm of the Spirit.

Few Christians, even those with many highly anointed visions, have ever experienced such a vision. I think perhaps one time I did, when the archangel Michael appeared to me. But I cannot say definitively if it was actually seeing, or if it was something spiritual portrayed to my understanding through images.

Considering the three types of visions, let me give an exhortation. Do not disparage yourself and the pictures you see in your mind, thinking, *I've never had a vision.* You may have had many but just did not understand that lower levels of visions are truly visions.

Open your heart and mind to the Holy Spirit. Believe He really does have access to your mind and can choose to act through your imagination. Let Him begin to show you things.

Venture to Trust God to Speak

Of course, you must test visions and dreams using all the tests we discussed for prophetic words. But do not let the thief use fear or the falseness of docetic theology to rob you of your birthright as a dreamer and visionary for God. Remember that Joel 2:28 promises that we will see visions and dreams by the power of the Holy Spirit, and verse 29 says that all of us servants qualify: "Even on the male and female servants I will pour out My Spirit in those days." He did not say "on some." The implication is "upon all."

In the opening chapters I shared many instances of seeing pictures the Holy Spirit gave me for protection, blessing, etc. I may be more gifted than some, and I know that I am far less gifted than many other prophets. Each one of us is gifted to one degree or another. No one is totally bereft of gifting or power in the Holy Spirit. We should recognize Paul's exhortation in Romans 12:6: "Since we have gifts that differ according to the grace given to us, *each of us is to exercise them* accordingly" (emphasis mine).

I hate it when brothers or sisters say: "Nothing like that ever happens to me. I don't ever see anything or hear anything from God. I guess I'm just a spiritual klutz." Remember the principle we spoke about earlier. If a Christian will just open up and try to receive and act on spiritual impulses, the Lord will be pleased and increase both anointing and ability. Gifts are like muscles; unused they atrophy. What do we learn from the parable of the man who buried his talent rather than risk using it? When we do not risk using our gifts, what we were given is taken away and given instead to one who is willing to risk and venture for the Lord. Do we assume that the admonition "Do not despise prophetic utterances" (1 Thessalonians 5:20) was only a warning not to reject prophecies said by others? I think it far more crucial that people learn not to despise their own efforts to prophesy, however bumbling in the beginning.

True, not all are called to be prophets. Prophets are equipped by the Lord for their calling with many and varied gifts. But we all *are* called to hear God, and dreams and visions are two primary ways to do that. But we cannot grow without risk. Listening to God draws us closer to Him and reveals His nature to us more and more as we stumble and fall and try again. Sweet fellowship with Him is worth whatever it costs our pride—and our fear.

God needs more and more servants who will give themselves as living sacrifices to the Lord (see Romans 12:1), so that He can pour out His gifts of dreams and visions. He wants a vast army of seers and hearers through whom He can bless, heal, prevent harm, defer harmful judgments, edify the Church, reveal convicting and evangelizing truths and prepare for what is coming.

Let me plead with every reader—venture, risk, try to hear God, open your mind to receive images from Him. When they begin to happen, do not shuck them off by saying, "Oh, that was just my silly imagination. God would not speak to little me. I don't want to go off half-cocked, presuming that what I see is from God when all that happened was that I ate too many onions for supper last night." You will have time enough later to balance things and check with wise friends. In the beginning, open up and flounder. All of us learn by trial and error. God's Kingdom is big enough that a few mistakes by you are not going to upset His vast timetable and plan. He will turn everything you offer into best wine for the feast (see John 2:1–10). Trust God that some of those pictures that come into your mind may truly be visionary gifts from Him.

Do Not Seek the Gift, but the Giver

On the other hand, our flesh can desire dreams and visions for inappropriate motives. People sometimes think that being recognized as a dreamer or a visionary gives them special status. Pride may fill their hearts. "Everyone who is proud in heart is an abomination to the LORD" (Proverbs 16:5).

I want to quote from a secular novel here, *People of the Earth*, by W. Michael Gear and Kathleen O'Neal Gear, because it expresses this idea well. Their heroine, White Ash, was called to become a dreamer for the salvation of her people. She feared it and did not want to become a dreamer. Wise old Singing Stones became her mentor. One of their conversations beautifully expresses the difference between wanting to be a dreamer and being called to be one:

> She lowered her eyes and pulled her shining black hair away from her face. "Everyone seems to think I'm a Dreamer except me. What happens if I do not *want* to be this Dreamer?"
>
> The wrinkles on Singing Stones' face pulled themselves into another pattern. "Oh, you *will not* want to. No one *wants* to be a Dreamer. That's part of the way Dreamers are—at least, the good ones. Any fool could wish to be a Powerful Dreamer, but he sees only the power and how it could do things for him. Make him an important person whom others look up to. That sort of thing. What the idiot does not understand is that you do not use Power. It uses you. Anyone who *wants* to Dream knows not what he asks—and is generally denied by Power in the end." He shook his head. "No, young White Ash. Dreaming is for those who *have* to dream."

How applicable to our study! Of course, God does not "use" anyone, but every true prophet knows that the Lord's anointing only flows through him. The prophet does not create it or manipulate it. In this sense, the power of the Holy Spirit does "use" him rather than the other way around. And prophets do "have" to dream and be the Lord's prophets, but not in the sense of being manipulated puppets. Rather, we often feel like crying out as Jeremiah did: "If I say, 'I will not mention Him, or speak anymore in His name,' then within me there is something like a burning fire shut up in my bones; I am weary with holding it in, and I cannot" (Jeremiah 20:9, NRSV). It burns within us, and in that sense we do "have" to dream.

Do not seek dreams and visions. Seek the Giver. Seek to serve. Gifts come as equipment for the serving. In the serving, then seek His visions. Humble yourself under the mighty hand of God, and He will exalt you.

Discern and Lay Down Guideposts of Warning

Please note that I quote from the Gears' book *not* because I recommend it. It is thoroughly New Age and speaks of "spirit guides," communicating with the departed and so on. I have purposefully quoted from it to teach that God can speak truth to us through the most unlikely sources. I do not at all mean that we can dabble in the occult. I had no idea what kind of book it was when I began to read it.

All of us inevitably will be exposed to impure things from time to time—movies we did not know would turn out to be so raunchy, illicit sex in TV programs, novels like the one I quoted above, people cursing in the booth next to us, friends sharing what turn out to be dirty jokes, etc. We need to learn not to be afraid of defilement. We are more than overcomers in Christ. We have gifts of discernment and are able to test all things (see 1 John 4:1–6). We wear Christ's armor (see Ephesians 6), and are protected by Him (see Psalm 91). Prayer cleanses us quickly— "the blood of Jesus His Son cleanses us from all sin" (1 John 1:7).

Moreover, and this is the reason I have quoted from this book, God knows when we are going to be in defiling situations, and He wants us to learn from them and to use them for His glory. My friend Cindy Jacobs had to read books about the occult and watch many defiling videos to warn the Body of occult evils, which she did in her book *Deliver Us from Evil*. After I was converted and renounced the occult, I had to study the occult in order to write knowledgeable warnings and teachings about healing from occult involvement in Mark's and my book *A Comprehensive Guide to Deliverance and Inner Healing*.

Some may yet question whether God would speak a true word through impure sources. Paul, writing to Titus to advise him about the Cretans, told him, "One of themselves, a prophet of their own, said, 'Cretans are always liars, evil beasts, lazy gluttons.' This testimony is true" (Titus 1:12–13). Here, Paul says that a prophet of another faith, himself polluted by laziness and gluttony, is yet able to present a true word from God!

This teaching is important if we are to be able to interpret not only the meanings God would have us see in the events of life but dreams and visions. This is an important function of prophets—to lift away the blinding veil of fear and reveal what good thing God may be saying to us through fearful dreams and frightening visions, and the hurtful events of life. It is a great joy for prophets to discern in reality how and where everything does truly work for good to those who love God, who are called to His purposes (see Romans 8:28).

Seek the Lord and devour His Word first. "Your word I have treasured in my heart, *that I may not sin against You*" (Psalm 119:11, emphasis mine). It is by His Word that we gain discernment:

> For the word of God is living and active and sharper than any two-edged sword, and piercing as far as the division of soul and spirit, of both joints and marrow, *and able to judge [other versions say "discern"] the thoughts and intentions of the heart.*
>
> HEBREWS 4:12, EMPHASIS MINE

By being soundly rooted in His Word, you shall be able to discern and to interpret dreams and visions. But remember that no one can grow as a prophet who interprets dreams and visions until the Lord vastly humbles him to seek only to serve his Lord and do what he was created to do.

What to Do with the Dreams God Gives

Now, what are we to do with the dreams God gives us? Jane Hamon, daughter-in-law of Bishop Bill Hamon, presents in *Dreams and Visions* the best opening statement I have found:

> In order to fully begin to investigate the messages contained in our dreams and visions, it is imperative that we begin to develop an understanding of symbolism. When a person dreams a dream or has a vision, they may have a clear picture of what God is trying to say to them because the revelation is very direct and straightforward, needing little or no interpretive skill to understand. In most cases, however, and for most individuals, dreams and even some visions may come forth in disjointed scenes, pictures and conversations that make little sense on their own.
>
> Most dreams are communicated through symbols such as people, places, things, and activities. This is where understanding the language of symbolism comes in. Some people dream short, concise dreams, and others dream as though they are watching a full-length movie. It does not matter what the length of the dream is, only what it contains and what it communicates.
>
> Dr. Gayle Delaney, who spends a great deal of time studying dreams from a scientific perspective, says, "Dreams are very much like poetry.

You understand them if you get the metaphor." Understanding symbolism is essential to dream interpretation. Symbolism is the most basic and elementary language there is. Ancient cultures recorded their history through the use of pictures and symbols.

Unfortunately, symbols tend to intimidate people into thinking that they are too difficult or too deep to understand. As mentioned previously, part of the reason for this is the attitude of our western culture, which has a basic lack of patience when it comes to symbolism.

This is not so in the Oriental cultures of the eastern world of which the Jewish people are considered to be a part. Jesus never hesitated to speak to His disciples using the language of symbolism. On many occasions He related truths through the use of parables, which were rich with symbolism. At times the parables had to be interpreted, since the meaning was veiled.

You may ask, why did Jesus not just say what He meant without concealing the meaning in symbols? This could be because there is a depth to symbols that mere words do not have. Symbols give a broader meaning to what is being described.

Sound familiar? I said almost the same things in chapter 10. I quote Jane Hamon here to make it clear that dreams and visions are to be regarded in the same way as all other forms of dark speech. The same cautions and advice apply. We need to ponder, pray, test and seek wise counsel. Both Pharaoh and Nebuchadnezzar had the wisdom to seek counsel from those reputed to be experts in the interpretation of dreams. We have seen a number of Christians, however, fall into trouble by quickly and rashly thinking they understood their dreams.

A man may dream of selling his car. He thinks that is a command from God and hastily sells it for far less than patience and wise business methods would obtain. If he had sought counsel, on the other hand, a wise interpreter would have questioned and mused with him. Perhaps the car that needed to be sold was his own ambitious nature, in exchange for the cross of Christ.

In another example, people, possibly psychotic, have had powerful dreams of killing their children. They read the story of Abraham's trying to sacrifice Isaac and felt compelled to kill their family—and some did so! God would never tell anyone to do such a thing. It goes against all He is and says. If a dream like this were in any degree truly from God, it would be a call to repentance, to kill on the cross the false children of passions and thoughts that had been given birth in the heart and mind.

Though that example is probably starker than any of our readers may experience, let its starkness call you away from impetuosity and isolation. Never act without counsel. And never act in haste.

A Prophet's Role in Interpreting Dreams

So far we have covered how to react when you receive a dream, basically repeating most of the advice given in chapter 10 concerning dark speech. But a function of prophets is to interpret dreams. We read more about that in the Bible than about prophets having dreams. Both Joseph and Daniel rose to power interpreting rulers' dreams. The kings of Israel often called for the prophets whenever they or an advisor had a dream or vision.

The following are words of counsel concerning this task.

Study the Topic

Study to show yourself a workman who does not need to be ashamed (see 2 Timothy 2:15). Study all the instances of dreams in the Bible, paying close attention to how the prophets interpreted them—for instance, the seven lean years eating up the seven fat (see Genesis 41). Learn whatever you can about symbolism. Read Jane Hamon's *Dreams and Visions* and Paula's and my *The Elijah Task,* in which entire chapters are devoted to dreams and visions, and the many other books now available on the topic.

Pray for the Gift of Interpretation

Pray for the gift of the ability to interpret dreams and visions. Then practice interpreting your own, where you are less likely to do harm to others while you learn by trial and error.

Find Mentors

Seek relationships with others who can mentor you. It is best if these are established prophets who have long practiced interpreting. But if you cannot find any, seek people who are full of common sense and wisdom, not necessarily the most mystically gifted. Down-to-earth people give us prophetic types balance and solid perspective.

Incidentally, the three wise men may have been wise enough to read heavenly portents in the stars, but they knew nothing about human nature! Of all the dumb things, they went to the reigning king to find out where the new king would be born! And God had to warn them not to return to the king when common sense ought to have made that abundantly clear. This is to say to us prophets that often, in the beginning, we are "so heavenly minded we are of no earthly use." We need to stick close to "earthy" people who have good balance and common sense until their way rubs off on us.

Pray for God's Wisdom

Pray for wisdom. It is one thing to understand a dream's possible meanings, and quite another to know how much to reveal. A good rule of thumb is that if immediate actions are required, and the dream or vision seems easily discerned, think about revealing its meanings. But if the dream seems to be speaking of something well in advance of needing to know, do not cut short the other's pondering time. Do not pridefully blurt out meanings and think you have done a good service. What good does it do for God to give the person something to pray and think about if you are going to spoil God's intentions with premature finality? Suggest possible meanings. Hint. Ask questions that cause further thinking.

Study the Methods of Other Modern Prophets

Study how other modern prophets interpret dreams. Listen and observe. Let me give you a case in point. Do you remember my example in chapter 10 about dreaming of snakes? I know it may be hard for some to think that being entwined by a snake could actually be something good, having to do with receiving wisdom. But here is a similar type of dream and its fascinating interpretation by Jane Hamon—about tarantulas!

While my husband and I were building a new home, I experienced a bit of anxiety regarding the finances needed for certain changes we had made. The most costly change was putting a tile roof on the house, rather than an asphalt one. In this time of faith stretching, I had the following dream:

173

THE TARANTULA ROOF

Everyone was excited because we were putting on our new tile roof. The excitement stemmed from the fact that the tiles were made of a new and innovative and costly material—they were the best! They were made of the dried preserved bodies of Tarantula Spiders! I was having a tough time seeing what was so exciting about these tiles. If you asked me, it was strange! Then I was going into the homes of people I knew, and they were raising baby tarantulas with great joy and excitement, feeding them, putting them to bed, etc. It was very strange to me.

I was perplexed by this dream and thought, "Surely this can't be an edifying meaning—everyone knows spiders are evil." I thought about the dream throughout the day, and late at night I lay in bed still praying and pondering the dream.

I decided to get up and look up Tarantula Spider in my Junior Encyclopedia Britannica. This is what it said:

In the middle ages it was believed that the bite of the tarantula spider caused a disease known as Tarantella, which was supposed to have symptoms of having an overwhelming, uncontrollable desire to dance!

It went on to say that this dance, the disease and the spider were all named after a town in Italy called Taranto. This town's name is very similar to the city in Canada called Toronto, which at the same time of this writing is a place of great outpouring of God's Spirit of joy.

The encyclopedia also mentioned that the bite of this spider is actually not harmful to humans. This spider is also the only spider that aggressively chases down its prey instead of waiting for it to fall in the web.

So the Lord used this dream to say that He was going to cover our home with joy and rejoicing (which was symbolized, strangely enough, by a tarantula spider). As people fear the spider's bite without cause, so I was moving in fear instead of faith and God was assuring me that my worry was without cause because His provision would be with joy and abundance.

The spiders were also being raised in the homes of our church people. God was encouraging me that this joy would be poured out in every home, as well as our church home, and that it would produce an aggression to go and track down their spiritual enemies and destroy them.

When the interpretation came, I was filled with joy and laughter, and suddenly I was full of faith, believing what God had already promised was true. Who would have ever thought a tarantula spider would bring joy and rejoicing?!

So many valuable lessons are embedded in this story:

A. Jane was frightened, but she did not panic and jump to the conclusion that she was being warned of some impending evil, though she thought of spiders as evil.
B. She thought about it, pondering all day and into the night.
C. She prayed for God to reveal what it meant.
D. She got up and did research. This was a very important key to discovery.
E. She was able to think figuratively.
F. She was able to see and repent of her fault, revealed by the dream to be her unfaith.
G. She was able to do what is called free association—tarantula, Tarantella, Taranto, Toronto where the dance of joy in the Holy Spirit was being experienced. And she was able to think in the Lord's way of speaking in puns.
H. Knowing her from her book—though I have not met her—I do not doubt that she talked about her dream and its possibilities with her husband, Bishop Bill and others.
I. In the end, she believed. Her faith was in a God who gives good gifts. Knowing His loving nature colored all her research and thinking. So many I know celebrate the supposed power of darkness, and that colors all their dreams, visions and interpretations.
J. She rejoiced, allowing God to bring His blessings to the max.

So, as shown by this example, study and follow the models God gives in others of the faith.

Be Obedient

Be obedient to what God commands or merely reveals in dreams. Teach others to do the same. Sadly, many times I have heard of warnings or promised blessing in dreams—and personal prophecies—to which the people did not respond in obedience. The blessing failed to come— as though God had sent the angel with the gift and we failed to pray him past the "prince of Persia" (Daniel 10:13). Or the disaster that could have been prevented struck.

Be Free of Sin and Stay in Prayer

Keep your spirit open and clear, free from sin and defilement, and tuned in by a daily life of prayer. Be expectant, alert and ready at any moment's notice, like a minuteman in the American Revolution. Teach and model the same.

Listen to Interpretations of Others

Involve others in interpreting. Do not pridefully scorn others. Listen to many. You may have to sift and toss many straws from many people before God's needle of truth pricks your mind with revelation.

Remember That Not All Dreams Are Spiritual

Do not think that every dream is spiritual and has great significance. Ecclesiastes 5:3 says, "For a dream comes with much business and painful effort, and a fool's voice with many words" (AMPLIFIED). In other words, if you are overwrought and busy, a dream may be telling you that and has little other significance—or no significance at all. And Jeremiah 23:25–27 says,

> "I have heard what the prophets have said who prophesy falsely in My name, saying, 'I had a dream, I had a dream!' How long? Is there anything in the hearts of the prophets who prophesy falsehood, even these prophets of the deception of their own heart, who intend to make My people forget My name by their dreams which they relate to one another, just as their fathers forgot My name because of Baal?"

Testers in mints learned to detect false money by handling true money all day, until they could sense the false quickly. You will learn by the feel of it when a dream is not what it pretends to be.

A friend of mine believed that the Holy Spirit vouchsafes every dream, that every dream is spiritual and safe. Wrong! God will not vouchsafe any area in us from sin. Not all dreams are significant, and not every spiritual dream is from the Holy Spirit (see Jeremiah 23:25–28). Keep your guard up, and teach others to do the same.

Practice Patience

Finally, be patient. Do not feel that because people burden you to solve their conundrums, you have to come up with answers. There is nothing shameful about saying, "I don't know." God may give you answers later on.

Seeking to Have Visions

All this we have been saying about dreams also applies to visions. But one aspect is different for each of the two. Normally, we do not try to have spiritual dreams. It is good to give ourselves to God, repeatedly, saying that we give Him permission to plant His dreams in our minds. But since we are asleep during dreams, we are not actively involved in trying to see. On the other hand, we can and should seek directly to have visions.

How? First, close your mind to all other spirits. That is, renounce and repent for any previous occult activity. Tell God you reject any influence other than that of the Holy Spirit. Tell Him you want to see whatever He wants you to see. Make yourself comfortable, so that distractions of the flesh do not interfere. Pray yourself into His presence. Usually you will want to know about something specific. For example, when my children were in danger, I would say, "Show me, Lord." It is more difficult to focus when you ask generally, "Show me whatever, Lord." Relax, and let Him float His images and pictures into your mind. Sometimes they are "still shots," but most often for me it is like watching a movie.

Our carnal minds are at enmity with God (Romans 8:5–8) and will cast up distractions. Do not fight your mind. That is what it wants. If you fight it, your carnal mind will then have won the battle of keeping you from seeing what God wants you to see. Your mind then remains in control of you, rather than the Holy Spirit. Ignore the mind's signals. If you find you have wandered off into a reverie or a daydream, do not bother scolding yourself. Ignore it, and haul yourself back to resting and trying to let Him place His images in your mind.

Do not confuse this process with Eastern meditation, which is based on resignation. Do not try to blank out your mind. Your mind is the citadel of your spirit. It is your conscious mind that the Holy Spirit uses to guard you. Blanking it, as in Eastern meditation, leaves you open to demonic invasion. Christian meditation is active. It purposefully and alertly seeks to meet with the Lord.

Do not ask to peer into the secrets of others. Ask to be shown what God is willing for you to see. The hallmark of God's Kingdom is courtesy. Satan's, on the other hand, is discourtesy. Trying to see what is forbidden quickly invites a demon of divination.

Practice Seeing Visions

Practice makes perfect, so practice seeing. Ways developed become customary roads. It becomes easier and quicker as you learn to recognize and celebrate what He is showing you.

Seeing spiritually, like any muscle or skill, grows stronger with use. God needs hundreds and thousands to whom He can come and say, "Look, child. See what is happening, or going to happen, and call My people to pray."

Often, the Holy Spirit uses visions to show Paula and me the places where we are invited to speak. We may have never been there before physically, but He shows us the place and what needs prayer before we arrive. Also, He calls us to pray for people and shows them to us. We see them grieving or fearing or praying, and we pray for them. Our prayers, then, are specific and accurate because of what He has shown. Phone calls then confirm every detail. Additionally, as I reported earlier, we have seen accidents about to happen, dangers lurking and blessings God wants to bring, such as prospective spouses.

If you are called to be a prophet, then you must study and practice— just as if you were called to be a pianist. If and when you have been faithful in small things, such as for individuals and churches, He will begin to call you and show you things of great import, for cities and states and nations. Then, you are capable of being called into the councils of God, as I explain in my book *Healing the Nations*, in the chapter entitled "The Councils of God."

A Final Word to Prophets on Dreams and Visions

A fundamental task of prophets is to guide the Body of Christ by what they dream and see by vision. This function will grow more acute as the times of tribulation mount. If you are a prophet, enlarge your stakes. Set your tent pegs further out (see Isaiah 54:2). Grow into the fullness of the calling that is upon you. A weary and hurting world awaits your arrival.

PART 3

PURPOSES AND TASKS OF PROPHETS TODAY

THIRTEEN

INTERCESSORY PRAYER

TASKS MAY NOT SEEM VERY DIFFERENT from functions. I am using the word *task* to refer to something larger than one function. Sometimes, many functions are required to accomplish one task. For example, listening to God, interpreting dreams and visions, blessing and protecting all may be required to accomplish one task of intercession.

The Purposes of Prophets

Functions accomplish tasks; tasks accomplish purposes. It is time we look at the purposes of prophets. In *Prophets: Pitfalls and Principles* Bishop Bill Hamon says:

> Prophets are special to the heart of God. They participate in all of God's plans and performances on planet earth. They are to prepare the way for the second coming of Christ by bringing revelation knowledge on the Scriptures that must be fulfilled before Christ can return. Thus, the restoration of the prophetic ministry and the company of the prophets is the greatest sign of the nearness of Christ's coming.

In *The Coming Prophetic Revolution* Jim Goll says:

The true purpose of the prophetic is to not only reveal the Man Jesus but to reveal the Lordship of Jesus. "No one can say, 'Jesus is Lord,' except by the Holy Spirit" (1 Corinthians 12:3). We cannot understand Jesus' Lordship and His right authority over our lives without the revelation of the Holy Spirit operating in our behalf. The revelation of Christ Jesus and His Lordship is the foundational purpose and focus of all prophetic revelation. If we are not fully grounded here, we will have no prophetic revolution.

Ernest B. Gentile, in *Your Sons and Daughters Shall Prophesy*, offers several statements regarding purposes of the prophet. Here are two:

From the divine standpoint, prophecy is God speaking His mind and sharing His words with mankind. From the human point of view the prophet is the conduit, channel or spokesman for those words, and in such use speech is elevated to the highest possible function. For the current of divine revelation to flow, there must be a live contact at both ends. The prophet-spokesman, obedient to God and sympathetic with man, was God's human contact.

The early Church embraced an astounding belief—one that could revolutionize today's Church if we would accept and buy it as our own. They were convinced that the Jesus who had walked among mankind in a literal body now resided among them in the invisible Person of the Holy Spirit. The Christ who had spoken to them through His own lips now spoke to His people through the inspired speech of His servants! They called this continuing voice of Jesus in the Church *prophecy*.

Exciting and dynamic, prophecy provides an essential benefit in our church programs for experiencing God and expanding Christ's Church. Prophecy is a vital part of the renewal of the Church, and Christians must become more enlightened and inspired about its function and use.

My own vision of the purposes of prophets and the prophetic movement is summarized in the two mandating Scriptures of Elijah House:

"Behold, I am going to send you Elijah the prophet before the coming of the great and terrible day of the LORD. He will restore the hearts of the fathers to their children and the hearts of the children to their fathers, so that I will not come and smite the earth with a curse."

MALACHI 4:5–6, NKJV

183

And He answered and said, "Elijah is coming and will restore all things."

MATTHEW 17:11

Father God purposes for Elijah prophets to be major players in restoring all things and presenting them as gifts to His Son (see Psalm 2:8). Turning the hearts of fathers and children to each other is crucial to that task and is the special province of Elijah prophets.

I believe every prophet alive today is called to be an Elijah prophet. Whatever else we are called to be and do, we are Elijahs. We are to walk in the spirit and power of Elijah. For this reason, this book is entitled *Elijah Among Us.*

On the other hand, God's purposes for His prophets and for the end time are probably too great for any one prophet's vision to encompass. To me, the statements quoted above, and all the many others of like stature we could quote, are coruscate facets of one diamond too brilliant and grandiloquent for any one of us to describe alone.

Thus, I believe Elijah is to return not as one person, but as the company of Elijah prophets who will restore all things. *I believe Elijah is returning now, as the company of prophets is being raised up to stand in his spirit, purpose and power. We are to prepare the way for the return of our Lord Jesus Christ.*

Intercessory Prayer

The Prophets' Role in Intercessory Prayer

Intercessory prayer is both a function of prophets and a major task. Prophets are essential to the work of end time intercession. Not only are prophets themselves to intercede, but the Body of Christ needs to know the specifics of when and what to pray about. Random and often fleshly originated prayers will not accomplish all that is needful. Any army needs a battle plan, cohesion and instant direction. God wants to inform His spiritual army of its battle orders. *The Lord's Elijah prophets are to hear our General (the Holy Spirit) and send His directions to all His officers and troops.*

The Lord wants His army of intercessors to be like the army of Joel 2:7–9:

> They run like mighty men,
> They climb the wall like soldiers;

And they each march in line,
Nor do they deviate from their paths.
They do not crowd each other,
They march everyone in his path;
When they burst through the defenses,
They do not break ranks.
They rush on the city,
They run on the wall;
They climb into the houses,
They enter through the windows like a thief.

The picture is of unity and disciplined order, no one doing his own thing or wandering off on fruitless tangents. Each is joined in efforts with others of like mind and heart—guided and directed, without wasted efforts, without jostling each other. They enter to plunder the evil one's riches like thieves, regaining for the Body what was stolen. That is the Lord's plan for any time, but most succinctly for this age just before the Parousia, the Second Coming.

Historically, before every great spiritual revival there has first been a vast revival of intercessory prayer. That is where we are right now in history. The great end time revival is about to begin. The Holy Spirit is moving in preparation. The army of intercessors is arising. To me, this means it is crucial that the Lord's prophets arise, learn who they are and what they are to do. A major reason for this book is to help God's Elijah prophets learn that they are more than those who give personal words; *they are the very life-link of heaven and earth, the transmitters who are to make cohesion out of chaos for all our prayer efforts.*

Elijah Prophets Call the People into United Prayer

Prophets must rise to such stature and cohesion that together they are able to sound clear trumpets calling the Body into concerted intercessory prayer for the nations and the great events of our time. Paul warned, "For if the bugle produces an indistinct sound, who will prepare himself for battle?" (1 Corinthians 14:8). So far we have yet remained too detached, too isolated from one another. But the Holy Spirit is at work, calling us together.

We see it beginning to happen in the many voices that call the Body into intercession for the peace of Jerusalem. The world totters on the

185

brink of a war that could become the prophesied climactic war of Armageddon, and many prophets are sounding the trumpets of prayer. Various groups of prophets are beginning to band together and network. For example, the Apostolic Council of Prophetic Elders, a group of well-known prophets, meets as often as their divergent schedules allow, to pool insights and to intercede for the nation and the world. These and many more are fledgling beginnings of formation.

C. Peter Wagner is the guiding apostolic voice in the founding of the World Prayer Center. The vision is magnificent. At this center in Colorado Springs, a group of people of every denomination from every level of faith can join in prayers of intercession and warfare for the issues of the world, great and small. In the basement of the building is a center of coordination and communication. Whenever something of import happens anywhere in the world, a call comes to the center, and in a few moments' time hundreds, perhaps thousands, of prayerful people are called and focused onto that trouble-spot needing prayer. This is one powerful way intercessors can be mobilized to function as that powerful army described in Joel 2.

Other such organizations are arising around the world. God is moving. At a large gathering in Colorado Springs, Cindy Jacobs proclaimed that the Lord revealed to her that the prayers ascending before the Lord in John's Book of Revelation were not simply something seen and accomplished two thousand years ago when John saw the vision, but a mighty concourse of heaven and earth praying together right now for the great climactic events of history.

For the first time in history, we are able to communicate with others around the world at a moment's notice. The many new forms of media and communication offer us means of information and cohesion never before available. Phones and faxes, Internet links, e-mail, and organizations like the World Prayer Center act as nerve centers and relay stations for the entire prophetic prayer army of the Lord. Ephesians 4:14–16 can happen in our time:

> As a result, we are no longer to be children, tossed here and there by waves and carried about by every wind of doctrine, by the trickery of men, by craftiness in deceitful scheming; but speaking the truth in love, we are to grow up in all aspects into Him who is the head, even Christ, *from whom the whole body, being fitted and held together by what every joint supplies,*

according to the proper working of each individual part, causes the growth of the body for the building up of itself in love.

EMPHASIS MINE

This is the first time in all of history that we can supply one another at a moment's notice, the first time we can really be fitted together! For the first time, each part can in fact contribute to the whole. As blood courses through our bodies, carrying life-giving oxygen and nutrients to every cell, now there is a river of communication flowing throughout the Body of Christ, carrying life-giving information. As nerve cells transmit signals that alert our physical bodies for action, summoning adrenalin and whatever is needed to function, so media cells transmit signals and summons throughout the Body of Christ. *The Elijah prophets are to be the cells next to the brain (the mind of God) that forward His messages throughout the Body.*

But how shall the prophet share the mind of God with His people in today's world? In small local intercessory prayer groups, the prophets can bring revelation: "This is what I see God wants to happen. Let's pray for it." Or, "This evil or bad thing is about to happen. Let's prevent it." Additionally, prophets who carry more than local authority can mobilize people in whole cities, regions, states or national and international situations. Prophets can call God's people to action through whatever media are available, mobilizing the Lord's intercessors through the Internet, e-mail, phones and faxes. And someday prophets may even hold such recognized stature that they will be able to utilize secular radio and TV stations to broadcast the Holy Spirit's summons far and wide.

If we prophets are obedient to our Lord, we shall see a mighty joining together, so that with one concerted voice we raise prophetic trumpet calls to the Body. This is perhaps the most exciting age in all of history, as God moves His players into position on the chessboard of history. We are almost to that time when the Lord will proclaim triumphantly to all the powers of darkness, "Checkmate!"

The Church's Role in Intercessory Prayer

First Corinthians 14:8 says, "For if the bugle produces an indistinct sound, who will prepare himself for battle?" The Lord is at work, purging His prophets, that they may give clear and distinct signals for the Body

187

of Christ. But the question is, if a prophet does trumpet a sure signal, who will get ready for battle? Of one fact I am sure. *None of this that I have just written can to any degree be fulfilled if there is not sufficient intercessory prayer support from the Body of Christ.* John's vision on the island of Patmos speaks of end time wonders being specifically affected by the intercessions of the saints:

> When He had taken the book, the four living creatures and the twenty-four elders fell down before the Lamb, each one holding a harp and *golden bowls full of incense, which are the prayers of the saints.*

> REVELATION 5:8, EMPHASIS MINE

> When the Lamb broke the seventh seal, there was silence in heaven for about half an hour. And I saw the seven angels who stand before God, and seven trumpets were given to them. Another angel came and stood at the altar, holding a golden censer; and much incense was given to him, *so that he might add it to the prayers of all the saints on the golden altar which was before the throne.* And the smoke of the incense, *with the prayers of the saints,* went up before God out of the angel's hand. Then the angel took the censer and filled it with the fire of the altar, and threw it to the earth; and there followed peals of thunder and sounds and flashes of lightning and an earthquake. And the seven angels who had the seven trumpets prepared themselves to sound them.

> REVELATION 8:1–6, EMPHASES MINE

As the angels sounded their trumpets one by one, what followed were the cataclysmic events of the summation of all history before the return of the Lord. Dutch Sheets speaks of the bowls, which are the prayers of the saints, in his marvelous book *Intercessory Prayer.* I am not pointing you to the particular pages about how the golden bowls need to be filled before the angels can sound their trumpets, lest you look them up and close the book. Read the book in its entirety. It is the requisite primer for the work that lies before all of us if the Lord's return is to happen with our involvement, rather than in spite of us.

How can the Church offer the sufficient intercessory prayer support necessary for the end times?

The Body must respond. Obedience must follow. It will not be enough for the Lord's Elijah prophets to learn how to serve if the Body of Christ shuffles off what is said and goes on with business as usual. If the Church is not faithful to respond in obedient prayer, the Lord will not say, "Well done," and open greater possibilities such as local and national television spots. And the leadership of the Church must set the example for others to follow. Sadly, so many times I have observed a prophet bringing a message to a local church and, though the word implored the people to fall to their knees in repentant prayer, the leader of worship or the pastor has responded, "That was great. Nice to hear a word from God. Now let's sing such-and-such a hymn." No one bowed in prayer. The prophet might as well not have spoken! But how exhilarating when leadership hears and immediately calls the Body into obedience! And how powerful it is when the Body responds!

How great it would be if every small group, local church, great conference and gathering had access to Elijah prophets who could discern, hear God and call the people into intercessory prayer. To me this is one powerful way Ephesians 4:14–16 can happen, as each part supplies its gifts and the Body of Christ receives and responds. Thus we are to grow into the fullness of maturity and power.

Pray for the rising of the Elijah company, and perhaps pray more for an obedient Church.

God's Humor in the Midst of the Serious Business of Intercession

I had thought to end this chapter on that high note, but sometimes I think the Lord wants to add a bit of humor. Julie Andrews sang that immortal line, "A spoonful of sugar makes the medicine go down," and sometimes I think God uses humor to make the lesson go down more easily into our hearts.

Jan and Rich O'Brien are our Elijah House staff members whose job it is to relay prophetic and other calls for intercessory prayer. They do a great job. This morning they mailed out a list of intercessory needs to all our intercessors. My own needs were the last on the list. Earlier, the intercessors had been called to pray because of my recent heart attack. Now the O'Briens were reporting and calling for further prayers. They meant for people to pray that the Lord would slow me down to a *lower activity level*, knowing my workaholic nature. But there was a typo. It actually read: *"John S. is doing well. Pray for the Lord's grace in dealing with John's lover activity level and different diet. Also pray for the Lord's comfort and strength*

189

for Paula." I guess Paula does need comfort and strength to deal with my lover activity level!

Isn't it wonderful that even in the seriousness of world-shaking calls, right while I was writing this chapter this morning, the Lord seemed to smile and say, "Relax, guys, it's not all that serious. I've already won the battle. Have some fun while you are about the business of serving Me."

FOURTEEN

RECONCILIATION

Now all these things are from God, who reconciled us to Himself through Christ, and gave us the ministry of reconciliation, namely, that God was in Christ reconciling the world to Himself, not counting their trespasses against them, and He has committed to us the word of reconciliation. Therefore, we are ambassadors for Christ, as though God were making an appeal through us; we beg you on behalf of Christ, be reconciled to God.

2 CORINTHIANS 5:18–20

GOD PURPOSES TO RECONCILE all the warring factions of mankind—families, churches, states and nations, ethnic and religious groups, etc. In the end, He shall have so accomplished His purpose that "They will not hurt or destroy in all My holy mountain, for the earth will be full of the knowledge of the LORD as the waters cover the sea" (Isaiah 11:9). Implausible as it may seem now, while more than 135 wars defile the earth, God will complete His work of reconciliation so that "they will hammer their swords into plowshares and their spears into pruning hooks. Nation will not lift up sword against nation, and never again will they learn war" (Isaiah 2:4).

What a great and enduring hope, guaranteed by the promise of prophetic Scriptures throughout the Bible! A hope modeled and died for by our Lord Jesus Christ. A hope for which countless saints through-out Christian history have been martyred.

As yet, we see little enduring fruit of reconciliation. Mankind con-tinues to tear itself apart on every level—from divorce to ethnic hatred to murder to political oppression and warfare. But "He will not be dis-heartened or crushed, until He has established justice in the earth" (Isa-iah 42:4). "The LORD will go forth like a warrior, He will arouse His zeal like a man of war. He will utter a shout, yes, He will raise a war cry. He will prevail against His enemies" (Isaiah 42:13). He is truly a wonder-ful, paradoxical Lord, whose ways are not our ways and whose thoughts are not our thoughts. Isn't it just like Him to use images of a mighty war-rior to describe how He will bring His climax of peace upon the earth?

Reconciliation Within the Church

Our Father God is beginning His mission of justice and peace by answering His Son's prayer in John 17, that those who believe in Him may all be one. Because judgment begins with the household of God, He is beginning His work of reconciliation by moving upon the Church. So the Holy Spirit is seeking reconciliation among His own, through His many ambassadors, to break down the strongholds of hubris that long have divided and set the arms of His Church against one another. Hubris is that exaggerated ego that caused many denominations, in the nine-teenth century especially, to split off from one another in jealousy and spiritual pride. Each declared to have a special revelation of truth no others possessed, and each believed it and it alone was right and would inherit eternity. Though pockets of this separatism still exist, praise God that the Church as a whole has broken free of such delusions and no longer honors divisive theologies, teaching and preaching.

Hundreds of issues of difference remain. Denominations quarrel about baptism. At what age should one be baptized—at birth or infancy, or only upon belief by those of accountable age? Should baptism be by sprin-kling or immersion? Who is qualified to baptize? And we have made the Lord's Supper into another divisive issue. We argue over what it means, what it is, who is invited and allowed to receive, and who is qualified to celebrate its rites. And some very acrimonious debates rage about our Lord's mother and her place and activity in the Church.

192

Years ago, Barbara Shlemon Ryan and I were called to minister inner healing in Tiffany, Ohio. There the Lord called us to enter into prayer together. When I was not teaching and we were not counseling as a team, we entered into prayer for the healing of the Roman Catholic-Protestant split throughout history, she as a Catholic laywoman and I as a Protestant pastor. Day after day, as representatives of our denominations, we repented together for everything the Lord could bring to our minds that had happened throughout history—war, disrespect and disallowance of each other's sacraments and services, hatred, animosity and jealousy, intermarriage troubles and divorce, family feuds, etc. In the midst of our praying, the Lord gave us a vision that we both saw together. It was of two long lines of people stretching out of sight, converging and walking in amicable pairs through an archway into glory.

From that moment on, I have worked and prayed for unity between Catholics and Protestants. It is a dominant passion of my life. The Lord has given me a deep love for both branches. In many ways and places, Paula and I have seen that vision happening, as Catholics and Protestants have held services together and accepted one another as brothers and sisters in Christ, whether they agree on every issue or not.

The Body of Christ is learning that unity is not coterminous with uniformity, and that we do not have to agree in order to be united as one. We are learning to focus on the Lord Jesus and agree to disagree, while serving together in one harness. Our Father is calling us to learn what it means that He truly is *our* Father.

Reconciliation: A Major Theme of Christian Life

Reconciliation is the calling and work of every Christian. As a prophet of the Lord, here in these pages I call every reader to join the Lord's cause in praying for and walking out unity in the Body of Christ. The world will not recognize Jesus as Savior and Son of God until and unless it sees us demonstrating who He is by walking in love for one another (see John 13:35).

Earlier I described how God expanded our vision of Malachi 4:5–6 by saying that the Jewish people are the fathers of Christians, Catholics are the fathers of Protestants and native people in any land are the fathers of colonists. The import of that was and remains a most impelling sum-mons to be His ambassadors for reconciliation.

Subsequently, God called me by a personal prophetic word into work-ing for reconciliation between natives and others all over the world. But that was not a call for me alone. Within that prophetic word was a prom-ise. I quote it exactly as God said it to me: *Through your prayers, all that was stolen from native people around the world will be restored.* The weight of that frightened me terribly, until I realized that *your* was not singular. It did not mean that through my prayers alone all would be restored. *Your* is plural. God's call was not for me alone—it was also a prophetic command to call and lead others into the work. Through the prayers of all who respond, God will restore all that the thief has stolen from native people around the world.

That prophetic promise was not confined to objects and land. The most important things stolen from native people are their identity, sense of worth, destiny and purpose. In our book *Healing the Nations*, readers can see in more detail how God is restoring what can be redeemed of native culture—songs, dances, music, arts, beliefs and understanding, etc.

As time passes, more and more Christians are responding to the call to pray and work for reconciliation. *It needs to become a major theme of Christian life*, until the prophecies of Isaiah are fulfilled in full.

The Prophet's Role in Reconciliation

Prophets are vital to our Father's work to establish unity. Prophets speak for God. We carry His authority. We are to be His ambassadors for reconciliation, giving direction to the entire Body of Christ who are truly His ambassadors.

A Prophet Must Speak Truth in Love

One point regarding prophets and the mission of reconciliation is unequivocal: *Whatever prophet calls for reconciliation, within the Church or anywhere else, is a true prophet of God. Whatever prophet calls for division and divisiveness is ipso facto a false prophet.* God's people must not listen to such a prophet. He or she should be rebuked, sternly if necessary: "Answer a fool as his folly deserves, that he not be wise in his own eyes" (Proverbs 26:5). Prophets, more than all others, must die to self in what we say, that every word is checked by the grace of the Holy Spirit. We must not add one tiny stick to the fires of human discourse, but at all times and everywhere be His ambassadors for reconciliation and not harm.

· There are no qualifications to this statement. Prophets and teachers can and should speak the truth in love, but the key word is *love*. There are ways to speak truth that heal rather than divide. Whoever has not learned how to do that should keep his mouth shut. "For lack of wood the fire goes out, and where there is no whisperer, contention quiets down. Like charcoal to hot embers and wood to fire, so is a contentious man to kindle strife" (Proverbs 26:20–21). We who are the Lord's Elijah prophets should burn the Lord's words indelibly upon our hearts, especially in this area of being His ambassadors for unity:

> A gentle answer turns away wrath, but a harsh word stirs up anger. The tongue of the wise makes knowledge acceptable, but the mouth of fools spouts folly.
>
> PROVERBS 15:1–2

> A soothing tongue is a tree of life, but perversion in it crushes the spirit.
>
> VERSE 4

> The mind of the intelligent seeks knowledge, but the mouth of fools feeds on folly.
>
> VERSE 14

> A hot-tempered man stirs up strife, but the slow to anger calms a dispute.
>
> VERSE 18

> A man has joy in an apt answer, and how delightful is a timely word!
>
> VERSE 23

> The heart of the righteous ponders how to answer, but the mouth of the wicked pours out evil things.
>
> VERSE 28

And then there are those powerful words from the apostle James, which are addressed to teachers but can be applied to prophets, as well:

> Let not many of you become teachers [or prophets], my brethren, knowing that as such we will incur a stricter judgment. For we all stumble in many ways. If anyone does not stumble in what he says, he is a perfect man, able to bridle the whole body as well. . . . So also the tongue is a small part of the body, and yet it boasts of great things. See how great a forest is set aflame by such a small fire! And the tongue is a fire, the very world of iniquity; the tongue is set among our members as that which defiles the entire body, and sets on fire the course of our life, and is set on fire by hell. For every species of beasts and birds, of reptiles and creatures of the sea, is tamed and has been tamed by the human race. But no one can tame the tongue; it is a restless evil and full of deadly poison. With it we bless our Lord and Father, and with it we curse men, who have been made in the likeness of God; from the same mouth come both blessing and cursing. My brethren, these things ought not to be this way. . . . Who among you is wise and understanding? Let him show by his good behavior his deeds in the gentleness of wisdom. But if you have bitter jealousy and selfish ambition in your heart, do not be arrogant and so lie against the truth. This wisdom is not that which comes down from above, but is earthly, natural, demonic. For where jealousy and selfish ambition exist, there is disorder and every evil thing. *But the wisdom from above is first pure, then peaceable, gentle, reasonable, full of mercy and good fruits, unwavering, without hypocrisy. And the seed whose fruit is righteousness is sown in peace by those who make peace.*
>
> JAMES 3, EMPHASIS MINE

Control of the tongue and pen has not been easy for me—or for any of us prophets—to learn, and far be it from me to say I have learned it altogether. I suggest that those who are in earnest, who very much want to fight and win the battle with their own unruly tongues, can profit greatly by reading a book entitled *Stop the Runaway Conversation* by Dr. Michael D. Sedler. But I must warn our readers, you have to be a happy masochist to study it all the way through. It flays you alive, and you do not come out alive—you die a pile of good deaths!

I belabor this point because we who are prophets are at once the most vulnerable to becoming critical and divisive—and the foremost called to lead the other way, to peace and reconciliation! Prophets have gifts of discernment. We see things others do not. It comes as part of the prophetic package to see evil and hate it with a purple passion!

For instance, idolatry is one of the things we prophets hate. It is the nature of Elijah, who called down fire upon the bullock of idolatry and slew the 850 prophets of idolatry. We feel it ricocheting throughout our hearts and minds when brothers and sisters idolize something that is otherwise good. For example, suppose our church has a tremendous worship experience where the presence of the Lord overshadows all. The following Sunday, the congregation seems to be worshiping God, and they think they are, but we know they have now fallen to worshiping last Sunday's experience! They would now use worship and the Lord to find that experience. Their feelings in worship have become the idol they are serving.

We see idolatry when God's people turn the Trinity into God, Jesus and the Bible rather than the Holy Spirit. Or: Father, Son and my traditions. We see it when people begin to idolize theology. Or most commonly, we see it when people fall to serving the idol of themselves serving God, rather than dying to self and living purely in and for Him.

How difficult it is to bite the tongue when we want to thunder against the things we hate! If we thunder when God did not call us to speak, or when He wants us to speak with grace and humbleness, we actually serve the idol of our own hatred of idolatry. We have then become that which we hate. And we have become agents of division rather than ambassadors of reconciliation.

A deep and abiding love for what our Lord loves—His Father's Kingdom and unity within it—must be born in us by His grace. Thus, each tiniest breach of unity by our foolish mouths causes us to groan with grief and repentance to the core of our being! Only then do we truly become ambassadors for reconciliation in Christ.

A Prophet Leads into Reconciliation

How shall everyday Christians be effective in praying for reconciliation if they do not know what to pray about? Of course, they will have some beneficial effect if they just pray blindly by faith. But how much better when keys of knowledge inform the heart and mind! *That is the task of the Lord's Elijah prophets—to inform God's people so that their prayers may be of maximum effect.*

Elijah prophets lead into reconciliation, giving revelation of what needs to be healed, when and how. Inner healing is the application of the Lord's blood, cross and resurrection life to every wound and resultant practice in individuals' lives. But groups of people also have need of inner healing. Tribes, states and nations all have histories of relationships. Often, these histories are hidden, unrecorded and unrecoverable except by revelation. Here is where prophets are crucial to the work. As in individuals, forgotten histories allow wounds to fester and practices to grow. Prophets are gifted to be seers, and God uses them to see the hidden events of history in order to bring about inner healing and, thus, reconciliation.

Sometimes I have walked into churches and felt the deposit of discord that has defiled them from within their history. The Lord has then shown me the faces of individuals or told me events in the church's history. Members have confirmed what the Lord showed me. Through such revelations, the Lord was able to point out to the church what needed to be repented of and prayed about for reconciliation.

Similarly, countless times God has shown me and others on our counseling staff details in a family's history. He tells us how a family's history has left a deposit and what that deposit is, and He gives us the wisdom and ability to lead into prayers of repentance, forgiveness and reconciliation.

Darrell Fields, a brother of native descent, found himself crying over a region of Pennsylvania. Both the Holy Spirit and careful research of secular materials revealed many events that he and others could pray about for the healing of Pennsylvania. Specifically, they were led to pray for the reconciliation of descendants of wounded natives and white colonists. I suggest reading his powerful little book, *The Seed of a Nation.*

Today's prophets must get their eyes open to the fullness of their tasks. Prayer groups need revelation so as to apply the balm of Jesus and His cross where history has left defiling deposits in relationships. Prayer groups need to learn how to invite and encourage prophets to become eyes and ears for those times when their own gifts seem too ineffective or blinded and deafened. Pastors need to learn how to invite the prophets in their midst to see into possible root causes for disruptions in relationships in their congregations and communities.

Reconciliation—The Foremost Task of Our Time

We have spoken of how prophets can be eyes and ears. But prophets also need the people as much or more than the people need them. We need the people's prayers, their love, acceptance and encouragement, and above all their invitation to perform among them as what we are—the Elijah prophets of the Lord. Mutual interdependency and cooperation between prophets and God's people must grow until each can be fully effective for the other. Then, God's ministry of reconciliation will gain a solid footing upon which His Church can stand. Only in this way can the prophets bring the message of reconciliation God wants them to bring, and only in this way can the people hear the message and respond.

Reconciliation is the foremost task of our time. Everything else finds its base there and flows from it. With reconciliation, brothers and sisters find and nurture the best in each other. Without it, we find and nurture the beast in each other. Without reconciliation, healed troubles break open again. Today's prophets are called to edify the Church, and what is that edification if it is not born in reconciliation and love for our Lord Jesus Christ and one another?

> If someone says, "I love God," and I hates his brother, he is a liar; for the one who does not love his brother whom he has seen, cannot love God whom he has not seen. And this commandment we have from Him, that the one who loves God should love his brother also.
>
> 1 JOHN 4:20–21

FIFTEEN

SPIRITUAL WARFARE

GOD'S FIRST PURPOSE in spiritual warfare is already accomplished. He won the war once for all through the death and resurrection of His Son. In His wisdom, He has left "mop up" operations for us so that His second purpose can be realized: By wrestling against the powers of darkness, we are to grow strong in Him and comprehend more fully what sacrifices Jesus Christ made for us.

Spiritual Warfare Is Fraught with Danger

Recognizing that it is God's purpose that we battle against the powers of darkness, we must recognize also that this war is deadly serious and fraught with consequences. For example, in the last several years, as the Elijah company has begun to arise so have Jezebels and Ahabs. Many Jezebels have torn churches apart—or tried to. John Paul Jackson's wonderful book *The Veiled Ploy* is a prophetic revelation of how Jezebels work as agents of the enemy, and how to defeat them. This book is spiritual warfare at its best and exemplifies the prophetic function of protecting God's people in the midst of warfare.

I doubt that any one of the Lord's prophets has been without persecution and emotional and physical attacks. Three times since I have had this heart attack, while writing this book, demonic forces have jumped on me during the night. They have tried to throw me into another heart attack and kill me so that I cannot finish the book. Paula and I have spent hours in prayer, casting away the demonic, refinding rest in our Lord. Hundreds of prayer warriors have been called into prayer for us and others.

But my situation is minimal compared to the fierceness of warfare going on around the world. It *is* a war. There *is* real danger. More martyrs are being made now than in all the history of the Church! In Sudan millions are being slaughtered for the name of Christ. Satan is whipping up the seas of hatred among the Muslim world, to hurl Islam into a "jihad" against Jews and Christians around the world.

The Lord's intercessors are greatly stressed and, in many cases, worn out. Who among us burden-bearing intercessors could not resonate with Nehemiah 4:10? "The strength of the burden bearers is failing [other versions say "wearing out"], yet there is much rubbish; and we ourselves are unable to rebuild the wall."

The good news is that, although personally we may experience defeat and even death here on earth, not one hair of our heads is lost eternally! God *is* faithful, and all will be turned to glory and rejoicing, if not here, then in eternal reward. Nothing is lost. For Christians, from the perspective of eternity, Satan has won no victories whatsoever and never will. But in the meantime there can be great suffering, tribulation and persecution.

The Prophet's Role in Spiritual Warfare

In a sense, every function of prophets is a part of their warfare—even in positive activities that may seem to have nothing to do with warfare, such as bringing blessing and healing. These establish the Lord's beachheads, so that His troops have a foothold in the enemy's territory. This entire book is an attempt to inform the Lord's prophets of the magnitude of their tasks in spiritual warfare and to call them to it, and to instruct the Church to receive prophets and enable them to function as God intends.

The Intelligence Wing of the Army of God

As I indicated earlier, prophets are intended to be the intelligence wing of the Lord's army. They are to carry God's messages from the General to His soldiers. They, more than others, are gifted to see the hidden stratagems and activities of the enemy. We can see this in what happened with the king of Aram (Syria). He sought again and again to capture the king of Israel, who was warned each time by Elisha. Finally the king of Aram called his servants and cried out, "Will you tell me which of us is for the king of Israel?" In other words, "Who's the traitor?" (2 Kings 6:11).

Throughout Old Testament history, the kings of Israel and Judah went to the prophets seeking guidance as to whether or not they should go up against the enemy. Not only were they told whether or not to go to war, but sometimes even when and how.

> When David inquired of the LORD, He said, "You shall not go directly up; circle around behind them and come at them in front of the balsam trees. It shall be, when you hear the sound of marching in the tops of the balsam trees, then you shall act promptly, for then the LORD will have gone out before you to strike the army of the Philistines."
>
> 2 SAMUEL 5:23–24

So far, modern prophets have not been given status to prophesy guidance for secular warfare, but perhaps that day will come. World leaders have sought guidance from many other sources. Hitler, like the pagan kings of old, sought guidance from astrologers—which was, of course, another of his sins. And our own beloved Abraham Lincoln allowed séances in the front room of the White House! Some of our presidents have sought the counsel of widely known pastors, like Billy Graham. But so far as I know, to date none has sought the counsel of well-known prophets.

In other arenas the guidance of prophets is sought. All the stories I told in chapters 7 and 8 about warnings and protection described prophetic guidance for pastors and leaders in the daily spiritual warfare of the life of the Church. John Dawson's and Cindy Jacobs' books *Healing America's Wounds, Taking Our Cities for God* and *Possessing the Gates of the Enemy* are great prophetic manuals on spiritual warfare for the sake of cities, regions and nations. My own book *Healing the Nations* is another device God has used to give guidance to the Body. C. Peter Wagner's new book, *What the*

Bible Says about Spiritual Warfare, is a powerful statement of the biblical principles behind spiritual warfare. The Lord's prophets are speaking out through books and teachings, laying the groundwork for the increasing warfare of these last days.

Drill Sergeants in the Church's Base Camps

Another function of prophets in spiritual warfare could be called the drill sergeants for the Church's base camps. Or perhaps the inspectors who come around to see how well the sergeants and trainees are doing. Learning to be an accurate, wise prophet is tough. It demands ability to live with repeated humiliation, as the errors of novice prophets become known and have to be dealt with. In chapter 16, I will speak of prophetic mentoring. I remember how dearly I appreciated and loved the men who gently chastised me. These men held me accountable not only for what I said, but how, when, whether or not in wisdom, and in what spirit I said it. Fortunately, my "drill sergeants" and "inspectors" were nothing like the usual cursing and shouting military men! But had I been stiff-necked and unwilling to receive counsel, refusing to change and obey, they would have become rightly tough and stern.

Guiding Principles for Warfare

I could tell many stories and refer to many other books about prophets' functions in the war, but by now readers have the concept in mind. From here on, I want to give some guiding principles for warfare—a drill sergeant's manual for training inductees, as it were.

Get Balance and Perspective

The Christian life is not all warfare. Life is a good heavenly Father raising children for fellowship with Him throughout eternity. There happens to be a war, but it is only one detail in the grand picture of history. Within that:

A. Satan is not God's equal and opposite number. He is a defeated fallen angel. War with him should not elevate him in our thinking to a too prominent place. That is the heresy of the third-century Manichaeans, who said that life is a contest between light and dark forces, the dark being almost equal to the light.

B. Satan is not omniscient (knowing everything) or omnipresent (present everywhere). Nor is he omnipotent (all powerful). He cannot read your mind. He does not know the future, as God does. His demons are not behind every bush or active in every practice in our old nature—though they can be in some. Nor are they the cause or inhabiting force of every disease—though perhaps of some.

C. Satan is not smarter or more active than God, and he should not be feared. Martin Luther's hymn says, "On earth is not his equal" and "Our striving would be losing; Were not the right Man on our side." But the right Man *is* on our side. "Your adversary, the devil, prowls around like a roaring lion, seeking someone to devour" (1 Peter 5:8). But he is *not* a lion, he goes about *like* one. Many have said his teeth and claws have been pulled. Bob Mumford says, "He is a great big bee—with no stinger." He can devour only those who turn from God, and those who believe he has the power to devour them. The Lord told me, after a protracted battle with the devil, *John, he could fight with you so long because you believed he could. He had to use your faith in him to have power.* Those who have learned the lessons of base camp know what John meant when he wrote, "I am writing to you, young men, because you have overcome the evil one" (1 John 2:13). I testified that in this time of weakness demonic forces have jumped on me three times, trying to kill me. But even in my weakness they could not bring harm because He is my strength, and, in that sense, at my weakest I am strongest.

Remember: Life Is Not Always Warfare

Even secular troops have times of R and R. Do not always be praying and seeking spiritual battles or demons to cast away. Keep your Sabbaths. Have some good earthy activities (I did not say "worldly"). Play games. Visit with friends, laugh and enjoy life. The Lord does so Himself. "He who sits in the heavens laughs" (Psalm 2:4). Do not stay up all hours, fighting spiritual battles, thinking yourself indispensable to the Lord's victory. Get plenty of sleep. "I lay down and slept; I awoke, for the LORD sustains me" (Psalm 3:5). Peter said, "Be of sober spirit, be on the alert" (1 Peter 5:8). But that does not mean to be tense and stressed out. The minutemen of American history were just normal guys tending their farms and businesses, but when the call came, they were ready. So it must be with us. We are to be the Lord's minutemen, ready at any minute to answer the Lord's call to battle—whether the call comes through His prophets or otherwise.

Study and Know the Scriptures

Scripture is your best weapon. Each time Satan tempted Jesus, He answered by quoting Scripture. Paul said the weapons of our warfare are powerful, capable of pulling down strongholds (see 2 Corinthians 10:4). Psalm 19:11, speaking of the virtue of the laws of God, says, "Moreover, by them Your servant is warned; in keeping them there is great reward." And Psalm 119:11 says, "Your word I have treasured in my heart, that I may not sin against You." If you have not devoured the Word of God until its verses leap from the treasure of the heart to your mind in most—if not all—circumstances, do not consider that you are ready to leave base camp for the warfare. You are not at all prepared and are a danger to yourself and those who depend upon you.

Be Under Authority

You have no authority unless you are under it. Be corporate. Be humble and willing to listen to others. Be dead to pride. The purpose of the Lord's base camp is to smash your pride and train you to be willing to listen to others and to obey those over you. "Obey your leaders and submit to them, for they keep watch over your souls as those who will give an account. Let them do this with joy and not with grief, for this would be unprofitable for you" (Hebrews 13:17). If you still think you know better than others and ought to be the captain of your own soul and master of your fate (a paraphrase from the poem "Invictus"), not only are you not invincible, but you are an arrogant fool who ought not to be let out of base camp until you have had at least another round of training. "Be of the same mind toward one another; do not be haughty in mind, but associate with the lowly. Do not be wise in your own estimation" (Romans 12:16).

Avoid Haste

Do not be in a hurry. Normally, the Lord will speak in plenty of time for all necessary preparations. Thus, do not be presumptuous. Wait for the Lord to confirm out of the mouths of two or three witnesses.

Do Not Be Afraid to Risk

When the Lord makes a list, He normally begins with the most extreme. For example, in a list of negatives, He names the worst first. In Revelation 21:8, when the apostle John listed those who will be in the lake of fire and brimstone, the first were the "cowardly and unbelieving" (other versions say "the faithless"). Then came the "abominable and murderers and immoral persons and sorcerers and idolaters and all liars." This Scripture suggests that God deems cowardice and faithlessness the worst kind of abominations. Cowards and people-pleasers endanger the entire troop—and sometimes whole battalions—of the Lord's warriors. When the call is confirmed and duty is upon you, do not be afraid to step forward in faith and enter the battle.

It is for good reason that Paul's most powerful advice to warriors begins, "Put on the full armor of God, so that you will be able to *stand firm* against the schemes of the devil" (Ephesians 6:11, emphasis mine), and again says, "Stand firm" (verse 14). Paula is fond of saying, "No one can be a little bit pregnant. And you do not stop halfway through delivery and say 'I don't want to be a mother anymore!'" Likewise, having enlisted in the Lord's army, you do not become a deserter.

Have Faith

Pray for "see-through faith." If someone stretches a wire across Niagara Falls and drives a motorbike across, you know it can be done. That's belief. Faith happens when he says, "Hop on, and we'll go back across," and you do it! Belief costs little. Faith always involves risk.

Behind this is something very basic and simple—trust in the Lordship of Jesus Christ. If you need a guarantee before you will step out, you do not have faith, and you do not yet belong on the lines of warfare. If you do not have faith enough to be at rest in Him, you will fall to striving in your flesh to make things happen. The flesh profits nothing, and you will fail. You must have enough experience in our Lord that you can be at rest in any and all circumstances, knowing He is the victor, whatever happens to you. "'Not by might nor by power, but by My Spirit,' says the LORD of hosts" (Zechariah 4:6).

"The horse is prepared for the day of battle, but victory belongs to the LORD" (Proverbs 21:31). A warhorse in that day stood for strength and power. Just as today a soldier might trust in the armor of his tank and feel invincible, men in those days felt powerful when they owned a well-trained warhorse. Today, whenever we put our trust in our intelligence, our years of experience, our courage, knowledge of the Word or even our faith, we have placed our trust in our own warhorse rather than the Lord. "'Not by might nor by power, but by My Spirit,' says the LORD of hosts." In the end, we are vouchsafed in warfare not by anything in us, good or bad, but simply by the grace of our Lord Jesus Christ.

SIXTEEN

OTHER PROPHETIC PURPOSES AND TASKS

LET US TURN NOW to four additional purposes and tasks of the prophet: forerunners, Nathanic prophets, calling other prophets and mentoring.

Forerunners

When God desires to begin a new work or lay down a new track, He selects a man or a woman for the task. Adam and Eve began the track for all mankind—Adam for men and Eve for women. Unfortunately, the track they laid was full of sin. As the forerunner, the first of all mankind to experience life, whatever Adam did set a track for all mankind to follow. "Therefore, just as through one man sin entered into the world, and death through sin, and so death spread to all men, because all sinned" (Romans 5:12). Paul went on to say that Jesus Christ was the first of the new, who set a fresh track for all to follow. Paul said that by Him, "much more did the grace of God and the gift by the grace of the one Man, Jesus Christ, abound to the many" (verse 15). Whatever a first one does opens doors of possibility and closes others.

208

The process could be likened to the effect of workers laying down a railroad track. Once the track is laid, trains on it can go nowhere else. Or the process could be likened to programming a new computer. Once it has been set, the computer follows that track indefinitely.

This does not mean that all of life is predetermined by what has gone before and that whoever follows another is captive, without free will. But it does mean that people have powerful *predilections, tendencies to act in pre-set ways*. Most people succumb to these predilections and act out whatever pattern was set for them.

What can happen to break these patterns? Forerunners are those who, by God's grace, break established patterns and forge new trails.

Does Scripture Contradict Itself?

A mystery of seeming contradictions exists in Scripture. On the one hand, Ecclesiastes 1:9 says, "That which has been is that which will be, and that which has been done is that which will be done. So there is nothing new under the sun." The scientific law of inertia states that things tend to continue as they were first initiated. What has been will be. Forerunners affect others because of this principle —things tend to continue as forerunners initiate them.

On the other hand is Isaiah 48:6–7, "You have heard; look at all this. And you, will you not declare it? *I proclaim to you new things from this time, even hidden things which you have not known. They are created now and not long ago; and before today you have not heard them, so that you will not say, 'Behold, I knew them'*" (emphases mine). On this basis, forerunners can and do initiate new patterns in God's Kingdom. There *are* new things under the sun.

I do not know that anyone can or should fully explain this principle, which seems utterly contradictory. God's ways are far beyond ours. But perhaps we can make some sense of it. To me it seems explainable if we look at the context of the statement. The writer of Ecclesiastes has been speaking of man and his works, and of the pre-set ways of God's creation. Given our human nature and the ways of nature, what he says is true— everything does go on as before. Human nature has not changed in all the millennia, nor has nature changed its course. In that sense, there truly is "nothing new under the sun." But that fact has never prevented God from intervening in His creation to alter the course of all mankind and nature. That is what the incarnation of Jesus Christ and His saving, redeeming work is all about. God came in Jesus to create a new path. *Jesus is the primary forerunner.* He set the new track and paved the way so that all of us can follow Him into the new.

Ecclesiastes 1 declares the stale pattern of the Old. Jesus brought the fresh revelation of the New. The two Scriptures are not truly contradictory. The first is the cry that calls for the second. Both are true in their own time and way.

Famous Forerunners

Our actions tend to fall into patterns. These sometimes become clothed in religious armor—we tend to think religious traditions are never to be changed lest we offend God. Religious traditions themselves were at one time forerunner beginnings. But as time passed, they tended to become ossified and falsely sacred. Jesus, as the Forerunner of our faith, continually struggled against and broke the bonds of the religious traditions of His day. He broke the bondages of Sabbath traditions when He healed a man's withered hand (see Luke 6:6–11), and when He and His disciples plucked and rubbed grain on the Sabbath day (see Luke 6:1–5). Paul, as the forerunner of faith to the Gentiles, broke free from the religious traditions of the circumcision party—in which he had been raised as a Pharisee.

Many forerunners dot the landscape of Christian history. All of us recognize a few of them. Martin Luther was the forerunner for the Protestant Reformation. At the same time Ignatius Loyola, founder of the Jesuit Order, was the Roman Catholic forerunner for a new expression of missionary evangelism to the world. William Penn was a forerunner in the relationship between American Indians and white colonists. John Wimber was a modern forerunner in the rediscovery of signs and wonders—miracles, healing, power evangelism, etc.

Our book *The Elijah Task*, a prophetic statement and reclamation of the functions and proper discharge of the prophetic office, made Paula and me forerunners in the rediscovery of the prophetic office. We also have been forerunners in the ministry of inner healing, a rediscovery of the process of sanctification and transformation. We have been among the forerunners in burden-bearing and intercessory prayer. Cindy Jacobs, C. Peter Wagner, Chuck Pierce and others have been forerunners in spiritual warfare. John Dawson has been a forerunner in the work of reconciliation among tribes and in cities and nations. Billy Graham was a forerunner in modern mass evangelistic crusades. Mike Bickle, Jim Goll, Tommy Tenney and a host of others have been pioneer forerunners in leading the Church into intimacy with the Father. John Arnott and others have been forerunners in renewal. Cindy Jacobs is at the moment of this writing powerfully engaged in the groundbreaking work of calling today's prophets together into relationship around the world.

And so it goes. I could list many more. God is raising up forerunners in many fields as He leads into preparation for the end times.

The Fathers Among Us

In biblical times, if a man became a pioneer in any field, discovering new techniques and knowledge, he was called a "father" of the field. For example, a man who found new methods to care for camels and became an expert in this field was called "the father of camels." A man who advanced knowledge and skill in the training of horses was called "the father of horses." Just so, Jesus is the Father of our faith. Isaiah 9:6 proclaimed, "And His name will be called Wonderful Counselor, Mighty God, *Eternal Father*, Prince of Peace" (emphasis mine). The appellation "Eternal Father" probably does not refer to Father God. The prophecy was declaring who Jesus would be. It is not proper theology to confuse the two; the classic Trinitarian formula is "The Father is not the Son, the Son is not the Father, nor is the Holy Spirit either one, but all three are God." But Jesus is the Forerunner, the Originator and, thus, the Eternal Father of the faith.

This means that whether male or female, God's forerunning prophets are the fathers of whatever movements they begin. Thus, Paula and I, the Hamons, Paul Cain and others are the fathers of the modern prophets. Paula and I, Francis MacNutt and a few others (too numerous to name) are the fathers of inner healing. And all the others listed above are the fathers of the movements they have been instrumental in founding.

A major thesis of this book is to turn the hearts of the fathers to the children and the hearts of the children to the fathers. We need to see and honor the fathers among us. Since all have received persecution and painful, unfair criticism, we are called into repentance and reconciliation to heal wounds and provide support, to enlist armies in each movement. The fathers need armies. They need steadfast volunteers who will not turn aside or betray. Bob Mumford said, "I used to have angel wings, but the backbiters ate them off!"

In our town was a certain Christian bookstore. People stopped in to relax and "gossip the Gospel." Anytime Jean Rainbolt heard someone say anything negative about a Christian leader in the community, she tracked it down. "Who told you that?" "Where did you hear that?" She would track each rumor and bit of gossip to its source, and shut up the gossipers with a tongue-lashing if necessary. The pastors of the town loved her! We need a host of Rainbolts if our forerunners are to be healed and we as the children are to receive the gift they are to us (see Ephesians 4:11).

I call us all to be reconciled to the fathers among us and to administer healing as children to the many wounded fathers. We need to honor, bless, pray for and support our fathers in Christ, and protect our forerunners—from slander, criticism, hatred and the wiles of the devil.

Forerunners Bear Great Responsibility

Being a forerunner is no light task. It is fraught with the weight of responsibility.

Paula and I are painfully aware that whatever we do and teach in the prophetic field or the field of inner healing can lead thousands astray. We have prayed, fervently, reverently, repeatedly, "Keep us on track, Lord. Do not let us get sidetracked from the Bible. Keep us in sound doctrine. Keep us morally pure."

We know of several churches in which leadership has fallen into moral sin. Because leaders are forerunners who can open doors either into blessing or harm, a plague of immorality, separations and divorces has run like a flood throughout these churches (see Numbers 25)!

On the other hand, I heard brother Winston Nunes say, "Billy Graham is light." He explained that Billy Graham set himself to do exactly what the Lord called him to do and has never deviated from it. Not even a breath of scandal has ever been attached to him or his ministry. Winston said, "Therefore, he is a light to the world." How many millions have been brought to the Lord and kept in Him because of this faithful forerunner! In Billy Graham, the Church has a beautiful modeling of what a forerunner-father should be. *We need to pray for our forerunner-fathers in Christ for their protection and purity of anointing so that they continue to bring blessing, and not harm, on all who follow them.*

Nathanic Prophets

Nathanic prophets are those gifted by God to know the secret sins of the people. The Father is not willing that any should perish. Therefore, He wants to bring to light what Satan would keep hidden. "But all things become visible when they are exposed by the light, for everything that becomes visible is light" (Ephesians 5:13). Whatever becomes visible can be dealt with. Bringing sin into light causes repentance to move from the general, "We have all sinned before Thee, O God," to the specific, "I did this sin. O God, forgive me."

Confession Brings Redemption

When I was a teenager, I did something wrong and guilt bothered my heart until I could not help but confess. So that night, I went to my father and said, "Dad, I did something wrong and I feel guilty about it."

Dad answered, "That's great, son, that you want to tell me. What did you do?"

So I said, "It's really bad, and I feel so bad about it."

His response was, "I know you feel bad about it, and I'm glad you have the courage to come and tell me," and then he said more forcefully, "but just *what* did you do?"

"Martha Jane [my younger sister] and I went to the carnival. I got hooked into a gambling thing, lost my money, and then got into the safe at your store and took $19.00 [a lot of money in those days] and lost that, too. I'm sorry, and I'll repay it."

Dad smiled and said, "What did you learn, son?" Seeing my heart, he reckoned that the pain of the experience had already accomplished what discipline would, so he just counseled and taught me—and I never forgot! Among the lessons was the realization that general repentance costs little and brings little relief. God wants us to be honest, straightforward and specific. What specifically becomes visible specifically becomes light.

To us, in this lawless age in which conscience has become dulled, that incident may seem trivial. Today, most of us would simply have shrugged off the $19.00 and gone "on our merry way," wondering why we were no longer so merry. To me, this is a mark of our society's defection from reverence for the Word of God and consequent dulling of conscience. Abraham Lincoln trudged three miles just to return a penny! If raised forty years later, would I have had such a conscience that I could not rest until I confessed to my father? I think not. How grateful I am for my father and for the time in which I was raised! What a commentary on the moral sickness of our age!

What would have happened had my theft remained hidden? My father would have spent hours trying to figure out why his books would not balance—and maybe would have accused someone else of taking or misplacing the money. Our sins are never isolated, affecting none other than ourselves. But, oh, how they do affect us! Guilt would have remained like a festering sore inside my heart. Having suppressed conscience that time, it would have become easier to sin and overlook it next time. I would have been launched upon the seas that lead eventually to a shipwrecked conscience (see 1 Timothy 1:19). And Satan would have had a foothold in my heart to accuse, torment and tempt.

For these reasons and countless more, Satan wants to keep our sins and our sinful nature hidden from us. So long as he can do that, whatever remains undealt with in our hearts lives in the darkness and serves him as a playfield. God knows that whatever becomes visible becomes light. He can then redeem it.

In His Love, God Uncovers Sin to Set Us Free

The problem is that either we do not know we have sinned, or, knowing, we neglect to confess quickly and maybe even forget the sin. A friend backed her car out of her driveway—right into the side of a delivery truck! She got out and saw that it was just a little dent. No one was around. She was in a hurry—to attend a spiritual meeting! So she drove off, thinking, *That kind of thing happens all the time in parking lots. They'll just have it fixed. Insurance will take care of it.* In a day or so, she had forgotten all about it.

Subsequently, this woman, who was renowned for her powerful gift of physical healing, began to lose anointing. She herself no longer felt good physically and was having trouble sleeping. She had sense enough to know that some kind of sin in her life was causing it all. Not having a Nathanic prophet available—or any prophets at all in those days—she sought to listen to the Lord. As she meditated, the picture of that small dent came floating into her mind. She thought, *Surely that could not be it, Lord. That was so small, and this trouble is so big.* But the gentle persistence of the Lord

214

told her she had better look into it. She phoned the company of the delivery truck and confessed what she had done. The manager said, "We are so glad you've called. That driver has been a good man for us, and when he could not explain how that dent got there, we thought he was lying and covering up. We could not believe any driver who got a dent like that would not know how it happened. We took the repair costs out of his salary and put a black mark on his record." She offered to pay for the repairs, apologized to the driver and asked for his forgiveness. Her healing anointing quickly returned, as did her health and ability to sleep like a baby.

God can speak directly to one's heart to point out sin, as He did for this woman. But He also often uses Nathanic prophets to uncover secret sin. A beloved member of our church prayer group, a very beautiful woman, fell into adultery with a pastor on exchange from a distant country. The moment it happened I was suddenly struck with illness and great grief and went to lie down in the middle of the afternoon. As I lay there and prayed, her face came before me, and the face of the pastor. I knew in my spirit what had happened. Paula and I prayed about it. The next morning I went to see her. As she handed a cup of coffee to me, I looked into her eyes. In that second I knew I was right—she had indeed fallen into adultery. She knew I knew. After a few moments of silent commiseration, in which she knew I was grieving for her, I said only the words, "Did you?" She burst into tears and blurted out through her sobs what she had done. Forgiveness and redemption were immediate. That is the function and work of a Nathanic prophet.

The same thing happened with another loved one in our church. Paula and I both felt ill at the same moment, and prayer allowed the Holy Spirit to reveal who had done what. Again, we prayed in love and compassion for the fallen one. She came to us and confessed.

Truly, if one member suffers, all suffer. We are one in the Lord, who cares about us with infinite grace and wants to reveal our sins, not because He is stern and judgmental, but because His heart of love wants to set us free from the snares of sin.

Ministers of Redemption Who Bring Healing

Nathanic prophets must be dead to judgmentalism. Their hearts must be suffused with His love and care for His people. They must be trustworthy with secret knowledge—Paula and I never told anyone what we knew about the sins of these daughters of the Lord. We have known many times who was gossiping, who was betraying secrets in a small group, who was full of envy and malicious slander, etc. Most often we simply prayed, grieved for the persons involved and repented before God for them, knowing that could lead to their own confessing. Often, the people in the group saw their sins and confessed. *We have never confronted harshly or judgmentally.*

Isaiah 4:2–6 presents a powerful message of the Lord purifying His Church by "the spirit of judgment and the spirit of burning" (verse 4). This message is followed by a tremendous prophecy that the Shekinah glory that was upon the Israelites as a cloud by day and fire by night will return upon the Church in all its assemblies (verse 5)! Remember that God's judgment is first mercy and kindness to heal and set straight. His fire burns away the dross of our lives.

Father God is preparing His Church as a resting place for His Son, and as a firebrand of holy love and healing for a torn and sinful world. His judgment begins with the household of God. The problem is that in so many Christian lives our sins and sinful nature lie hidden in our hearts. The Church is far from being pure, and certainly is not yet a beautiful bride prepared and adorned for her husband. Our Father wants to raise up countless Nathanic prophets whose hearts never condemn but only make visible for relief and healing transformation (see Romans 12:2). *Nathanic prophets must above all be ministers of redemption, who heal and reconcile and set the crooked straight.*

Christian Counseling Can Be a Nathanic Task

"The Spirit of the LORD will rest on Him, the spirit of wisdom and under-standing, the spirit of counsel and strength, the spirit of knowledge and the fear of the LORD" (Isaiah 11:2). Our prayer ministers at Elijah House are Nathanic prophets who operate under the anointing of Isaiah 11:2. Not all are prophets, but all work under that anointing invoked by Paula and me as the forerunners. They see what is hidden in clients' lives and work by the blood and cross to set free and transform. As people share their stories, the Holy Spirit's gifts of knowledge and perception enable our counselors to see hidden motivations and character structures, and often specifically what has happened in people's lives that they have for-gotten. In this way, our Nathanic prophets make visible what has been hidden and in darkness, for the purpose of bringing God's healing.

Just today, in confidence Paula and I had lunch with our daughter, who is also one of our staff counselors. Ami shared with us on this very subject, a counseling experience she had had. A woman had come to her who continually knocked herself out sacrificially for her family and could not understand why everyone in her family fled from her. She could not see the hidden motivations that defiled all she did and caused her family to react negatively. Ami had to tell the woman lovingly but firmly she was not the purely loving person she thought herself to be. Through Ami's wise counsel, the Holy Spirit revealed to the woman that she was not actually loving her family for their sakes, but rather, she was laboring for them out of performance orientation and duty. Her hidden sinful nature caused her to manipulate and control her family, which was why they all fled from her. This mother had not suffered sufficient death of self and, thus, could not see what her family really needed from her. She just performed dutifully, missing their hearts by miles. Ami's example perfectly demonstrates how Christian counseling that is grounded in the Holy Spirit is a prophetic Nathanic task.

Nathanic Prophets Must Confront in Love

We who counsel are quite familiar with Nathanic prophecy; we live it every day in the office. But it needs to get out of the office and into widespread application throughout the Body of Christ. Brothers and sisters in prayer groups often see and gently reprove, but it needs to happen more frequently. I do not mean that pop psychology and criticism should be unleashed amongst the Lord's prayer groups. Remember that all such confrontation is to be exercised in the gentle, tactful and considerate nature of our Lord. But neither should considerations for courtesy, or the fear of what people might think of us if we confront, deter us from speaking the truth to one another in love. We often have said, "If your prayer group is always 'nice' and 'safe,' it's probably dead!" Brothers and sisters who love one another not only "do not let friends drive drunk" but confront with gentleness, tact and wisdom. We need to enter into agreements in our groups that give permission to our brothers and sisters to "speak the truth in love" to us, to set us free to mature in the Lord—in holiness. We need to learn how to invite and cherish rebuke. "Whoever loves discipline loves knowledge, but he who hates reproof is stupid" (Proverbs 12:1).

Most importantly, today's prophets are often under bondage to speak only "that which edifies the church," an often-voiced demand upon prophets—as though confrontation and transformation somehow do not edify! I can think of little that is more cogent for edification than being hauled up short and delivered from hidden, sinful ways. I remember when a teenager in our church said to me, "Pastor, I'd become a servant of the Lord, except I'm afraid I'd become like you!" That hurt at the time—but it hurt in a good way! Today I'm so grateful for his loving me enough to tell me truth about myself—I was such a workaholic, so serious and "religious" that this young man (and how many others?) did not want to become what I was modeling. A wise proverb says that if you rebuke a wise man he will love you for it, but if you rebuke a scoffer you will only get yourself abuse. Still today, almost fifty years later, I think of that young man with fondness and gratitude.

Let's set our prophets free to be Nathans to us. Let us praise God for them, and love them for it.

Prophets Calling Others to the Office

Our book *The Elijah Task*, as well as the writings of the Hamons, Ernest B. Gentile and others, discusses the ways God calls His prophets. So I will not expound in much detail, as those books cover the topic more fully. But we must address the topic here.

Isaiah was called sovereignly, in a mighty visitation in the Temple on the Day of Atonement. In our time, Bob Jones, Todd Bentley and others experienced similar sovereign callings. Jeremiah was called before his birth, as were Paul Cain, John Paul Jackson, myself and many others. Many simply found themselves doing the works of prophets. In all cases of true prophets, sooner or later the Body of Christ confirmed the person's standing in the office.

But established prophets also call other prophets. That is one of the tasks of prophets.

Prophets Must Be Very Cautious in Calling Others

Prophets must be very careful about proclaiming such callings. First, we must be absolutely sure that the one we are calling is indeed the one

218

God intends to be called. In addition, we must be circumspect about such questions as, "Is this the right time to call this person?" "Is it the right place and way?" "Should the call be given in public or privately?" Some prophets love to go about giving personal words elevating others in God's service, sometimes to be prophets or evangelists or even apostles. May I plead with established prophets not to be hasty about this? May I warn that giving such words can be highly pleasing to the flesh, both to the recipient and to the prophet?

Paul, speaking of this as the "laying on of hands," warned not to "lay hands upon anyone too hastily and thereby share responsibility for the sins of others; keep yourself free from sin" (1 Timothy 5:22). Two chapters before this, he had laid out carefully the qualifications for an overseer in the Church—actually the same for any leaders, only more stringent for prophets. In chapter three, verse six he said: "and not a new convert, so that he will not become conceited and fall into the condemnation incurred by the devil." Taken together, these two passages mean that if we exalt new converts and they fall into reproach, we share that reproach. We have become a part of their sinning. We elevated them into it and bear responsibility for it. As I said earlier, I have seen men quit their jobs or leave their families, or do many other foolish things, impelled by immaturity in the reception of prophets' words.

As I testified earlier, Father God spoke to my mother before my birth about my calling, but she and my father had the wisdom not to tell me until I came of age and received my own calling. Even then, it plunged me into foolish strivings—or rather, I plunged myself. Be aware of the impact of what you prophesy. Be most circumspect about presenting prophecies that promise high elevation in God's service. Even if the person is more mature and does not rush into foolish responses, usually the Lord may take years and years to fulfill that word, and "Hope deferred makes the heart sick" (Proverbs 13:12). So, if you must give such a word, surround it with words of wisdom that caution the recipient:

1. to prepare his heart for testing;
2. to wait upon the Lord's timing and not fall into disappointment and disillusionment if the Lord's fulfillment tarries; and
3. not to act hastily but to wait for confirmations.

Before you give a word that another is called to the office of a prophet—or any other office—check with brothers and sisters first to see if they bear witness to what you think you hear.

Years ago, Paula and I taught in a Christian summer camp. Many came and asked for baptism by immersion. We went to the enclosed pool at the university that hosted the camp. Among the applicants was our own dearly beloved godson, Greg Thompson. As each person was being led out to me in the water, Paula, a recognized prophetess in the Church, listened for a Scripture that could be a remembrance and a blessing for them, and even a guidance for their lives. As the time approached for Greg to enter the water, Paula kept hearing the Lord say, *Hebrews 7:17, "You are a priest forever according to the order of Melchizedek."* Knowing this would mean a call to be an ordained minister, she was afraid to read it. What if this were an error, or worse, a presumption out of her own heart's love for Greg? Could she risk changing Greg's life from then on? Quickly, she conferred with several elders. But they all witnessed to it. This was indeed the Lord's call. With great trepidation she read it aloud, "Thou art a priest for ever after the order of Melchizedek" (KJV). The Lord opened my eyes, and I physically saw a sheet of fire fall out of heaven! It hit the water with a loudly audible and very real snap! The power knocked a woman to the ground. All felt it. And then, I baptized Greg.

After this event, Greg's father suffered a debilitating illness. Greg had to earn his way through college and seminary. Many times he became discouraged, but he kept plugging on. At one time I had to go to see him and scold him into persevering. All of us knew why the Lord had given him his calling so dramatically—without it he might not have had the determination to keep on trying. Today, Greg is pastor of a thriving Vineyard Church in Aurora, Colorado, and has been the Vineyard overseer for a large region of the West.

I shared this story to display the caution and wisdom God gave to Paula. She was not puffed up with pride that God would give such a word through her. Rather, she was filled with holy fear and caution. She checked with elders who could confirm or deny the word. God confirmed with a dramatic sign, witnessed by all there. No one could doubt Greg's call to become a minister, least of all Greg.

Again, I call for all prophets to be more circumspect when giving words that could drastically change lives than they are when giving any other kind of word. I do not mean to be harsh but feel I must report that we who are prophets have too often seemed much more cavalier and careless about this aspect of our ministry than God would have wanted—or we should have known better than to have allowed.

Many times I have "seen" a child in the Spirit when he stands before me. I know there is a calling upon his life. I may speak to his parents, and sometimes to him, to say the calling is there. But most often, unless stringently commanded, I will not say to what office, even though I may know it. Very seldom do I reveal the entire calling to the very young. There will be time enough later, as in my case, to discover what the calling may be. The times I have been led to reveal in full to a person, the word was almost invariably a confirmation, since the person had already been called in his childhood. This also was the case with the prophet Samuel.

Is it enough? Have we heard the cautions? The lives of God's people must not be damaged by our foolishness. And the purposes of the Lord's Elijah prophets must not be caused to lose credibility because we have been prideful, incautious and maybe even presumptive.

Once Called, Always Called

A word to those who receive high callings: Whenever God calls a servant to a high office, he must not turn back from it. Thou art a priest or prophet or teacher or whatever, *forever*. God Himself, later on, may change the calling to something higher—or He may demote, release or retire His servant. But only God, not human wishes or decisions, can change a calling. So many times, as a counselor in Christ, I have grieved over men who either never answered or left their callings. From then on, it was as if they were wandering in dry places, while the river of God's anointing and blessing ran someplace else.

In biblical days when a call came to be a holy man for God, recipients knew they were to leave everything behind, even filial duties to father and family, and follow the one who called. For this reason, Scripture records that when Jesus called Peter, Andrew, James and John, "immediately they left the boat and their father, and followed Him" (Matthew 4:22). They were never, ever to return to fishing. To do so would be a grievous sin, which was exactly the sin Peter led the disciples into after Jesus arose from the dead! "Simon Peter said to them, 'I am going fishing.' They said to him, 'We will also come with you.'" (John 21:3). Of course, they caught nothing—anointing had fled. Jesus appeared on the beach and had breakfast ready for them, because to eat together in Eastern culture is to express forgiveness.

But forgiveness was not pardon. Jesus also disciplined. In the biblical country if you rebuke someone once, that is simply a rebuke. If you rebuke twice for the same thing, that is humiliating. If three times, that was crushing! Therefore, Peter was grieved when Jesus asked him the third time whether he loved Him more than these fish (John 21:17). He knew he was being crushed. In our own lives, if we have begun to turn back or even just away from God's plan for us, we ought not to be surprised if more than one event happens to rebuke us, or if the third event is crushing. To our godson Greg, I was the second warning, his own conscience having been the first. Thank God he never needed a third!

Paula and I have seen financial reverses, illnesses and even death of loved ones happen to those who were turning back from their callings. It is not that God is such a tyrant that He kills if we do not obey. Rather, when we walk apart from Him, not only does blessing ebb, but also the protective shield of God's favor is shattered. Father God grieves when our defection brings harm into our own lives and those of our families— we prevented His grace.

When Elijah called Elisha, he threw his mantle over him, which was the accepted way of calling in those days (see 1 Kings 19:19). At first Elisha demurred, asking if he could first kiss his father and mother (verse 20). He was not simply asking if he could just run home and give them a goodbye kiss. It was the duty of sons to close their parents' eyes and give them a kiss when they died. Elisha wanted to wait until his parents died; then he would follow Elijah. That was a sinful response, because a call to serve the Lord professionally supercedes filial responsibility. So at first Elijah rejected him, saying, "Go back again." But then Elijah relented and gave him a second chance, reminding him of the importance of what he had just done, "For what have I done to you?" (verse 20). Elisha realized his sin, killed his oxen, broke up their yokes and held a barbeque for all his family and friends. This meant he was properly burning his bridges behind him. He could never return to farming. Since all the people ate with him, they shared in the covenant of salt—they would never, ever speak against his calling or reprove him for leaving his duty to his parents.

This is also why a calling to ministry is so precarious. It calls us to leave our duty to our parents and follow the calling first of all. I think I reported elsewhere that in my junior year of university my parents' store failed, and they asked me to come home and help them close it out. Though I had always been obedient to them and had come home on weekends to clean up the store, this time I said no. The Lord's calling superceded all other responsibilities. The Pharisees wrongly used this and said that whatever duty should be performed for their parents was "Corban," meaning, given to God (Mark 7:11). They, therefore, excused themselves from caring for their parents. But they were not called to be holy men and had no right to use this provision as an excuse for their lack of responsibility to their parents, and Jesus rebuked them for it.

Prophets, realize that when you call someone to high office, you disrupt entire family structures and behavior. For example, if you call a man to become a Roman Catholic priest who can never marry, his parents will lose all hope of ever having grandchildren! If you call a Protestant to become a minister, you may be calling a man away from the family business his father has long hoped he would take from his shoulders. And a wife may be subjected to hardship financially while her husband studies to become ordained—and afterward. Is she also called? Does she want to become a minister's wife? Think well, and pray, seeking confirmations before speaking. Make sure it is the Lord calling, and not yours.

Mentoring

Tyro, or novice, prophets need mentoring. Historically, mentoring is a long-developed, practiced art. Our American seminaries actually began under a mentoring model. For example, young men called to the ministry lived with Presbyterian Tennant families to be trained by them. In Roman Catholic and Anglican churches, for centuries men and women were mentored under what they called spiritual directors. This is still practiced in many places today.

Sister Linda Koontz, formerly of Spokane, took me before Bishop Topel, who was then the Roman Catholic Bishop of Spokane and its environs. She asked permission for me as a Protestant pastor to be accepted as spiritual director for nuns in his diocese! The Bishop knew of my record among them, trusted me and asked only, "What would you do if one of my nuns confessed something to you?" Though I know that within my heritage I have full authority to pronounce forgiveness, I

223

respected his beliefs and responded, "I would send her to a priest for the sacrament of confession and for absolution." Bishop Topel then did the unheard-of thing—he granted permission for nuns in his diocese to come to me as a Protestant pastor for spiritual direction! I did that for a number of years and still carry fond memories from those times.

Not Enough Mentoring in the Church

But mentoring as a whole has too much become a lost art in the Church. Secular professions and businesses intern newly hired recruits with veteran employees. Even restaurants practice this, as new waiters are trained alongside practiced servers. A little mentoring is done in our churches, but far too little. We have been too individualistic and private, too unwilling to be advised and governed by others.

Mentoring is a great responsibility. Bishop Bill Hamon founded a school for the purpose of mentoring and takes his responsibilities for those under him very seriously. Mike Bickle held the same responsibility for the prophets in the Kansas City Fellowship. Others have founded schools for prophets.

In biblical days, mentoring was conducted under the "green tree." Full explication of this can be found in *The Elijah Task*. Suffice it to say here that the green tree extends branches from which tendrils reach down and send roots into the ground to become extra trunks for the tree. Thus, one tree could expand over a quarter-mile area. The banyan tree is similar, one of which spreads over an entire block in La Haina on the island of Maui. Deep shade from such a tree provided comfort in an extremely hot land, and so, established prophets chose such places to teach the younger, who literally "sat at the feet" of their instructors.

The green tree also was called the tree of heaven. No one planted it or cared for its nurture. It became a symbol of God's provision and protection. People running from bandits or blood avengers could flee under it and be safe from all harm—no one would dare to harm another under the green tree. Prophetic training was thus conducted in a safe place, apart from the cares and problems of the world. And as established prophets were the "trees" from which tyro prophets took root and branched, the many expanding branches of the tree symbolized how the prophets would expand and themselves become green trees for others.

If the corps of Elijah prophets being called and raised by the Lord today is to mature securely into its purposes and tasks, we must rediscover and establish much more mentoring than presently exists.

Warnings and Advice on Mentoring

Understanding the need for and the proper ways of mentoring is a first step, and is a reason for this book. But entire books and manuals are needed on the subject. Here, let me simply provide a list of warnings and advice.

1. Mentors are spiritual fathers and mothers.

Mentors raise God's children to adulthood. Hundreds of maturing Christians relate to Paula and me as their spiritual parents. Several rules are supremely important:

A. Mentors as fathers and mothers must never reduce people to or look upon them as infants, or as inferior to themselves. They are to respect them as valuable adults and equals, to be treated as such.

B. As fathers and mothers, mentors give unconditional love, often supplying what was lacking in childhood in families of origin. They never berate or belittle. A man came from England for a time of healing with Paula and me. While he was here, one of our spiritual sons accidentally deleted my entire chapter 9 that I had just written by inspiration. If our consultants could not reinstate it in the computer, we knew we would not recover it. Soon after, this same spiritual son dropped my cordless phone into the hot tub! I laughed with my spiritual son, understanding his embarrassment, forgiving without an iota of reproach. It was mentoring for the Englishman to see how I responded, as his own father had been harsh and unforgiving. My spiritual son told the man, whom he was now counseling for me, that he knew that when he blew it, I would still love him. He was secure in the fact that no matter how many mistakes he made, he could not fall out of my love. This is a major task of father-mentors—to undergird with unconditional love and security.

C. Unconditional love is not to be confused with permissiveness or licentiousness. Father-mentors hold people accountable, but never in ways our gracious Lord would not employ. Father-mentors examine what and how people are doing things, advise, reprove and explain why something is either not good or acceptable.

225

D. Father-mentors carry people in the heart, as Paul did: "I hold you in my heart" (Philippians 1:7, AMPLIFIED). As natural fathers are responsible before God for their children—for their provender, physical protection, welfare and raising in the Lord—spiritual parents are to the same degree responsible to carry their children before God in intercession. They bear their children's burdens to the Lord as in Galatians 6:2. As natural parents do, spiritual parents weep for their children when they suffer, and they rejoice with and for them. Their task is not to be *over* them—to control, boss or manipulate—but to be *with* them in spirit. Spiritual parents stand alongside their children so that they may know the incarnate love of our Father. The child needs to know that there is someone who will fight for him or her spiritually as fiercely as a mother bear would for her cubs.

E. Father-mentors pray for inner healing for their children, so that in as many areas as possible their loved ones are transformed into the nature of our Lord Jesus Christ.

F. Finally, father-mentors release. They look into the hearts of their children to see what God would have them become, and then they release them into it. *They must not simply turn out cookie-cutter copies of themselves.* They are to die to what they want or would like their children to become and bring forth what God wants. They may not see what the person is to become, and that may even be better, for they run less risk of controlling and manipulating. For example, Paula and I founded Elijah House on certain principles for ministering to the hearts of others. Then the Lord said, *I want you to train these people and then let them find their own ways.* This is a very important point: *Fathers and mothers must not stifle the creativity of their followers.* Just last week Elijah House held a reunion for graduated internees. Our counselors taught refresher lessons. Three of them started with information we had provided, and then they added other materials. One incorporated Mark Virkler's teachings on a particular subject, another demonstrated some of the materials of a method employed by Ed Smith, and a third added to our revelations on a certain subject. Some were afraid I would be offended. *Many founders insist that things be done their way or no way at all.* Visitors were surprised that I applauded what they were doing. They had stuck to the original principles and used their own creativity and the materials of others to come up with something better. To paraphrase Jesus' words: *Greater works than I do will you do after Me—but only if spiritual fathers and mothers die to themselves and release their disciples into their own creativity.* Spiritual fathers do not overprotect their own ideas and ways, nor confine their spiritual children to their own limited views.

2. Mentors are teachers.

They spend time teaching and explaining. They know the value of repetition. An old adage says we retain about 10 percent of what we hear once, 40 percent of what we hear twice, and about 60 percent of what we hear three times. Add to that the fact that we retain about 50 percent of what we see. But we retain about 80 percent of what is acted out. An old southern preacher who received no formal training in university or seminary was once asked how his people knew the Bible and spiritual things so well. He said, "First I tell 'em what I'm gonna tell 'em. Then I tell 'em what I tell 'em. And then I tell 'em what I told 'em. And then they know." What he did not say was that he also lived it virtuously among them day by day. Spiritual mentors teach by repeating the important lessons and by modeling them, helping to ensure that their children retain.

They often teach mainly by question and answer. This is to invite their learners into the process of discovery. They do not want to spoon-feed information and then have it repeated back to them verbatim. Rabbis taught by questions and answers in biblical days, and prophets under the green tree employed the same method. In the twentieth century, Rabbi Ernst Jacob, who taught my university classes in Old Testament history and the prophets, often reverted to questions and answers.

Spiritual mentors learn to applaud wise answers, and particularly those that show the student has comprehended the material enough to answer creatively in his or her own words. They celebrate imagination and applications in unique ways.

3. Mentors examine their students' "diet" and practices.

They want to know what their children read. Sometimes they may say, "Try reading some of the desert fathers. You need to expand your perspective." Or, "You've been too serious lately. Take some time off. Rest and play awhile." Or, "I want you to read a stanza of the 119th Psalm every night before you go to bed. Meditate on it and pray it into your heart. Keep at it until you've gone all the way through the psalm." Mentors may tell them it is because they want them to grow into increased reverence for the laws of God. Or if they want them simply to learn obedience, they may not explain why at all.

If disciples refuse or prove to be lazy, mentors may reprove, but they will never coerce or manipulate. Each disciple grows at his or her own rate of determination or lack thereof. The mentor will grieve and intercede, and may eventually terminate the discipling if the student proves to be continually irresponsible.

4. Spiritual mentors oversee, applaud and chastise behavior.

They may invite the student to chat awhile, encouraging him or her to talk about all the little events that have happened in the family and among friends. Then comes a time of pleasant questioning: "What did that mean to you?" "Why do you suppose that happened?" They commiserate when that is needed. When trust has established restfulness and lack of fear, the director may turn the questioning inward: "Can you see and describe what your own feelings and motives were when those things happened?" Like a shepherd who examines his sheep's faces at the end of the day for blood-sucking ticks, the mentor examines the student and then helps the student learn how to examine himself or herself. He applauds honesty and praises keen and accurate perceptions, until together they ferret out life-sucking hurtful emotions and reactions. Together they look at possible root causes for whatever behaviors were not pleasing to the Lord. Teaching may then metamorphose into the inner healing described above.

5. Mentors in Christ examine all of life by the plumb lines of the Bible, proper doctrine and the nature of our Lord and His Father.

They are gentle executioners, bringing to death on the cross whatever is not consonant with those three plumb lines. As they talk with their disciples, what they say and do models how to discern, how to live, how not to live, how to test all things and how to die rightly on the cross (see Galatians 2:20; 5:24). Years ago, the evangelist Tommy Tyson did that for me. I do not suppose he consciously acted as a father model, but his behavior was that for me anyway. Whenever we got together I would trot out my latest speculations and theories. Sometimes he would gently question me until I could see that my ideas did not quite match up to the Lord's standards. Most often, he did not have to say anything. I could tell by his pained expression that I had better rethink that one! Tommy is quite roly-poly and full of humor and simple wisdom. I used to say that Tommy was a most comfortable rock to bounce off of. Tommy was the kind of mentor we all need—someone we can test against who is "comfortable," whose ways bear no harm and who models reproof that makes you feel good rather than put down.

6. Mentors should seek to do themselves out of a job.

Their purpose is to be so transparent that people move easily through them to the cross. As I said before, they do not want to turn out "cookie-cutter copies" of themselves. Rather, they want to find and release all that their spiritual children are to be in Christ.

Thus, spiritual mentors are called to continuous death on the cross, so that people do not latch onto them rather than the Lord. They do not want to create dependent people, or codependency. Sometimes psychological transferences do occur in the process of training, but each mentor should learn to recognize these and handle them with wisdom and discretion. More about transference can be found in several of our books and in those of many others. It is not my purpose to discuss that condition fully here. Rather I will simply say that it can happen, it can be handled, and mentors need to learn how to recognize and deal with it appropriately in the Lord's way.

In the end, mentors release people into maturity. The relationship of mentor-"mentee" ends, and they learn to stand alongside each other as friends. Jesus meant something like this when He said to His disciples that no longer would He call them servants but friends. Their relationship changed to a different basis, more that of companionship than that of Master-servant.

7. Mentors look to that time when the Lord shall present us all, one by one, before the Father.

Above all, he wants the Lord to be filled with pride as He presents us. Mentors know that they need to build with gold (the wisdom and nature of our Lord), silver (precious knowledge of the Word and the Way of Life) and precious stones (talents and skills, developed and released into service for the glory of the Lord). They know that whatever is built with wood, hay and stubble will be burned up as life tests us all. Therefore, mentors want to burn away the dross while relating with their spiritual children, knowing there is still time to rebuild with materials that will endure beyond time into eternity.

8. Mentoring also involves humbling.

Novice prophets desperately need mentors. Paula and I have grieved over many budding prophets who never came to full bloom either because there were no mentors or, more regrettably, because they refused the corrections of the mentors God provided. I know Bishop Bill Hamon and many other mature prophets share the same grief. You may recall our quote about the man who refused the correction of Bishop Bill's team and my reference to my beloved friend who rejected the prayers of our ministerial group. It is a grievous situation when prideful people—prophets among them—will not humble themselves to hear the teachings of others, much less their rebukes. But those who have learned to profit from receiving mentoring and its humbling become great mentors for others.

Unfortunately, the errors of the earlier shepherding and discipling movement have caused many to become unnecessarily afraid of God's true gift of mentoring. But remember what I said above about spiritual cowardice. The mistakes of others must not be allowed to become an excuse for what God presently calls us to do.

Established prophets under the green tree trained their students not simply by questions and answers. They also gave them insurmountable tasks to do, precisely to crush their pride in failure. Or they gave them humiliating tasks to humble them. For this reason, when King Jehoshaphat asked if there was a prophet from whom to inquire, one of his servants replied, "Elisha the son of Shaphat is here, *who used to pour water on the hands of Elijah*" (2 Kings 3:11, emphasis mine). We modern Westerners think nothing of helping out by doing what is often considered "women's work." *But in the biblical countries of that time, no male would ever be caught doing women's work!* That would be utterly humiliating—even crushing—to male pride. Mentoring prophets commanded their students to do the menial women's task of pouring water over their hands after they had eaten. Jehoshaphat's servant was telling the king that he could trust Elisha—he had been properly humbled and brought to death in his pride (see Matthew 21:44).

Knowing this, I used to take team members with me on teaching tours and immediately hurled them into tough situations, speaking and praying for people. Actually, though I grieved for their errors, I also privately rejoiced when they stumbled. I knew the humbling would build in them a true—and even desperate—hunger to learn how to do things right, even if that meant humiliation and having to learn to receive and cherish rebuke. Those students became strong and able to stand on their own. Our prayer counselors at Elijah House still train our internees by allowing them to minister, and then sitting down with them to critique and correct. Humble internees profit and grow. The prideful fail.

For this reason Peter exhorted young Christians to endure being raised by others: Let us all come to Him as living stones and be "*built up* as a spiritual house for a holy priesthood, to offer up spiritual sacrifices acceptable to God through Jesus Christ" (1 Peter 2:5, emphasis mine).

How I pray that budding prophets today may come to cherish stern and humbling rebukes. This self-serving generation seeks pleasant and easy ways to comfort the flesh. But it is not the vastly gifted whom God seeks to become His trusted servants. It is only those whom chastisement and suffering have slain on the cross of Christ.

Are you willing?

Mentoring Is Vital to the Office of the Prophet

It is not true that we can take nothing with us into heaven. We take into heaven whatever we have become in this life. We will indeed be changed in the twinkling of an eye, but whatever is of gold, silver and precious stones in us will not be lost but will be transformed into greater glory. Thus, we have great need for mentors. Pastors are shepherds for the flock. Mentors are God's gifts to His officers in all the offices. Mentors are shepherds who mentor and guide beyond what pastors of lay flocks are trained to do.

Tyro prophets need mentoring until they have grown to capacity to mentor others. Mentoring is an important function of prophets if the Body of Christ is to mature into the fullness of Christ.

Pray that the Lord will raise up His mentors—and that we who are so often filled with the pride of our office may have the grace and humility to allow God's spiritual mentors to do their job among us. Let us all come to Him as living stones and be "built up as a spiritual house for a holy priesthood, to offer up spiritual sacrifices acceptable to God through Jesus Christ" (1 Peter 2:5).

SEVENTEEN

THE COMING WAVE

ON JANUARY 20, 1994, the Holy Spirit fell with great power on the Toronto Airport Christian Fellowship—and that began an outpouring upon the entire world. This has been one of the greatest moves of the Holy Spirit in Christian history. Since then, more than five million people from all over the world have traveled to Toronto to experience the flow of the Holy Spirit as God the Father has poured out His love upon His children. Still happening today, it has proved to be transferable and highly contagious. Christians have caught the blessed infection of the Holy Spirit and the love of Father God and carried them home, until many centers of renewal have sprung up around the world.

Three years later, John Arnott, founding pastor of Toronto Airport Fellowship and the father of the renewal, had a vision of a second great wave of the Holy Spirit coming upon the Church. He saw it as a great tsunami rising up in the sea, about to burst upon the shore. At the same time, independently, I saw exactly the same vision. Others saw and prophesied much the same thing.

To date it has not yet happened—perhaps because the price of prayer has not been paid. More likely, I think, it has not yet been the Father's timing. I have not heard the Lord say, but I sense that something else has to happen, a precursor to the fullness of spiritual renewal the Lord has in store for us. But it *is* coming. The second great wave of the Holy Spirit will be the first of this century and perhaps the greatest revival ever. It is rapidly approaching.

This New Wave—How Is It Different?

Of course, many great waves, or movements, of the Holy Spirit have occurred throughout Christian history. Even prior to the time of Christ, the Holy Spirit has moved dramatically upon mankind many times since Adam. The Exodus, for example, was surely one of the greatest, most spectacular actions of God in all of human history. The subsequent conquest of Palestine was attended by military miracles that have not been seen since, such as the walls of Jericho falling down. In the days of good King Josiah, God moved to restore faith in Israel and to cleanse out the old leaven of idolatry and witchcraft. And was there ever a greater move of God than in the time of John the Baptist and our Lord Jesus Christ?

In Christian history—that is, since the time of Christ—many moves of God have taken place. Perhaps the most well known are the simultaneous rise of the Reformation and the Jesuit missions that reached across the world in the sixteenth century, and the first and second great awakenings in America. God has not left Himself without witness in any age.

What is different now, unique to this time, is the proximity of the Lord's return. Many think the coming wave may be the last great revival that is to sweep in the final great harvest before the end of history. I do not think so. A great revival, yes, but the Church is certainly not yet a bride adorned and prepared for her Husband. Right now, though glories abound, we are a tattered and sinful mess.

The Church Will Be Cleansed and Adorned

The Lord is rapidly cleansing His Church, and I am sure that is one of the great hallmarks of the coming wave. This is a time of purging and cleansing greater and more thorough than the days of Josiah or the Reformation or the renewal in the Roman Catholic Church. In Isaiah 4:2–6, Isaiah prophesied about this very aspect of the coming wave. We know this is so because he begins his prophecy with "In that day." He is referring to the last days before the return of the Lord.

In that day the Branch of the LORD will be beautiful and glorious, and the fruit of the earth will be the pride and the adornment of the survivors of Israel.

ISAIAH 4:2

This verse is Hebraic thought-rhyme, saying the same thing twice in different ways. Jewish believers see this and the following verses as a tremendously hopeful prophecy—that after all the pogroms and holocausts are over, God will restore Israel's survivors to glory, as in the days of God's Shekinah presence in the desert. That may be, and I hope it is so, but that does not prevent us Christians from also seeing it as a prophecy about us. Jesus is the Vine; we are the branches (see John 15:5). The prophecy is that we who are the branches and the fruit of the earth (see Romans 8:18–22) will be beautiful and glorious. Whether completed in this great coming wave or remaining for succeeding waves to finish, the Church will be purged, cleansed, transformed and beautiful. This shall be one of the most remarkable signs of the coming wave—that God the Father will cleanse and transform His people as a bridal gift to His Son.

The Church Will Be Sanctified by Faith, Not the Law

It will come about that he who is left in Zion and remains in Jerusalem will be called holy—everyone who is recorded for life in Jerusalem.

ISAIAH 4:3

To Christians, Jerusalem is not only the city of our Lord: It is also our residence in our Lord's heart as His Zion, His people who are "recorded for life" (see Luke 10:20). We will be called "holy."

Throughout history, every great revival has been attended by a call to holiness. Regrettably, every past revival has ended when Christians have mistaken Old Testament holiness for the New. Old Testament holiness was a striving to live up to the Law in order to win acceptability in the sight of the Lord. Noble as the attempts were, they inevitably ended in frustration and failure. We can never become righteous that way. Old Testament holiness was self-centered and selfish. One strove to be righteous for one's own end—acceptance.

New Testament holiness is utterly otherwise. We do not have to strive to live up to the Law to win acceptance. We are already acceptable and received into the bosom of our Father by the merits of Jesus' righteousness for us on the cross. Now, we attempt to live honorably, not to gain anything for ourselves, but to express our love for Him and all mankind as an easy outflow of His Spirit within.

New Testament holiness is Love hanging on a cross for the sake of all others. Among us, it is love in action, unmindful of self. Old holiness is a farm tractor, washed, waxed and polished, sitting in a field, looking good, doing nothing. New Testament holiness is that same tractor plowing a field to feed others, getting dusty and dirty in the process, holding to the lines of righteous obedience in order to plow straight for others' sake, not to gain anything for itself. It does not care to look good—that is already taken care of by the Lord.

Unfortunately, in each previous renewal the fires of love have all too soon become banked, and the call for holiness has devolved from the New to the Old. Pharisaism and legalism have then dimmed the flame of revival, eventually killing it.

This time, in the coming great wave, God wants His Church to be filled with love. He wants us to pour out ourselves in service to others and keep ourselves pure morally, not for the Old reasons, but so as not to disgrace the Lord or hamper His move upon mankind for salvation. The coming great wave is to be marked by the Church at last learning to abide in New Testament holiness, without falling back into the Old.

For this reason the outpouring of the 1994 wave has been a rediscovery of God the Father's loving nature. Ever since 1994, we have increasingly been called into the Father's presence and into intimacy with Him. In the coming wave, the Father's love will consume us with transport into blessed intimacy. Only so shall we avoid falling back into the mistakes of the church at Galatia, whom Paul chastised for seeking to follow the Law rather than walking by the Spirit (see Galatians 3–5).

The Second Wave Will Be a Time of Judgment and Burning

When the Lord has washed away the filth of the daughters of Zion and purged the bloodshed of Jerusalem from her midst, *by the spirit of judgment and the spirit of burning . . .*

ISAIAH 4:4, EMPHASIS MINE

This second great wave, more than any previous, will be a time of judgment and burning. This wave will come in fire, perhaps even as fire descended upon the disciples at Pentecost. John the Baptist prophesied that the Lord would baptize us "with the Holy Spirit and fire" (Matthew 3:11). To date, we have seen the latter day outpouring of the Holy Spirit "on all mankind" (Joel 2:28), but very little, if any, baptism in fire. *The coming wave will bring fresh outpouring of the Holy Spirit and at last the baptism of fire!*

But remember, God's first and desired judgment is His mercy and kindness, setting straight whatever manifests darkness in our lives. Inner healing will cease to be looked upon as a questionable adjunct to the faith, perhaps even an aberration. It will be seen as the *sine qua non* of continuing maturation in the Lord. What has been thought of as something needful only to those who "could not make it" will be seen as what it is—one of the primary means the Holy Spirit employs for the sanctification and transformation of every Christian. Sanctification and transformation will be the natural and only safe ground of all who continue to walk in the fires of His love.

In this work of purging by fire and judgment, God's Nathanic prophets who understand and decipher the deceptions of the human heart will become crucial. *Purging and fire only become blessing and joy where ministry turns them into mercy and kindness.* Where Christians do not avail themselves of such ministry, or cannot find it, the Lord will accomplish the same purging and sanctification the hard way, by pain and suffering.

The Second Wave May Manifest the Shekinah Glory of God

Then the LORD will create over the whole area of Mount Zion and over her assemblies a cloud by day, even smoke, and the brightness of a flaming fire by night; for over all the glory will be a canopy.

ISAIAH 4:5

This is the glorious promise that the same visible cloud by day and fire by night that guided the Hebrew people in the desert will be upon the Church, wherever it assembles. Observers will call out fire departments, thinking church buildings are on fire!

Referring to verse 4, note that it happens only "when the Lord has washed away the filth." The Shekinah glory will rest whenever and wher-

236

ever judgment and burning (sanctification and transformation) have been allowed to do their work to the fullest.

I do *not* know that the Shekinah glory will descend within this second great wave. Much, *much* changing of hearts must happen first. I do know prophetically that the requisite cleansing and changing will begin in this second great wave. I pray that enough will catch the vision of sanctification and transformation that His presence may come in this move of God.

The Next Wave Will Be Marked by Joy

"For over all the glory will be a canopy" (other versions say "will be a defense"). The bride of a man is his glory, as The Song of Solomon illustrates. We are the bride of Christ; therefore we are His glory. Over us is His canopy, His protection. Those who walk in the judgment and fire of this coming great wave will walk at ease, knowing themselves to be under His protection. *Knowing* is too weak a word. *Experiencing, living in, thrilling in the comfort of, at rest in* would be more like it. It shall be a time of unadulterated blessing for those fortunate enough to be caught up in it, a time of inexpressible rejoicing (see 1 Peter 1:8).

This coming wave will be marked by joy as no other in history. In the 1994 outpouring of the Holy Spirit, the Church was surprised by fits of laughter that burst out of those who had fallen under the influence of God's Spirit. It was as though the Church, which had fallen into the seriousness of the faith and had lost the childlike ability to delight in the Lord, had to be broken open to uncontrollable laughter. What had been too long suppressed burst like a submerged ball being shot high beyond comprehension and control. But joy in this coming wave will be resident, constantly within, bubbling to the surface not uncontrollably but in winsome smiles and chuckles that sometimes erupt in holy laughter from the sheer joy of being in the loving presence of the Father and the Son.

The Second Wave Will Bring with It Refuge and Protection

There will be a shelter to give shade from the heat by day, and refuge and protection from the storm and the rain.

ISAIAH 4:6

237

This second wave will not lose its life in selfish legalism. Its adherents will find their continuing joy, their ability to continue to abide, in ministering His love to all they meet.

God is not raising up an army to take it home before the battle. He is preparing a special people, a corps who know Him, so that as the long-prophesied time of tribulation approaches and its sufferings increase He can say to the torn and battered of the world, "Here! Run here, under the covering of My Church, whom I have prepared as a mother hen's wings for you for this very time." It is not that God so hates the world He can hardly wait to get the Church out of it so He can beat up on it. It is that God so loved the world that He sent the Son, that all who believe in Him might be saved—and it is still the same today. He is still sending the Son, through all His purged and transformed believers, who can become shelter and healing for a world that richly deserves nothing but destruction.

This wave will be a move of God to save the lost, but not merely by conversion in great revivals. The coming wave will be an expression of the Father's love that does not end with conversion—it will begin there. Its defining mark will be deep ministry to the heart that transforms from loss and degradation to glorious living. Salvation will come to mean what it does mean—not mere conversion, but transformation of heart and mind and spirit into the glorious possibility of living as He lives, free and giving to all others.

The Second Wave Will Have a Solid Foundation

Perhaps the second great wave has not yet come because its prophets and apostles have not yet arisen to assume their places. Ephesians 2:20 says that the Church is "built on the foundation of the apostles and prophets, Christ Jesus Himself being the corner stone." As a child, I was taught that meant that Jesus and the apostles and prophets lived two thousand years ago and built the foundation of the Church. But the Lord told me, *I am the present cornerstone because I am presently living. In like manner, the present apostles and prophets are meant to be the present foundation of the Church. The Church has been weak because its foundation has been absent.*

Listen to Psalm 82:5: "They do not know nor do they understand; they walk about in darkness; all the foundations of the earth are shaken." Apostles and prophets bring revelation and direction. The Church has

238

been much too blind and stumbling, walking about in darkness, simply because its apostles and prophets have not been there.

"If the foundations are destroyed, what can the righteous do?" (Psalm 11:3). In the coming wave, not only will God's apostles and prophets arise, as they are beginning to do, but they also shall find their place and status. They shall then be able to serve as the foundation of the Church and the righteous will have the guidance required to be effective. For this reason, I have written the many chapters in this book about blessing, healing, protection, warning and personal words, dreams and visions, etc. Other prophets, and now the apostles, are writing and speaking, equipping the Church as never before for its end time tasks. This is the Father's expression of Ephesians 4:11, a gift to the Church to equip the saints for the work of ministry. It shall no longer be that the righteous shall walk about in darkness. God is raising up His messengers.

The Second Wave Will Be Marked by Healing of the Earth

His messengers, in this coming wave, will lead into the healing of the nations and the healing of the earth. For that reason I wrote *Healing the Nations*, and many are writing similar books—notably those already mentioned by John Dawson and Cindy Jacobs. Years ago, Winkie Pratney wrote a marvelous book, *Healing the Land*, and now Judith Monticone has written a volume also called *Healing the Land*. And the last book I am commanded to write is to be *The Healing of the Earth*. God the Father is moving to heal His world, to present the nations and the earth as gifts to His Son.

Receive the Prophets, and Respond

How much shall be accomplished by, or during, this coming wave, I cannot say. I know all will be done, but perhaps much awaits another great wave—or will await our Lord's return, to be accomplished only after His Parousia. I want to celebrate the Father's purposes and His eminence, as He acts among us and in the earth. I call the Church to look up, to expect and receive the maturation of His prophets and apostles, and to respond in obedience.

The End Is Not Yet

While this book was in the final editing process, a new book by Chuck Pierce and Rebecca Wagner Sytsema came out, entitled *The Future War of the Church*. I found it glorious and challenging—though I might quarrel a bit with the authors about the title. Since the terrible tragedy of the destruction of the twin towers of the World Trade Center on September 11, 2001, it seems the book could more aptly have been entitled *The Present and Terrible War of the Church!* I close by quoting from it.

> And you will hear of wars and rumors of wars. See that you are not troubled; for all these things must come to pass, *but the end is not yet.*
>
> MATTHEW 24:6, EMPHASIS ADDED

If, as Jesus says, the end is not yet, then we must rise up and enter into the *now* of God. Because we have not reached that final time when the culmination of all things has occurred, we must learn to operate in the present—for what we do now will determine our future. Isaiah 46:9, 10 says:

> Remember the former things of old, for I am God, and there is no other; I am God, and there is none like Me, declaring the end from the beginning, and from ancient times things that are not yet done, saying, "My counsel shall stand, and I will do all My pleasure."

When the Lord makes a declaration, you can be sure He already knows the end of the thing. It is the process of that prophetic declaration, or divine promise, that we will look at in this book.

God already knows the end. Recognize that you are on a path of life; it is set before you. You are urged to press along that path and endure that path until you reach the end. There are big boulders and potholes along the way, and oftentimes the path needs to be cleared before you can even begin. Know that your Father in heaven is going to watch over you from the first step until you reach the finish line, because He already knows the end.

With this reality understood, we should never lose faith or hope along the path. The real issues along the path are who God is and what His purpose is from the beginning until the end. He says, "I am the Alpha and Omega, the Beginning and the End, the First and the Last" (Revelation 22:13). He is saying to you, "I AM. I AM, and I can make you well able to accomplish My purpose here on the earth."

240

BIBLIOGRAPHY

Arnott, John. *The Father's Blessing*. Lake Mary, Fla.: Creation House, 1995.

Cannistraci, David. *The Gift of Apostle*. Ventura, Calif.: Regal, 1996.

Dawson, John. *Healing America's Wounds*. Ventura, Calif.: Regal, 1994.

———. *Taking Our Cities for God*. Lake Mary, Fla.: Creation House, 1989.

Gear, W. Michael and Kathleen O'Neal Gear. *People of the Earth*. New York: Tor Books, 1992.

Gentile, Ernest B. *Your Sons and Daughters Shall Prophesy*. Grand Rapids, Mich.: Chosen Books, 1999.

Goll, Jim W. *The Coming Prophetic Revolution*. Grand Rapids, Mich.: Chosen Books, 2001.

——— *Wasted on Jesus* Shippensburg, Pa.: Destiny Image Publishers, Inc., 2000.

Hamon, Dr. Bill. *Prophets and Personal Prophecy*. Shippensburg, Pa.: Destiny Image Publishers, Inc., 1987.

———. *Prophets: Pitfalls and Principles*. Santa Rosa Beach, Fla.: Christian International, 1991.

———. *Prophets and the Prophetic Movement*. Santa Rosa Beach, Fla.: Christian International, 1990.

Hamon, Jane. *Dreams and Visions*. Santa Rosa Beach, Fla.: Christian International, 1997.

Jacobs, Cindy. *Deliver Us from Evil*. Ventura, Calif.: Regal, 2001.

———. *Possessing the Gates of the Enemy*. Grand Rapids, Mich.: Chosen Books, 1991.

———. *The Voice of God*. Ventura, Calif.: Regal, 1995.

Jackson, John Paul. *Selling Our Children's Souls*. Fort Worth, Tex.: Streams Publications, 2000.

———. *The Veiled Ploy*. Fort Worth, Tex.: Streams Publications, 2001.

McClung, Floyd Jr. *The Father Heart of God*. Eugene, Ore.: Harvest House Publishers, 1985.

Monticone, Judith. *Healing the Land*. Vol. 1. Mitchell, Australia: Healing the Land, 1999.

Owens, Jimmy and Carol. *Heal Our Land*. Grand Rapids, Mich.: Fleming H. Revell, 1997.

Petrie, Alistair. *Releasing Heaven on Earth*. Grand Rapids, Mich.: Chosen Books, 2000.

Pierce, Chuck, and Rebecca Wagner Sytsema. *The Future War of the Church*. Ventura, Calif.: Renew, 2001.

Plummer, Kristin. *Receiving a Prophet*. Bogota, N.J.: self-published, 1997.

Pratney, Winkie. *Healing the Land*. Grand Rapids, Mich.: Chosen Books, 1993.

Sandford, John and Paula. *The Elijah Task*. Tulsa, Okla.: Victory House, Inc., 1977.

Sandford, John Loren. *Healing the Nations*. Grand Rapids, Mich.: Chosen Books, 2000.

Sedler, Michael D. *Stop the Runaway Conversation*. Grand Rapids, Mich.: Chosen Books, 2001.

Sheets, Dutch. *Intercessory Prayer*. Ventura, Calif.: Regal, 1995.

Tenney, Tommy. *The God Chasers*. Shippensburg, Pa.: Destiny Image Publishers, Inc., 1998.

Torres, Hector. *The Restoration of the Apostles*. Nashville, Tenn.: Thomas Nelson, 2001.

Wagner, C. Peter. *Apostles and Prophets: The Foundation of the Church*. Ventura, Calif.: Regal, 2000.

———. *What the Bible Says about Spiritual Warfare*. Ventura, Calif.: Regal, 2001.

INDEX